AI Techniques
for Game
Programming

PREMIER PRESS

GAME DEVELOPMENT

AI Techniques for Game Programming

Mat Buckland

PREMIER PRESS

GAME DEVELOPMENT

Premier
Press

Publisher: Stacy L. Hiquet

Marketing Manager: Heather Hurley

Managing Editor: Heather Talbot

Series Editor: André LaMothe

Acquisitions Editor: Mitzi Foster Koontz

Project Editor/Copy Editor: Jenny Davidson

Technical Reviewer: André LaMothe

Interior Layout: Danielle Foster

Cover Designer: Mike Tanamachi

CD-ROM Producer: Jenny Davidson

Indexer: Sharon Shock

Proofreader: Marge Bauer

ISBN: 1-931841-08-X

Library of Congress Catalog Card Number: 2002108325

Printed in the United States of America

02 03 04 05 BH 10 9 8 7 6 5 4 3 2 1

Premier Press, a division of Course Technology

2645 Erie Avenue, Suite 41

Cincinnati, Ohio 45208

For Sharon—whose light never fades.

Foreword

Welcome to *AI Techniques for Game Programming*. I think you're going to find that it just might be one of the most useful books on game programming that you've ever picked up.

Mat first came to my attention back in 2000 or so when he began posting in the GameDev (www.gamedev.net) forums on various aspects of game AI, answering questions of all kinds. He quickly garnered attention and praise from his fellow posters, particularly when he posted two tutorials he'd done on neural networks and genetic algorithms for public consumption. Mat saw a need for AI technologies such as these to be more accessible to game developers in hopes that they might incorporate them into their games, and his tutorials and patient answering of questions in the GameDev forums were obviously a way to try to make that happen. It is with some pride that I find myself now writing a foreword for a book on the subject; may it be the first of many.

Content of This Book

This book is fundamentally about making better games. It focuses on doing this by making the computer opponents smarter, more capable, and more *human*. This is an area of knowledge that has only been getting attention in any meaningful sense for the past decade or so.

As this book goes to press, developers can look around and find the game industry exploding with activity, reaching out to new audiences, and evolving like never before. As new consoles and PC platforms flood the market, developers find themselves faced with an abundance of riches in terms of memory, CPU speeds, connectivity options, and video resolutions. These new capabilities provide the game developer with endless possibilities—and endless decisions for trade-offs and focus. Should the new game step up video resolution another notch, or should we focus on making the collisions more realistic? What about speed—can we do what we want to do with the standard machines in a year and a half when we're ready to hit the market? How can we make our product *different* from our competitor's down the street?

Great game AI is one obvious way to make your game stand out from the crowd, and the flood of books and articles on the subject bears this out. Good quality game AI is no longer something to be done as long as it doesn't hurt the framerate—it's now a vital part of the design process and one which can make or break sales, just like graphics or sound. Developers are doing everything they can to investigate new AI technologies that they can assimilate to help build better, smarter game AIs. They want to explore new ideas that might take AIs to the next generation, an era in which games don't just provide an interesting opponent but one in which they can *talk* to the player, *interact* with legions of online adventurers, and *learn* from game to game to be a more cunning and twisted opponent the next time around.

Of course, these new AIs have to help make the game sell better, too. That's always the bottom line—if a game doesn't sell, it doesn't really matter how good its AI is.

Making Smarter Games

This book focuses on exploring the relatively (to the game industry, anyway) "exotic" technologies of *genetic algorithms* and *neural networks* and how the developer might use them in his games. This has been a notoriously tough area to get developers interested in for a number of reasons. Most developers feel that their current techniques are just fine and are easy to debug. The standard *finite state machine* (FSM) and *fuzzy state machine* (FuSM) have done a great job of providing robust, easy-to-debug AIs that have led to hit games from *Age of Empires* to *Quake*. They work, and with enough code time, they can be built to cover almost any situation.

They're also sadly predictable in so many ways, and that's where developers are beginning to run into the Law of Diminishing Returns. Building an FSM to handle the innumerable possibilities inherent in some of the new games can be mind-boggling, the number of choices an AI must evaluate is overwhelming. To the human player, there might be two or three potential decisions which are "obviously" better—but what if the guy who coded the AI the Saturday night before the game's final version was sent to the publisher didn't think about those? The player sees the AI faced with a terrific decision upon which the entire fate of the game hangs—and it chooses incorrectly. Or worse than that, it chooses *stupidly*. A few instances of that and it's pop! The CD is out of the drive and the player has moved on to something else.

Suppose instead that the player faced a computer opponent that didn't have a blind spot, that a game didn't have a special combination of features that would render the AI brain-dead once the player discovered it. Suppose instead that the player faced an AI that might actually *adapt* to the player's style over time, one that played better and smarter as the player learned more about the game.

This kind of adaptation, or *learning*, is something of a Holy Grail for developers and players alike, and players clamber for it whenever they're asked what they'd most like to see next. Gamers want to be challenged by an AI that actually adapts to their style of play, AIs that might anticipate what the player is most likely to do and then do something about it. In other words, an AI that plays more like another human.

To the Future

That's where some of the more interesting AI technologies, such as the ones covered in this book, come in. These technologies bring a more *biological* focus to the normally dry, logic-like realm of AI, giving the developer tools through which she might construct computer opponents that think like the players do. Using these techniques, a developer might build an AI that is smart enough to try a few different things to see what works best rather than simply selecting options from a menu of whatever the programmer thought to include. It might analyze the relative strengths and positions of its opponent's forces, figure out that an invasion is near, and reposition forces to intercept it.

The benefits that are possible don't just affect the player's ability to have a good time. Properly built, an AI that learns can have real impacts on development and test time on the part of the programmer, because he no longer has to build and test dozens or hundreds of fragile, special-case AI logic. If the AI can instead be given a few basic guidelines and then learn how to play the game by watching expert human players, it will not only be more robust, it will simply play a better game. It's like the difference between *reading* about basketball and actually *playing* it.

Does that mean that Mat has done all the hard work here, and all you have to do is copy and paste his code into your latest project to build an AI that plays just like any human player? No, of course not. What is presented here is a guide, a framework, a baseline for those of you who don't know anything about these more exotic AI technologies and are looking for a new angle for your next project. Maybe you haven't had the time to research these possibilities on your own or perhaps you were just turned off by the more "academic" explanations found in other texts or around the Web.

The chapters that follow explore these technologies in an easy-going, friendly way. The approach is *by* a game developer *for* a game developer, and Mat maintains that focus throughout.

AIs that can learn and adapt are an emerging technology that clearly point the way to better games, more satisfied gamers, and, most importantly, more sales.

Steven Woodcock
ferretman@gameai.com

Acknowledgments

First and foremost, I'd like to thank the love of my life, Sharon, for her patience, understanding, and encouragement while I was writing this book. Not even after the umpteenth time I turned away from my keyboard, blank-eyed, muttering "sorry, what was that you just said?" did she once throw a plate at me.

Thanks to Mitzi at Premier for babysitting me through the whole process and for all her help with my often ridiculous queries (even if she does think Yorkshire-men sound like Jamie Oliver!). A big thanks also to Jenny, my editor, who has been awesome, to André who has combed my work for bugs, and to Heather for correcting all my mistakes and for suitably "Americanizing" my text.

Many thanks to Gary "Stayin' Alive" Simmons who suggested I write a book in the first place, to all the fans of my Internet tutorials whose e-mails provided daily encouragement, to Steve "Ferretman" Woodcock for taking the time to write the foreword, and to Ken for answering my many queries regarding NEAT.

And of course, I shouldn't forget Mr. Fish and Scooter, who always made sure I had a warm lap and a runny nose whenever I sat down to write.

About the Author

After studying Computer Science at London University, **Mat Buckland** spent many years as a Risk Management Consultant. He finally grew bored with all the money and corporate politics, made a bonfire of his designer suits, and went to work for a developer producing games for Gremlin Software. This paid a lot less but was a whole lot of fun—besides he got to wear jeans on weekdays! He now works as a freelance programmer and AI consultant. Mat has been interested in evolutionary computing and AI in general since he first read about these techniques back in the early '80s. He is the author of the ai-junkie.com Web site (www.ai-junkie.com), which provides tutorials and advice on evolutionary algorithms.

Contents at a Glance

Contents

CHAPTER 2
FURTHER ADVENTURES WITH
WINDOWS PROGRAMMING ••••••••••••••••••••••• 35

Part Two
Genetic Algorithms 87

CHAPTER 5
BUILDING A BETTER GENETIC
ALGORITHM ••••••••••••••••••••••••••••••••• 143

CHAPTER 6
MOON LANDINGS MADE EASY •••••••••••• 177

Part Three
Neural Networks 231

Part Four
Appendixes 413

LETTER FROM THE SERIES EDITOR

Being the series editor for the Premier *Game Development* series leaves me little time to write books these days, so I have to find people who really have a passion for it and who can really deliver the goods. If you have read any of my game programming books, you know that I always include heavy coverage of AI—from state machines to fuzzy logic—but I have never had time to write a complete book just on AI. Alas, we set out to find the perfect author to write the best game AI book in the world. And now that the book is done, I can't believe it, but we did it! Mat has not only written the book as I would have, but far exceeded my expectations of going that extra mile to bring you something that is timeless and will have far-reaching impact on the gaming community, as well as other areas of engineering, biological computation, robotics, optimization theory, and more.

I have never seen a book that has put neural nets and genetic algorithms together and made real demos with them that do real things. For 20 years, I have been using this stuff, and I am amazed that no one else has realized how easy it all is—this is not rocket science; it's just a new way to do things. If you look at all the academic books on AI, they are totally overkill—tons of math, theory, and not a single real-world program that does something other than let you type in some coefficients and then watch a couple iterations of a neural net or genetic algorithm work—useless.

When I set out to do this book, I wanted someone that not only knew his stuff inside and out, but was an awesome programmer, artist, and most of all, a perfectionist. Mat and I worked on the table of contents for quite some time, deciding what should be covered. Also, we absolutely both agreed that this book had to be graphical and have real examples of every single concept; moreover, we knew the book had to have tons of figures, illustrations, and visuals to help bring the concepts down to Earth. In the end, I can say without a doubt *"this is the best book on applied AI in the world."*

I dare anyone to show me a better book that teaches the concepts better than Mat has and brings them down to an understandable level that anyone can learn and put to use today. I guarantee you that when you finish this book, whether you are a programmer, an engineer, a biologist, a roboticist, or whatever, you will immediately put these techniques to work and shoot yourself in the foot for not doing it sooner—this book is that amazing.

Also, this book will give you the tools you need to use AI techniques in the real world in areas such as robotics, engineering, weapons design, you name it. I bet about 6 months after the release of this book, there are going to be a lot of really dangerous *Quake* bots out there on the Internet!!!

In conclusion, I don't care what field of computing you are interested in, you can't afford not to know what's in this book. You will be amazed and delighted with the possibility of making "thinking machines" yourself—machines that are alive but based in a digital world of silicon. They are no different than us—their domain and capabilities are different, but they are still alive depending on how you define life. The time of *Digital Biology* is upon us—new rules of the definition of life, what it means, and so forth are here—humans and organic organisms based in the physical world do not have unilateral reign of the concept of living or sentience. As Ray Kurzweil said in the *Age of Spirtual Machines*, "In 20 years a standard desktop computer will outpace the computational abilities of the human brain." Of course, this statement takes nothing but Moore's Law into account; it says nothing of quantum computing and other innovations which are bound to happen. My prediction is that by 2050, the computational abilities of a chip that can fit on the tip of a needle that costs 1 penny will have more power than all the human brains on the planet combined. I will probably be completely wrong; it will probably have 1,000,000 times that power, but I will be a pessimist for now.

So the bottom line is this: We are truly at the dawn of a new age where living machines are going to happen; they are inevitable. And understanding the techniques in this book is a first step to getting there. That is, the application of simple rules, evolutionary algorithms, and basic techniques modeled after our own biology can help us create these machines, or more ironically our *future ancestors*.

André LaMothe
Series Editor for the Premier *Game Development* Series

Introduction

Considering how many fools can calculate, it is surprising that it should be thought either a difficult or a tedious task for any other fool to learn how to master the same tricks.

Some [calculus] tricks are quite easy. Some are enormously difficult. The fools who write the text-books of advanced mathematics—and they are mostly clever fools—seldom take the trouble to show you how easy the easy calculations are. On the contrary, they seem to desire to impress you with their tremendous cleverness by going about it in the most difficult way.

Being myself a remarkably stupid fellow, I have had to unteach myself the difficulties, and now beg to present to my fellow fools the parts that are not hard. Master these thoroughly, and the rest will follow. What one fool can do, another can.

Silvanus P. Thompson

Introduction to Calculus Made Easy, *first published in 1910*

Home computers have come a long way from the days of the Sinclair ZX80. The speed of hardware keeps getting faster and the cost of components keeps falling. The quality of the graphics we see in games has improved incredibly in just a few short years. However, to date, that's where almost all the effort developing games has been spent—on eye-candy. We've seen very little improvement in the AI of our favorite computer opponents.

Times are changing, though. Hardware has now gotten to the point where game developers can afford to give more clock cycles to the creation of AI. Also, games players are more sophisticated in their tastes. No longer do people want the dumb monsters to be found in old favorites like *Doom* and *Quake*. No longer do they want their computer-controlled game characters blindly stumbling around trying to find paths that don't exist, getting stuck in corners, dropping resources where they shouldn't, and bumping into trees. Games players want a lot more from their games. They want to see believable, intelligent behavior from their computer-generated opponents (and allies).

For these reasons, I firmly believe the development of AI is going to take off in a big way in the next few years. Games like *Black & White* and *Halo* have wooed us with their AI, and games players are screaming for more of the same. What's more, completely new genres of games based around AI and A-Life have started to appear in the past few years, like Steve Grand's *Creatures*, which, much to his and everyone else's surprise, has sold over a million copies. And if you think that's a lot of copies, take a look at the sales of *The Sims* by Electronic Arts. To date, *The Sims* and the add-on packs have sold over 13 million copies! That's a lot of revenue, and it is a perfect indication of how much interest there is in this type of technology. The trend can only continue.

There are many techniques for creating the illusion of intelligence, but this book concentrates on just two of them: *Genetic Algorithms* and *Artificial Neural Networks*. Both these technologies are talked about a lot and they are definitely a "hot" topic at the moment, but they are also often misunderstood. Take neural networks, for example. It's not uncommon to see developers who believe neural nets are incredibly complex things, which will consequently take up too much processor time and slow down their game. Or conversely, they may be far too enthusiastic about a neural network's capabilities and as a result get frustrated when their plan to create a sentient HAL-like being fails! I hope this book will help allay some of these misconceptions.

The passage quoted in this section from the introduction of Silvanus Thompson's acclaimed book, *Calculus Made Easy*, seemed the perfect way to start my own book (thanks, Silvanus!), because neural networks and genetic algorithms, just like calculus, can be very difficult topics for the novice to start out with—especially for someone who hasn't spent much time treading the hallowed halls of academia. Almost all the books out there are written by academics, for academics, and are consequently full of strange mathematical formulas and obscure terminology. Therefore, I've written the sort of book I wished would have been available when I first got interested in these subjects: a book for fools written by a fool. Believe me, if I'd had a book like this when I first started out, it would have saved me many hours of frustration trying to figure out what all the academics were talking about!

Over the years, I've read many books and papers on this subject and hardly any of them give any real-world examples, nothing solid you can grasp hold of and go "*Ah! So that's what I can do with it!*" For example, your average book on genetic algorithms might give you a problem like this:

Minimize the function

$$f(x_1,...,x_5) = x_1 \sin x_1 + 1.7x_2 \sin x_1 - 1.5x_3 - 0.1x_4 \cos(x_4 + x_5 - x_1) + 0.2x_5^2 - x_2 - 1$$

where

$$-100 \leq x_1,...,x_5 \leq 100$$

I mean, fair enough, it's a problem you *can* solve with a genetic algorithm, but it's practically meaningless to us mere mortals. Unless you have a good mathematical background, this type of problem will probably seem very abstract and will most likely make you feel immediately uncomfortable. Reading any further will then feel like *work* rather than *fun*.

But if you are given a problem like this:

> *Let me introduce you to Bob. It's not a good day for Bob because he's hopelessly stuck in a maze and his wife expects him home shortly to share a meal she's spent all afternoon preparing. Let me show you how you can save Bob's marriage by using a genetic algorithm to find the directions he must follow to find the exit.*

Your brain has an anchor point—something it can relate to. Immediately you feel more comfortable with the problem. Not only that, but it is an *interesting* problem. You *want* to know how it's going to be solved. So you turn the page, and you learn. And you have fun while you're learning.

These are the sort of problems I've used to illustrate the concepts described in this book. If I've done my job correctly, it will be immediately obvious how you apply the ideas to your own games and projects.

I'm making only one assumption about you, the reader, and that is that you know how to program. I don't know about you, but I find it frustrating when I buy a book only to discover there are parts of it I don't understand, so I have to go and buy another book to explain the stuff in the first one. To prevent any similar frustration, I've tried to make sure this book explains everything shown in the code—from using the Windows GDI, matrix, and vector mathematics to physics and 2D graphics. I know there's another side to this coin and there'll be some of you who already know the graphics, physics, and the GDI stuff, but hey, you can just skip the stuff you know and get straight on to the exciting stuff.

NOTE

Building the Demo Programs

The demos are a cinch to compile. First copy the source code to your hard drive. If you use Visual Studio, simply click on the project workspace and take it from there. If you use an alternative compiler, create a new win32 project (*make sure winmm.lib is added in your project settings*), and then add the relevant source and resource files from the project folder before pressing the compile button. That's all there is to it. No additional paths, DirectX, or OpenGL to set up.

In all the examples, I've kept the code as simple as possible. It's written in C++, but I want C programmers to be able to understand my code, too. So for this reason I have not used any groovy stuff like inheritance and polymorphism. I make use of the simpler features of the STL (Standard Template Library), but where I do introduce an STL feature, there will be a sidebar explaining that feature. The whole point of using simple code is that it does not obscure the principle I'm trying to explain. Believe me, some of the stuff this book covers is not easy to grasp at first, and I didn't want to complicate matters by giving you examples in cleverly written code. I have done my utmost to bear in mind that old management consultant's favorite acronym: K.I.S.S (**K**eep **I**t **S**tupidly **S**imple).

So without further ado, let's start the adventure…

PART ONE

WINDOWS PROGRAMMING

Chapter 1

Chapter 2

CHAPTER 1

In the Beginning, There Was a Word, and the Word Was Windows

And Then Came Word, and Excel, and...

Customer: "I've just installed Windows 3.0."

Tech: "Yes."

Customer: "My computer isn't working now."

Tech: "Yes, you said that."

A Little Bit of History

Long ago, back in a time when *Airwolf* was considered exciting, and everyone walked around with a Rubik's Cube in their hands, a man named Bill Gates announced the coming of a new operating system developed by his company, Microsoft. The year was 1983, and the operating system was to be called "Windows." He initially decided to call his baby "The Interface Manager," but fortunately for Bill, his marketing guru convinced him that Windows would be a better name. The public was kept waiting for a long time, because although Gates had demonstrated a beta version of Windows to IBM in late 1983, the final product didn't hit the shelves until two years later.

Windows 1.0

Windows 1.0 (shown in Figure 1.1) was awful—clunky, slow, and buggy, and most of all, downright *ugly*. And on top of that, there was practically no support for it until Aldus released PageMaker in 1987. PageMaker was the first WYSIWYG (What You See Is What You Get) desktop publishing program for the PC. A few other programs came along soon afterward, such as Word and Excel, but Windows 1.0 was never a consumer favorite.

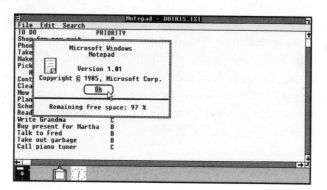

Figure 1.1

Groovy!

Windows 2.0

By the time Windows 2.0 was released, the user interface had begun to look much more like the GUI of a Macintosh computer. Apple, miffed at the resemblance, filed a lawsuit against Microsoft alleging that Bill had stolen their ideas. Microsoft claimed that an earlier agreement they had with Apple gave them the right to use Apple features, and after four years, Microsoft won the case. Therefore, Windows 2.0 (shown in Figure 1.2) stayed on the store shelves, but it sold poorly, because there was very little support from software developers. After all, what's the use of an operating system if there's no compatible software?

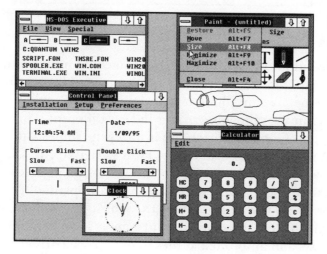

Figure 1.2

Windows begins to look more familiar.

Windows 3.0/3.1

Windows 3.0 (shown in Figure 1.3) was released in 1990. It boasted support for 16 colors (wow!), icons (bigger wow!), and had a much improved file manager and program manager. Although it was still bug ridden, for some reason programmers took a liking to this new version of Windows and plenty of software was developed for it. Microsoft addressed a lot of the problems and released Windows 3.1 in 1992; it was *much* more stable and also had support for stuff like sound and video. Three million copies were sold in the first two months. Soon afterward, Microsoft released Windows 3.1—Windows for Workgroups, which introduced network support, and Microsoft was well on their way to the big time.

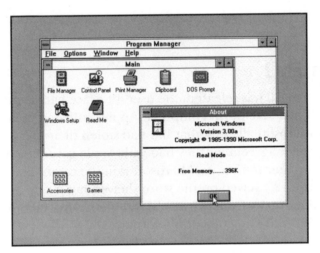

Figure 1.3

I bet this brings back some memories.

Windows 95

This version of Windows was the first version you could install without having to install MS-DOS first. It looked great, and it was a proper 32-bit multitasking environment. I remember installing it in the company of some friends. The first thing we did was run the same screensaver in four different Windows at the same time. My friends and I looked at each other with wide smiles and simultaneously said "Cooool!" A new era was born. Games even started to run fairly quickly under Windows. This was amazing, because prior to Windows 95, games written to run under Windows were a joke. They were slow, ugly, and plain-old boring. Everybody knew that a *proper* game had to run under DOS, or it just wasn't a game. Well, Windows 95 changed all that. No longer did gamers have to muck about endlessly with their config.sys and autoexec.bat files to obtain the correct amount of base and extended memory to run a game. Now we could just install, click, and play. It was a revelation.

Windows 98 Onward

Successive generations of Windows have built upon the success of Windows 95. Windows has become more stable, more user friendly, and easier to program for. DOS is a thing of the distant past, and nowadays, all games are written to run under the Windows environment. In its many guises—Windows 98, Windows ME, Windows 2000, and Windows XP—it is the single-most dominant operating system in use today. This is the reason my code was written to run under Windows, and this is the reason I'm going to start this book by teaching you the fundamentals of Windows programming. So let's get going!

Hello World!

Most programming books start by teaching readers how to code a simple program that prints the words "Hello World!" on the screen. In C++, it would look something like this:

```
#include <iostream>
using namespace std;

int main()
{
  cout << "Hello World!\n";
  return 0;
}
```

When run, this straightforward program will display an output that looks like Figure 1.4.

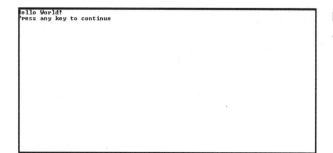

Figure 1.4

"Hello World" in a console.

Now I'm going to stick with tradition and show you how to get those familiar words up on your screen and inside a window.

Your First Windows Program

Here we go! Strap yourself in and prepare yourself for the ride! Initially, Windows programming may give you a few headaches, but I assure you once you've written a few programs of your own, it won't seem too bad. In fact, you may even grow to like it. So, without further ado, here's how you get "Hello World!" to appear on your screen in Windows.

```
#include <windows.h>

int WINAPI WinMain(HINSTANCE hInstance,
                   HINSTANCE hPrevInstance,
                   LPSTR     lpCmdLine,
                   int       nCmdShow)
{
  MessageBox(NULL, "Hello World!", "MsgBox", 0);
  return 0;
}
```

If you type this program into your compiler and run it (or just click on the HelloWorld1 executable from the accompanying CD-ROM), a little message box will appear on the screen, which will wait for you to click on OK before it exits. See Figure 1.5. If you *are* going to type in the code, make sure that you create a win32 project and not a console application in your compiler's IDE. Otherwise, the code will not compile, and you'll be stuck at the first hurdle.

Figure 1.5

A simple "Hello World" example.

As you can see, the first difference is that the entry point to the program is not good ol'

```
int main()
```

but the strange looking beast:

```
int WINAPI WinMain(HINSTANCE hInstance,
                   HINSTANCE hPrevInstance,
                   LPSTR     lpCmdLine,
                   int       nCmdShow)
```

Let's go through this one step at a time.

You can basically ignore the WINAPI part. It is just a macro defined in WINDEF.H, like this:

```
#define WINAPI _stdcall
```

And that tells the compiler how to create machine code in a way that is compatible with Windows. If you omit it, your program may still compile and run, but you should get a warning during compilation. The bottom line is you should always make sure your WinMain function includes WINAPI. Now on to those strange-looking parameters...

The first parameter, hInstance, is an *instance handle.* This is basically an ID given to you by Windows at run time that uniquely identifies your program. Occasionally you will make a call to one of the many Win32 API functions, and you will be required to pass your instance handle as a parameter. Windows uses this handle to identify your program among any other programs which may be running at the same time.

The second parameter is also an instance handle, but nowadays this is always set to NULL. In the past, it was used in 16-bit Windows applications for opening several copies of the same program, but it is no longer necessary.

lpCmdLine is similar to the DOS main() function's argc and argv[] parameters. It's simply a way of passing command-line parameters to your application. A LPSTR is defined in WINNT.H as a pointer to a character string. When you run your application from the command line, the string lpCmdLine will contain everything you typed, except the program name. So, for example, if your program is called MyGame.exe, and you typed in **MyGame /s/d/log.txt**, lpCmpLine will contain the characters, "/s/d/log.txt".

The final parameter, nCmdShow, tells your program how it should be initially displayed. There are many different parameters for this, which are summarized in Table 1.1.

When a user creates a shortcut to your application on the desktop or in the start menu, he can specify how the application should open. So, if the user decides he wants the window to open maximized, nCmdShow would be set to SW_SHOWMAXIMIZED.

Okay, I've explained WinMain, now it's time to take a look at the line:

```
MessageBox(NULL, "Hello World!", "MsgBox", 0);
```

This is simply a call to one of the thousands of Win32 API functions. All it does it print a message box to the screen in a style defined by several parameters. This little

Table 1.1   nCmdShow Options

Parameter	Meaning
`SW_HIDE`	Hides the window and activates another window.
`SW_MINIMIZE`	Minimizes the specified window and activates the top-level window in the system's list.
`SW_RESTORE`	Activates and displays a window. If the window is minimized or maximized, Windows restores it to its original size and position (same as `SW_SHOWNORMAL`).
`SW_SHOW`	Activates a window and displays it in its current size and position.
`SW_SHOWMAXIMIZED`	Activates a window and displays it as a maximized window.
`SW_SHOWMINIMIZED`	Activates a window and displays it as an icon.
`SW_SHOWMINNOACTIVE`	Displays a window as an icon. The active window remains active.
`SW_SHOWNA`	Displays a window in its current state. The active window remains active.
`SW_SHOWNOACTIVATE`	Displays a window in its most recent size and position. The active window remains active.
`SW_SHOWNORMAL`	Activates and displays a window. If the window is minimized or maximized, Windows restores it to its original size and position (same as `SW_RESTORE`).

function comes in very handy; it's a particularly good way of passing error information to the user. If you have a function that you think is error prone, you can simply do something, such as:

```
if (error)
{
  MessageBox(hwnd, "Details of the error", "Error!", 0);
}
```

Let's take a look at the function prototype:

```
int MessageBox(HWND    hWnd,       // handle of owner window
            LPCTSTR lpText,        // address of text in message box
            LPCTSTR lpCaption,     // address of title of message box
            UINT    uType);        // style of message box
```

hWnd is the handle of the window you want your message box to be attached to. You'll be using handles frequently in your Windows programming, and I'll discuss them in detail soon. In the HelloWorld1 program, hWnd is set to NULL, which means the message box will be attached to the desktop.

lpText is a null terminated string containing the message you want displayed.

lpCaption is a null terminated string, which is displayed as the caption to the message box.

Finally, uType is the style the message box is to be displayed in. There are loads of styles available, defined in groups of flags that you can combine to create even more styles (see Table 1.2). Look in your win32 documentation for the complete listing.

Table 1.2   Message Box uType Styles

General Settings

Flag	Meaning
MB_ABORTRETRYIGNORE	The message box contains three push buttons: Abort, Retry, and Ignore.
MB_OK	The message box contains one push button: OK. This is the default.
MB_OKCANCEL	The message box contains two push buttons: OK and Cancel.
MB_RETRYCANCEL	The message box contains two push buttons: Retry and Cancel.
MB_YESNO	The message box contains two push buttons: Yes and No.
MB_YESNOCANCEL	The message box contains three push buttons: Yes, No, and Cancel.

Icon Types

Flag	Meaning
MB_ICONWARNING	An exclamation-point icon appears in the message box.
MB_ICONASTERISK	An icon consisting of a lowercase letter i in a circle appears in the message box.
MB_ICONQUESTION	A question-mark icon appears in the message box.
MB_ICONSTOP	A stop-sign icon appears in the message box.

To combine the flags, you use the logical OR. Therefore, to create a message box with OK and Cancel buttons, which appears with a stop-sign icon, you would set the uType value to MB_OKCANCEL | MB_ICONSTOP. Easy.

Like most Win32 function calls, MessageBox will give you a return value. In the HelloWorld1 example, the return value is of no concern, and you ignore it, but often you will want some feedback from the user. The MessageBox function returns zero if there is not enough memory to create a message box or one of the following:

IDABORT	Abort button was selected.
IDCANCEL	Cancel button was selected.
IDIGNORE	Ignore button was selected.
IDNO	No button was selected.
IDOK	OK button was selected.
IDRETRY	Retry button was selected.
IDYES	Yes button was selected.

That wraps up the first lesson. Okay, I'll admit, I haven't actually showed you how to create a proper application window yet, but I wanted to lead you in gradually. I bet, though, that you've been wondering about all those weird looking variable name prefixes, such as lp, sz, and h. Well, Microsoft programmers all use a programming convention called *Hungarian Notation*, and it's probably a good idea to chat about that before I delve any further into the mysteries of Win32 programming.

Hungarian Notation: What's That About?

Hungarian Notation is the brainchild of a Microsoft employee named Dr. Charles Simonyi. It's named Hungarian Notation because, you guessed it, Charles is from Hungary. Basically, it's a naming convention that prefixes each variable name with letters that describe that variables type, and then a short description of the variable that commences with a capital letter. For example, if I needed an integer to keep a record of the score in a game, I might name it iScore. Hungarian Notation was invented out of the necessity of creating a coding standard that Microsoft programmers could adhere to. Imagine the mess a company could get into if all its programmers used a different naming convention...

Although this system seems cumbersome, and some of the names look like a language from a far-off country, once you adopt it you'll probably find it's actually very useful. I say probably because there are programmers who loathe this type of notation, and you may be one of them. The Usenet is filled with threads arguing the pros and cons of Hungarian Notation; it's amazing how so many people can be emotive about the subject. After all, in the end, it comes down to personal preference (unless you work for Microsoft, then you have no choice). Whatever your view though, you are going to have to learn the convention if you are going to program in Windows. That's the bottom line. So what do those prefixes mean? Well, Table 1.3 lists the more common ones:

Table 1.3   Hungarian Notation Prefixes

Prefix	Type
sz	pointer to first character of a zero terminated string
str	string
i	int
n	number or int
ui	unsigned int
c	char
w	WORD (unsigned short)
dw	DWORD (unsigned long)
fn	function pointer
d	double
by	byte
l	long
p	pointer
lp	long pointer
lpstr	long pointer to a string
h	handle
m_	class member
g_	global type
hwnd	Window handle
hdc	handle to a Windows device context

So now when you see variables such as g_iScore, szWindowClassName, and m_dSpeed, you'll know exactly what they are describing. As you'll discover when you look at my code, I have adopted my own version of Hungarian Notation, because I find it incredibly useful—as do thousands of other programmers. With Hungarian Notation, you can look at someone else's code and immediately understand all the variable types without having to refer back to their definitions. I have to add here that I do not use Hungarian Notation for every variable. If a variable is used in a small function, I'll use whatever I think is appropriate, because it should be obvious what the variable is. For example, if I'm writing a function that will take an error string as a parameter and display a message box, I would declare it like this:

```
void ErrorMsg(char* error);
```

and not like this:

```
void ErrorMsg(char*  szError);
```

In addition, I prefix all my classes with the capital letter C and all my structs with the capital letter S (now that's what I call thinking!). I also use my own convention, based on the Hungarian style, for things like 2D/3D vectors and the STL vector class. So a typical class definition might look like this:

```
class CMyClass
{
private:

  int           m_iHealth;
  S2DVector     m_vPosition;
  vector<float> m_vecfWeights;

public:

  CMyClass();
};
```

Got it? Okay, let's go dance with the devil...

Your First Window

Before you can create a window, the first thing you must do is create your own *window class* and then *register* it, so that the operating system knows what type of window you want displayed and how you want it to behave. Windows can be any size and they may or may not have borders, scroll bars, and menus. They may include buttons or toolbars and they can be any color. The options are almost endless. Even the little message box I just created was a type of predefined window. What you most often want, however, is a window into which you can place text and draw graphics, and this is what I'm going to show you how to create now. The code to accompany the next few pages is in the HelloWorld2 project on the CD-ROM.

Registering Your Window

The type of window you want is defined by creating your own window class structure. To do this, you must fill in a WNDCLASSEX structure. This structure looks like this:

```
typedef struct _WNDCLASSEX {
    UINT     cbSize;
    UINT     style;
    WNDPROC  lpfnWndProc;
    int      cbClsExtra;
    int      cbWndExtra;
    HANDLE   hInstance;
    HICON    hIcon;
    HCURSOR  hCursor;
    HBRUSH   hbrBackground;
    LPCTSTR  lpszMenuName;
    LPCTSTR  lpszClassName;
    HICON    hIconSm;
} WNDCLASSEX;
```

Argh! I hear you scream—more weird parameters! Oh yes, you're going to be seeing this sort of thing quite a lot from here on in. But stay calm, and try not to panic. Take a few deep breaths if you need to. I assure you everything will be okay in the long run. Let's go through each member in more detail.

cbSize holds the size, in bytes, of the structure. You set this to

```
cbSize = sizeof(WNDCLASSEX);
```

NOTE

Windows used to use a structure called WNDCLASS, but Microsoft made some improvements and designed the newer WNDCLASSEX structure. You'll see EX added to quite a few structure names for the same reason. You can still use the older structures, by the way, but there's not much point. It'd be like entering a 1930s sports car into a present day Formula One race. (Well, maybe the difference is not *that* extreme, but you get my point.)

Always make sure you set it, or when you register your class, Windows will spit it right back out at you.

`style` is the style the window will appear in. You set it by choosing several flags and logically `OR`ing them together—just like you can do for a message box. The most common configuration for the style is:

```
style = CS_HREDRAW | CS_VREDRAW;
```

which tells the Windows API that you want your window redrawn whenever the user changes the height or the width. There are quite a few style options that you'll find listed in the Win32 API help file.

`lpfnWndProc` is a function pointer to the *Windows Procedure*. I'll be talking a lot more about this shortly. That will be when things start to get *really* interesting.

`cbClsExtra`/`cbWndExtra`: You needn't worry about the parameters. You will nearly always set these to zero. They exist to allow you to create a few more bytes of storage space for your Windows class, if you so require (which you probably won't).

`hInstance`: Remember the `hInstance` parameter from `WinMain`? This is what the Windows class structure is asking for. You just fill this field in using the `hInstance` you get from `WinMain`.

```
hInstance = hInstance;
```

`hIcon` is a handle to the icon that you want your application to use. It is displayed when you use Alt+Tab to task switch. You can either use one of the default Windows icons, or you can define your own and include it as a *resource*. I'll be showing you how to do that in the next chapter. To get a handle to an icon, call `LoadIcon`.

This is how you would use one of the default icons:

```
hIcon = LoadIcon(NULL, IDI_APPLICATION);
```

`hCursor`: You guessed it—`hCursor` is a handle to the cursor the application will display. Normally, you would set this to the default arrow cursor. To obtain a handle to a cursor, you call `LoadCursor` like this:

```
hCursor = LoadCursor(NULL, IDC_ARROW);
```

`hbrBackground` is a field used to specify the background color of the client area of the window you create. The client area is the bit of the window that you actually draw and print to. The `hbr` prefix means that it's a "handle to a brush." A brush is something Windows uses to fill in areas with color or even with predefined patterns. You can define your own brushes, or you can use one of the stock brushes already defined by the API. So, if you want your background to be white, you would set this field to

```
hbrBackground = (HBRUSH)GetStockObject(WHITE_BRUSH);
```

I'll be discussing brushes in a lot more detail in Chapter 2, "Further Adventures with Windows Programming."

lpszMenuName is used to set the name of the menu—if you require one. If you don't require pull-down menus, such as edit, save, and load, you can set this to NULL. I'll also be showing you how to create menus in the next chapter.

lpszClassName is the name you give to your Windows class. This can be anything you like. Let your imagine run wild.

hIconSm is a handle to the icon that will appear in the task bar and in the top left-hand corner of your Windows application. Again, you can design your own and include it as a resource, or you can use one of the default icons.

After you've created your Windows class, you need to register it by calling RegisterClass. You pass this function a pointer to the WNDCLASSEX structure. Taking the example from the HelloWorld2 program on the CD-ROM, the whole thing looks like this:

> **TIP**
>
> It's worth mentioning at this point that very few programmers actually remember all these parameters. What most of us tend to do is keep a basic Windows template file we can cut and paste from whenever we start a new project. It makes life much easier.

```
//our window class structure
WNDCLASSEX      winclass;

// first fill in the window class structure
winclass.cbSize          = sizeof(WNDCLASSEX);
winclass.style           = CS_HREDRAW | CS_VREDRAW;
winclass.lpfnWndProc     = WindowProc;
winclass.cbClsExtra      = 0;
winclass.cbWndExtra      = 0;
winclass.hInstance       = hInstance;
winclass.hIcon           = LoadIcon(NULL, IDI_APPLICATION);
winclass.hCursor         = LoadCursor(NULL, IDC_ARROW);
winclass.hbrBackground   = (HBRUSH)GetStockObject (WHITE_BRUSH);
winclass.lpszMenuName    = NULL;
```

```
winclass.lpszClassName  = g_szWindowClassName;
winclass.hIconSm        = LoadIcon(NULL, IDI_APPLICATION);

 //register the window class
if (!RegisterClassEx(&winclass))
{
  MessageBox(NULL, "Class Registration Failed!", "Error", 0);

  //exit the application
  return 0;
}
```

This creates a Windows class with a white background, no menu, the default arrow cursor, default icon that knows to redraw the window if the user alters the size. Notice when registering the class, I've made use of that nifty little MessageBox function to inform the user of any errors.

Creating the Window

Now that you've registered a Windows class, you can get on with the business of actually creating it and displaying it to the user. To do this, you must call the CreateWindowEx function. You guessed it—that means filling in another load of parameters. Let's take a look at the function prototype:

```
HWND CreateWindowEx(
    DWORD     dwExStyle,      // extended window style
    LPCTSTR   lpClassName,    // pointer to registered class name
    LPCTSTR   lpWindowName,   // pointer to window name
    DWORD     dwStyle,        // window style
    int       x,              // horizontal position of window
    int       y,              // vertical position of window
    int       nWidth,         // window width
    int       nHeight,        // window height
    HWND      hWndParent,     // handle to parent or owner window
    HMENU     hMenu,          // handle to menu, or child-window identifier
    HINSTANCE hInstance,      // handle to application instance
    LPVOID    lpParam         // pointer to window-creation data
);
```

Table 1.4   Extended Windows Styles

Style	Description
WS_EX_ACCEPTFILES	Specifies that a window created with this style accepts drag-drop files.
WS_EX_APPWINDOW	Forces a top-level window onto the taskbar when the window is visible.
WS_EX_CLIENTEDGE	Specifies that a window has a border with a sunken edge.
WS_EX_DLGMODALFRAME	Creates a window that has a double border; the window can, optionally, be created with a title bar by specifying the WS_CAPTION style in the dwStyle parameter.
WS_EX_CONTEXTHELP	Includes a question mark in the title bar of the window. When the user clicks the question mark, the cursor changes to a question mark with a pointer. If the user clicks a child window, the child receives a WM_HELP message. The child window should pass the message to the parent window procedure, which should call the WinHelp function using the HELP_WM_HELP command. The Help application displays a pop-up window that typically contains help for the child window.
WS_EX_WINDOWEDGE	Specifies that a window has a border with a raised edge.

dwExStyle is used to set flags for any extended styles you may want. I've listed some of the available styles in Table 1.4, but it's unlikely you'll be using any of them for your first few Windows programs. If you don't require any, just set this parameter to NULL.

lpClassName is a pointer to a string, which contains the name of your Windows class. In this example, and in all my future examples, this will be set as g_szWindowClassName.

I always set up my Windows class name and my application name as two global strings, g_szWindowClassName and g_szApplicationName, right at the top of main.h. I do it this way because it makes changing the names at a later date much easier—I only have to look in one place.

lpWindowName is the title you want to appear at the top of your application. In my examples, this is set to g_szApplicationName.

Table 1.5　Windows Styles

Style	Description
WS_BORDER	Creates a window that has a thin-line border.
WS_CAPTION	Creates a window that has a title bar (includes the WS_BORDER style).
WS_HSCROLL	Creates a window that has a horizontal scrollbar.
WS_MAXIMIZE	Creates a window that is initially maximized.
WS_OVERLAPPED	Creates an overlapped window. An overlapped window has a title bar and a border.
WS_OVERLAPPEDWINDOW	Creates an overlapped window with the WS_OVERLAPPED, WS_CAPTION, WS_SYSMENU, WS_THICKFRAME, WS_MINIMIZEBOX, and WS_MAXIMIZEBOX styles. Same as the WS_TILEDWINDOW style.
WS_POPUP	Creates a pop-up window. This style cannot be used with the WS_CHILD style.
WS_THICKFRAME	Creates a window that has a sizing border.
WS_VSCROLL	Creates a window that has a vertical scrollbar.

dwStyle contains the flags that set the styles for your window. There are loads of styles to choose from. Table 1.5 lists some of the more common styles.

The x, y values set the upper-left hand corner of your window. Don't forget that in Windows the y value at the top of your screen is zero and increases as you move down the screen. See Figure 1.6.

nWidth and nHeight set the width and height of your window. I usually #define these values as WINDOW_WIDTH and WINDOW_HEIGHT in the file named defines.h.

hWndParent is a handle to the parent (or owner) of your window. If this is your main application window, set this to NULL; this tells Windows that the desktop is the parent.

hMenu is a handle to the menu you select to appear at the top of your application. I'll discuss menus later on in the chapter, but for now, set this parameter to NULL.

hInstance: You just pass in the hInstance from WinMain.

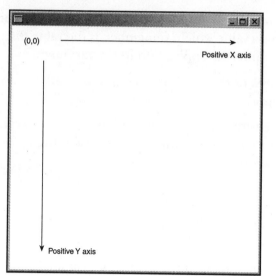

Figure 1.6

The topsy-turvy Windows axes.

lParam is used when you want to create a Multiple Document Interface window, but for now, you can just forget about it and set this value to NULL.

Phew! That's it—you are almost home and dry. This is what the completed CreateWindowEx call from HelloWorld2 looks like:

```
hWnd = CreateWindowEx (NULL,                   // extended style
                    g_szWindowClassName,    // window class name
                    g_szApplicationName,    // window caption
                    WS_OVERLAPPEDWINDOW,    // window style
                    0,                      // initial x position
                    0,                      // initial y position
                    WINDOW_WIDTH,           // initial x size
                    WINDOW_HEIGHT,          // initial y size
                    NULL,                   // parent window handle
                    NULL,                   // window menu handle
                    hInstance,              // program instance handle
                    NULL);                  // creation parameters
```

There's just one last thing you have to do: make the window visible to the user by calling

```
ShowWindow (hwnd, iCmdShow);
UpdateWindow (hwnd);
```

ShowWindow takes two parameters. The first is the handle of the window you want to show, which in this case is the window you just created, hWnd. The second parameter is a flag that specifies how the window is to be shown and whether it is to be minimized, normal, or maximized. Use the `iCmdShow` value which, remember, is the value the user chooses when he creates a shortcut or puts the application in his start menu.

`UpdateWindow` then causes the client area of the window to be painted with whatever brush you specified for the background.

Now, because you have registered a custom Windows class, before your program exits, you must make sure you *unregister* the class. You do this by using the `UnregisterClass` function. It looks like this:

```
BOOL UnregisterClass(
   LPCTSTR lpClassName,   // pointer to class name string
   HINSTANCE hInstance    // handle to application instance
);
```

Now all you do is pass this function the name you used for your custom Windows class and its `hInstance`, and the job's done.

And there you have it—your first window! There is one small problem, however. Compile the HelloWorld2 example and run it. If you have quick eyes—very quick actually—when you run HelloWorld2.exe, you'll see a window flash up for a split second and then close again. Therefore, if you want to use the newly created window, you are going to have to find a way of keeping it on the screen. And you can't do that by creating an endless loop after `UpdateWindow`. If you did, you would see your window, but you wouldn't be able to do anything with it at all. You wouldn't even be able to close it! Therefore, you need another solution, and fortunately, that solution is provided by the marvelous, magical *Windows Message Pump*.

The Windows Message Pump

Whenever you open an application, Windows is working in the background—moving your cursor, checking to see if you've resized or moved any Windows, checking whether you task switch, checking if you minimize or maximize the application, and so on. It manages to do all this because Windows is an *event-driven* operating system. Events, or *messages* as they are more often called, are generated when the user does something, and they are stored in a *message queue* until the active application processes them. Windows creates a message whenever you move a window, close a window, move your cursor, or press a key on your keyboard. Therefore, the programmer, that's you, has to find a way of reading the messages from the queue and processing them. Do this by using a Windows message pump immediately after `UpdateWindow(hWnd)` like this:

```
//this will hold any windows messages we grab from the queue
MSG msg;

//entry point of our message pump
while (GetMessage (&msg, NULL, 0, 0))
{
  TranslateMessage(&msg);
  DispatchMessage(&msg);
} //end message pump
```

The `msg` variable holds the messages and is a structure that is defined like this:

```
typedef struct tagMSG {
    HWND    hwnd;
    UINT    message;
    WPARAM  wParam;
    LPARAM  lParam;
    DWORD   time;
    POINT   pt;
} MSG;
```

`hwnd` is the handle to the window the message is directed at.

`message` is the message identifier. There are loads of these, and almost all of them start with `WM_`. So, for example, when your application window is first created, Windows puts a `WM_CREATE` message on the message queue, and when you close your application, a `WM_CLOSE` message is generated. You can find most of these identifiers listed in `WINUSER.H`. As your knowledge of Windows programming progresses, you'll learn how to handle more of these and even how to create your own custom messages. Some of the more common message identifiers are listed in Table 1.6.

`wParam` and `lParam` are two 32-bit parameters that contain additional information about the message. For example, if the message is a `WM_KEYUP` message, the `wParam` parameter contains information about which key has just been released, and `lParam` gives additional information, such as the previous key state and repeat count.

`time` is the time the message was placed in the even cue.

Table 1.6 Common Windows Messages

Message	Description
WM_KEYUP	This message is dispatched whenever the user releases a non-system key.
WM_KEYDOWN	As above but when the key is pressed (no surprises there).
WM_MOUSEMOVE	This message is sent whenever the cursor is moved.
WM_SIZE	This message is dispatched when the user resizes a window.
WM_VSCROLL	This message is sent whenever the vertical scroll bar is moved.
WM_HSCROLL	I'll let you guess this one.
WM_ACTIVATE	This message is sent to both the window that is being activated by the user and the window that's being deactivated—the value of wParam tells you which.

pt is a POINT structure, which gives the coordinates of the mouse at the time the message was placed in the queue. The POINT structure looks like this

```
typedef struct tagPOINT {
    LONG x;
    LONG y;
} POINT;
```

Now that you understand what a message is, let's go through the message pump one line at a time.

```
while (GetMessage (&msg, NULL, 0, 0))
{
```

GetMessage is a function that retrieves a message from the message queue. If there's not a message in the queue, it waits until there is one. It then obtains the message by passing a pointer to a MSG structure for Windows to fill in. The second parameter is the handle of the window for which you want to retrieve messages. In this example, you want to handle all messages being passed to Windows, therefore you set this parameter to NULL. The third and fourth values are additional filters you needn't be concerned with here, so just set them to zero. If the message received by GetMessage is anything other than WM_QUIT, GetMessage returns a non-zero value. When the message has been received by GetMessage, the message is removed from the queue.

```
TranslateMessage(&msg);
```

When you press a key down, you get a `WM_KEYDOWN` message, and when you release
that key, Windows generates a `WM_KEYUP` message. If you press the Alt key, you generate a `WM_SYSKEYDOWN` message, and when you release a key that was pressed when the
Alt key was held down, you get a `WM_SYSKEYUP` message. You can see how the message
queue can quickly get clogged up with messages if the user is using the keyboard a
lot. `TranslateMessage` combines these keyboard messages into one `WM_CHAR` message.

```
DispatchMessage(&msg);
```

Okay, so now you understand how to retrieve the messages from the message queue,
but you still don't know what to do with them, do you? Well, that's what
`DispatchMessage` is for. Remember a few pages back when you were registering the
Windows class, and you had to fill in the `lpfnWndProc` field with a function pointer to
a `Windows Procedure`? Well, that function—which was named `WindowProc`—is a callback
function to which `DispatchMessage` sends the message. `WindowProc` then handles that
message in whatever way you see fit. For example, if the user presses a key, the
message pump puts a `WM_KEYDOWN` message in the queue, and `WindowProc` then performs the necessary function for that key press. If the user resizes the window, a
`WM_SIZE` message will be sent to your `WindowProc`, and, if you coded it correctly, your
display will be resized accordingly.

Therefore, the application will remain in the message pump loop, endlessly handling messages until the user closes the window and a `WM_QUIT` message is generated—at which point `GetMessage` returns zero and the application exits the message
pump and shuts down. If the last few sentences were a little confusing, don't
worry—by the time you finish the next section, it will all make sense.

The Windows Procedure

At this point, you can pat yourself on the back. You've come a long way in just a few
pages, and there's only one more thing to learn before you've got the basics of
creating a Windows application under your belt: the *Windows procedure*.

A Windows procedure is defined like this

```
LRESULT CALLBACK WindowProc(
    HWND    hwnd;       //handle to window
    UINT    uMsg;       //the message identifier
    WPARAM  wParam;     //first message
    LPARAM  lParam;     //second message
};
```

LRESULT is a type defined for the return value of a Windows procedure. Normally, if all goes well, this will be a non-zero value.

CALLBACK is used to inform Windows that WindowProc is a callback function and is to be called whenever Windows generates an event that needs handling. You don't have to call your Windows procedure WindowProc by the way, you can call it anything you want, I just happen to always call mine WindowProc.

> **NOTE**
> It's possible to have several windows open simultaneously, each with a different handle and separately defined WindowProcs to handle their respective messages.

hwnd is the handle of the window you are handling messages for.

uMsg is the message ID of the message to be processed. It's the same as the message field in the MSG structure.

wParam and lParam are the same as the lParam and wParam contained in the MSG structure and contain any additional information about the message you may require.

So, let's take a look at the simple Windows procedure I've written for the HelloWorld3 program:

```
LRESULT CALLBACK WindowProc (HWND   hwnd,
                            UINT   msg,
                            WPARAM wParam,
                            LPARAM lParam)
{
  switch (msg)
  {

    //A WM_CREATE msg is sent when your application window is first
    //created
    case WM_CREATE:
    {
      PlaySound("window_open.wav", NULL, SND_FILENAME | SND_ASYNC);
      return 0;
    }
    case WM_PAINT:
    {
      PAINTSTRUCT ps;
```

```
    BeginPaint (hwnd, &ps);

    //**this is where we do any drawing to the screen**

    EndPaint (hwnd, &ps);
    return 0;
  }
  case WM_DESTROY:
  {
    // kill the application, this sends a WM_QUIT message
    PostQuitMessage (0);
    return 0;
  }

  }//end switch

return DefWindowProc (hwnd, msg, wParam, lParam);
}//end WindowProc
```

As you can see, the WindowProc turns out to be one big switch statement. The WindowProc shown here only handles three messages: WM_CREATE, WM_PAINT, and WM_DESTROY, but if you run the program, you'll see this is sufficient to give you a window that you can move around the screen, minimize, maximize, and even resize. See Figure 1.7. It even plays you a wav file when you open it, as a little treat for getting this far! Great, eh? You're really on your way now.

Let me take some time to go through each part of the WindowProc.

Figure 1.7

Your first window.

The WM_CREATE Message

A `WM_CREATE` message is generated when you first create your window. The message is grabbed by the message pump and sent to `WindowProc` where it is handled by the `switch` statement.

```
case WM_CREATE:
{
  PlaySound("window_open.wav", NULL, SND_FILENAME | SND_ASYNC);
  return 0;
}
```

In this example, when the program enters the `WM_CREATE` part of the switch statement, it uses the handy `PlaySound` feature of the API to play a wav file as the window opens up. Because I've used it, I'll take a few lines to explain that function for you. The definition of `PlaySound` looks like this:

```
BOOL PlaySound(
  LPCSTR  pszSound,
  HMODULE hmod,
  DWORD   fdwSound
);
```

`pszSound` is a string, which specifies the sound to play. If this value is set to `NULL`, any currently playing sound is stopped in its tracks.

`hmod` is a handle to the executable file that contains the wav as a resource. I'll be going into resources in the next chapter. Here though, I'm just specifying a filename, so you can set this parameter to `NULL`.

`fdwSound` is the flag used for playing sound. See your documentation for a complete list, but here I've used `SND_FILENAME`, which tells `PlaySound` that

> **NOTE**
>
> You must include the Windows multimedia library to use the `PlaySound` function. Therefore, make sure your compiler links to winmm.lib in your project settings before you attempt to compile the HelloWorld3 example.

`pszSound` is a filename, and `SND_ASYNC` makes sure the sound is played asynchronously. This means that the `PlaySound` function will start playing the sound and then return immediately.

The WM_PAINT Message

A WM_PAINT message is generated whenever the system makes a request to paint a portion of the application's window. A lot of newcomers to Windows programming think that Windows magically takes care of your window once it has been created, but this is not the case. Every time a user moves another window in front of your own or minimizes/maximizes/resizes your window, a WM_PAINT message is dispatched and you have to handle the repainting. The good news is that Windows handles the region that needs to be repainted. If only a portion of your window is overlapped and then uncovered, Windows knows not to redraw the whole window and will only redraw the portion that was overlapped. The region that needs repainting is usually referred to as the invalid region or the update region. See Figure 1.8. Once a WM_PAINT message is dispatched, and the call to BeginPaint has been made, Windows knows the region has been validated and any other WM_PAINT messages (that may have accumulated) are removed from the message queue.

```
case WM_PAINT:
{
  PAINTSTRUCT ps;
  BeginPaint (hwnd, &ps);

  //**this is where we do any drawing to the screen**

  EndPaint (hwnd, &ps);
  return 0;
}
```

The first thing to do when handling a WM_PAINT message is to create a PAINTSTRUCT. This structure is used by BeginPaint to pass the information needed to paint the Windows. Let's take a look at the PAINTSTRUCT definition:

```
typedef struct tagPAINTSTRUCT {
    HDC   hdc;
    BOOL  fErase;
    RECT  rcPaint;
    BOOL  fRestore;
    BOOL  fIncUpdate;
    BYTE  rgbReserved[32];
} PAINTSTRUCT;
```

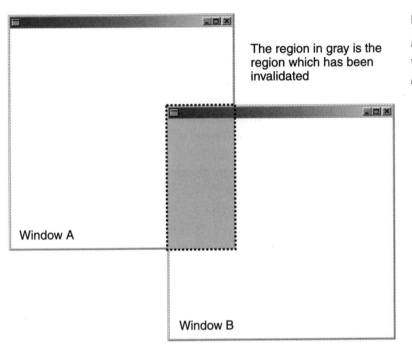

Figure 1.8

How an overlapping window produces an invalidated region.

The region in gray is the region which has been invalidated

Window A

Window B

`hdc` is a handle to a device context. For the purposes of this chapter you can ignore it, but you'll be using device contexts frequently in the next chapter to start drawing into the window.

`fErase` tells the application whether or not the background should be repainted in the color you specified when you created your Windows class. If this is non–zero, the background will be repainted.

`rcPaint` is a `RECT` structure that tells the application which area has been invalidated and needs repainting. A `RECT` structure is a very simple structure defining the four corners of a rectangle, and it looks like this:

```
typedef struct _RECT {
    LONG left;
    LONG top;
    LONG right;
    LONG bottom;
} RECT;
```

The remainder of the parameters are reserved for use by Windows, therefore you can ignore them.

When you call BeginPaint, the PAINTSTRUCT, ps, is filled in and the background is usually redrawn. Now is the time to do any drawing to the screen, and then tell Windows you have finished drawing by calling the EndPaint function.

The WM_DESTROY Message

This is a very important message, because it tells you the user wants to close the application window. The normal way of dealing with this is to call PostQuitMessage(0), which will put a WM_QUIT message in the message queue. Remember, the GetMessage function used in the message pump will return zero if it finds a WM_QUIT message, and the application will terminate.

> **TIP**
>
> If you don't use PostQuitMessage(0) to send a WM_QUIT message, the application window will close, but your program will still be running! This is one of the ways applications hide away in your taskbar.

```
case WM_DESTROY:
{
  PostQuitMessage (0);
  return 0;
}
```

What about the Rest?

Although you now know how to handle three of the messages, you may be wondering what happens to all the other messages sent to the WindowProc that do not get handled by you. Well, fortunately, Windows has a wonderful function called DefWindowProc, which deals with any messages you don't handle yourself. So, you return from your WindowProc like this:

> **TIP**
>
> Although programs don't generally call Windows procedures directly, you can choose to put messages on the queue yourself (and therefore have them handled by your WindowProc) by using the SendMessage function. You can find details of this function in your Windows API documentation.

```
return DefWindowProc (hwnd, msg, wParam, lParam);
```

and Windows will handle the extraneous messages for you. Good, eh?

Keyboard Input

Before I finish this chapter, I want to cover basic keyboard handling. When you depress a key, you generate a WM_KEYDOWN or WM_SYSKEYDOWN message, and when you release a key, you generate a WM_KEYUP or WM_SYSKEYUP message. The WM_SYSKEYUP and WM_SYSKEYDOWN messages are used for keystrokes that are generally more important to the Windows operating system than to the application. This type of message is produced when the user presses Alt+Tab or Alt+F4, for example. For now, you don't need to be concerned with the WM_SYSKEYUP or WM_SYSKEYDOWN messages, just let the DefWindowProc do its job and handle those for you.

For all of these messages wParam holds the virtual key code of the key being pressed and lParam contains additional information, such as the repeat count, the scan code, and so forth. I won't be using any of the information contained in the lParam in this book.

Virtual Key Codes

In the old days, programmers had to write code to read keystrokes straight from the hardware of the keyboard. Each different type of keyboard produces its own code for each key; these are known as the *scan codes*. This meant that every manufacturer had their own setups and, therefore, the code for a "c" keystroke press on one keyboard could be the code for a "1" on another! Obviously, this was a real pain in the backside. Fortunately, Windows solved the problem by introducing *virtual key codes*. This way you don't have to worry about the hardware, and you can just get on with the programming. Table 1.7 lists some of the most common virtual key codes used in games.

If the user presses a number or a letter, the virtual key code is the ASCII code for that letter or number.

Therefore, all you have to do to read keyboard input is to code a message handler for the WM_KEYDOWN or WM_KEYUP messages. I've added a simple WM_KEYUP message handler in the HelloWorld4 code example to check for the Escape key being pressed. If it detects that the Escape key has been pressed, the program will be exited. Here's what the relevant section of the WindowProc looks like:

```
case WM_KEYUP:
{
  switch(wParam)
  {
    case VK_ESCAPE:
```

Table 1.7   Commonly Used Virtual Key Codes

Key	Description
VK_RETURN	Enter
VK_ESCAPE	Escape
VK_SPACE	Spacebar
VK_TAB	Tab
VK_BACK	Backspace
VK_UP	Up Arrow
VK_DOWN	Down Arrow
VK_LEFT	Left Arrow
VK_RIGHT	Right Arrow
VK_HOME	Home
VK_PRIOR	Page Up
VK_NEXT	Page Down
VK_INSERT	Insert
VK_DELETE	Delete
VK_SNAPSHOT	Print Screen

```
  {
    //if the escape key has been pressed exit the program
    PostQuitMessage(0);
  }
 }
}
```

As you can see, you first check for a WM_KEYUP message and then create a switch based upon the wParam part of the message. That's the bit that holds the virtual key code. If the Escape key (VK_ESCAPE) is detected, the PostQuitMessage(0) call is used to send a WM_QUIT message, and the application terminates.

Another way of grabbing information from the keyboard is by using the GetKeyboardState, GetKeyState, or GetAsnyncKeyState functions. These can be very handy functions, especially when you're writing games; you can test for key presses anywhere in your code, and you don't need to go through the message pump. GetAsyncKeyState is probably the most useful, because you can use it to check if just a single key has been depressed. Its prototype looks like this:

```
SHORT GetAsyncKeyState(
  int vKey    // virtual-key code
);
```

To test if a key is pressed or not, pass the function the virtual key code of that key and test to see if the most significant bit (the leftmost bit) of the return value is set to 1. So, if you wanted to test for the spacebar being pressed, you'd do something like this:

```
if (GetAsyncKeyState(VK_LEFT) & 0x8000)
{
  //rotate left
}
```

If you are curious about the other two functions, look them up in your documentation, although it's unlikely you'll ever need them in practice.

Tah Dah!

And that's it! Your first Windows program is completed. Okay, so it doesn't do anything but sit there and wait for you to move it or close it, but I bet you feel a terrific sense of achievement for getting this far. I know I did when I first started Windows programming. And I can assure you, almost everything you learn from here on will be a *whole* lot more fun.

CHAPTER 2

Further Adventures with Windows Programming

"I cannot articulate enough to express my dislike to people who think that understanding spoils your experience... How would they know?"

Marvin Minsky

At last, on to the fun stuff! Deep down inside, the little kid in us all loves to draw and paint, and that's exactly how I'm going to start this chapter. You learned how to create a window—your blank canvas—in the previous chapter so now all I have to do is show you how to make use of the Windows drawing, painting, and text tools. Once you've had some fun with those, I'll show you exactly what *resources* are and how to use them to create your own menus, icons, mouse cursors, and so on. By the time you've finished this chapter, you'll have enough knowledge of Windows programming to understand the code examples used in the rest of the book—and then I can move on to the business of genetic algorithms and neural networks. There will be the occasional extras I'll have to cover with you later, but I'll go into those at the appropriate time.

The Windows GDI

The part of Windows that is responsible for drawing graphics to the screen is called the Graphics Device Interface, or GDI for short. This is a collection of many different functions that can be called. It includes functions for drawing shapes, drawing lines, filling in shapes, drawing text, clipping, setting the color and width of your drawing tools, and so on. The graphics you can display in a window can be divided up into four different areas:

- **Text.** The text parts of the GDI obviously play a very important role. I mean, where would you be if you couldn't output text? Fortunately, the GDI comes with a comprehensive suite of text formatting and output tools so that you can create and write text to the screen in just about any way you choose.

- **Lines, shapes, and curves.** The GDI provides ample support for drawing straight lines, curved lines (Bezier curves), primitive shapes (such as rectangles and ellipses), and polygons. A polygon is simply a shape made up from a series of connected points; the last point being connected to the first point to complete the shape. To draw, you first have to create a *pen* to draw with, and then you draw the required shape with that pen.

- **Bitmaps.** The GDI provides many functions for handling bitmaps. You can load bitmaps, resize bitmaps, save bitmaps, and copy bitmaps from one place to another. This copying is usually referred to by game programmers as *blitting*.

- **Filled Areas.** In addition to pens to draw with, you can also create your own *brushes*. Brushes are used to fill in regions and shapes on the screen.

In addition to providing functions for drawing and outputting text, the GDI also has many functions for defining regions and paths, handling clipping, defining palettes, and outputting to other devices, such as printers. To go into the GDI in all its magnificent detail would be a mammoth undertaking so all I'm going to do is teach you the very basics. But don't worry, even with the basics you can do loads of cool stuff—as you will see.

> **NOTE**
>
> The GDI is well known in the gaming community for being slow. And slow it is compared with APIs, such as OpenGL or Microsoft's DirectX. But I've chosen to use it for my examples because it's simple to use and understand, fast enough for our requirements, and, more significantly, my code isn't going to be cluttered with confusing references to a complex API.

Device Contexts

Device Contexts, or DCs as you'll come to know them, play a very important role in the process of drawing graphics and text using the GDI. Before you can draw to any graphics output device, such as your screen, a printer, or even a bitmap in memory, you have to get a *handle to a device context* for that device. You'll find with Windows that if you want to use something, you have to get a handle to it first. There are handles to brushes, pens, cursors, desktops, the instance to your window (remember hInstance?), icons, bitmaps… the list goes on and on. I suppose handles are a bit like licences. You need a driver's licence to drive a car and a liquor licence to serve beer; likewise, you need to obtain a handle to the particular type of object or device that you want to manipulate. So you ask Windows, "Hey, is it okay for me to use this window to draw on?" and Windows will give you a licence—the handle to that window—so you can use it.

So How Do You Get a Handle?

There are a few ways to get a handle to a device context, or an HDC as I shall now refer to them. One of them you've already seen, but you've probably forgotten all about it—I know I would have, so let me jog your memory.

Remember creating the WM_PAINT message handler in Chapter 1? The first thing created was a PAINTSTRUCT for Windows to fill in with the details of the window. This is what the PAINTSTRUCT looked like:

```
typedef struct tagPAINTSTRUCT {
    HDC  hdc;
    BOOL fErase;
    RECT rcPaint;
    BOOL fRestore;
    BOOL fIncUpdate;
    BYTE rgbReserved[32];
} PAINTSTRUCT;
```

Now you can see that the first field, hdc, is the HDC. So, if you do any painting within the WM_PAINT section of your WindowProc, you can use hdc as the handle to your window.

There's another thing I didn't tell you in the last chapter: When you make a call to BeginPaint, it fills in the PAINTSTRUCT for you, as well as returning an HDC. So an alternative way of grabbing the HDC would be something like this:

> **NOTE**
>
> The handle received from a PAINTSTRUCT is only valid for drawing within the region defined by the RECT, rcPaint. If you want to draw outside this area, you should use an alternative way of grabbing an HDC.

```
case WM_PAINT:
{
    PAINTSTRUCT ps;
    HDC hdc;
    hdc = BeginPaint (hwnd, &ps);

    //**this is where we do any drawing using your hdc

    EndPaint (hwnd, &ps);
    return 0;
}
```

You don't *have* to do all of your drawing in the WM_PAINT section of the WindowProc, however. You can draw at any time, as long as you get permission from Windows by obtaining an HDC. You can grab an HDC anytime by using the GetDC function:

```
HDC hdc = GetDC(hWnd);
```

in which `hWnd` is the handle to the window you want the HDC for. Whenever you create an HDC like this, you must always remember to release it when you are finished using it. You do that by using the `ReleaseDC` function.

```
ReleaseDC(hWnd, hdc);
```

I didn't call `ReleaseDC` in `WM_PAINT` because the function `EndPaint` releases the DC automatically. If you don't release the HDCs you create, you'll start to get resource leaks and your program will probably start doing all sorts of unpleasant things. It may even crash your system. Consider yourself warned.

If you'd like, you can grab an HDC that applies to your entire window (including the system menu and title bar areas), not just the client area. You do this by using `GetWindowDC`.

```
HDC hdc = GetWindowDC(hWnd);
```

And if you really need to, you can even obtain an HDC for the entire screen if you use `NULL` as the argument in `GetDC`.

```
HDC hdc = GetDC(NULL);
```

Cool, huh?

Okay, so now you've learned how to get HDCs; now let me show you how to use them…

Don't Forget!

The thing a lot of newcomers forget is that Windows does not monitor the redrawing of the window for you. Therefore, if you *do* draw outside the `WM_PAINT` section of your `WindowsProc`, you have to make sure that whatever you draw gets redrawn if the display needs updating (for example, if the user drags another window across your own or minimizes and maximizes your window). Otherwise, your display will look messy in no time at all. This is a lesson most of us learn the hard way!

Tools of the Trade: Pens, Brushes, Colors, Lines, and Shapes

When I was a child—way back in the seventies—there was a *really* strange craze for a couple of years. I mean, you get exciting crazes like the Frisbee and skateboarding, and you get fun crazes like the SpaceHopper, and even puzzle crazes like the Rubik's Cube. Only a few, however, are *really* strange. And this craze, I remember, was just that. Wherever you went, wherever you looked, you started to see these pictures on walls made from pins or nails and cotton. They came in lots of different guises, but the simplest was made by getting a rectangular piece of wood, hammering nails at regular intervals up the left-hand side and along the bottom and then attaching the cotton to the nails. If you think of the nails as representing the Y-axis and X–axis, a separate piece of cotton would be attached from the first nail on the X-axis to the last nail on the Y–axis, and then from the second nail on the X-axis to the next to last nail on the Y–axis, and so on until you got something resembling the curve shown in Figure 2.1.

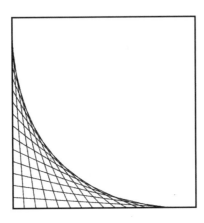

Figure 2.1

A strange passion for curves.

Do you remember them? Kits helping you create more and more sophisticated patterns started to be sold by the thousands. Almost everyone had one. Eventually, just before the fad died out, there were even huge 3D ones you could buy. Ah, such memories…

"Hold it!" I hear you say, "What does this have to do with the Windows GDI?" Well, the first program will be emulating those wonderful works of art. You are going to create your own masterpiece by just drawing a few lines, and it's going to look like Figure 2.2:

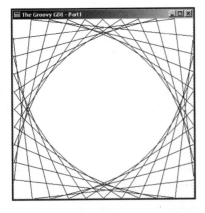

Figure 2.2

Magnificent lines.

You can find the source for this in the GDI_Lines1 project folder on the CD. To create all those magnificent lines, all I had to do was make some changes to the Windows procedure you saw in Chapter 1. Here are the parts of the altered WindowProc:

```
LRESULT CALLBACK WindowProc (HWND    hwnd,
                             UINT    msg,
                             WPARAM wParam,
                             LPARAM lParam)
{
    static int cxClient, cyClient;
```

Two static integers are defined to hold the size of the client area of the window. The client area is the area of the window into which you draw—the area excluding the title bar, any scrollbars, and frame. Any calculations required for the drawing are performed using these values so that if the user resizes the window, the display is rescaled accordingly.

```
    switch (msg)
    {
    case WM_CREATE:
      {
          RECT rect;
          GetClientRect(hwnd, &rect);
          cxClient = rect.right;
          cyClient = rect.bottom;
      }
      break;
```

When the window is first created, you need to determine the width and height of the client area. To do this, create a RECT and pass it to the GetClientRect function, along with a handle to the window. Then extract the information contained in rect and use it to set cxClient and cyClient. Now you know exactly how big the canvas is.

Now on to the drawing. Take a quick look at the WM_PAINT handler, and then I'll talk you through the relevant parts.

```
case WM_PAINT:
{
    PAINTSTRUCT ps;
    BeginPaint (hwnd, &ps);

    //how many lines per side we are going to draw
```

```cpp
const int NumLinesPerSide = 10;

//calculate the step size for the line drawing based upon the
//the window dimensions
int yStep = cyClient/NumLinesPerSide;
int xStep = cxClient/NumLinesPerSide;

//now do some drawing
for (int mult=1; mult<NumLinesPerSide; ++mult)
{

    MoveToEx(ps.hdc, xStep*mult, 0, 0);
    LineTo(ps.hdc, 0, cyClient-yStep*mult);

    MoveToEx(ps.hdc, xStep*mult, cyClient, 0);
    LineTo(ps.hdc, cxClient, cyClient-yStep*mult);

    MoveToEx(ps.hdc, xStep*mult, 0, 0);
    LineTo(ps.hdc, cxClient, yStep*mult);

    MoveToEx(ps.hdc, xStep*mult, cyClient, 0);
    LineTo(ps.hdc, 0, yStep*mult);

}
    EndPaint (hwnd, &ps);
}
```

As you can see, the drawing is fairly straightforward. Note that all the points used in the drawing are calculated from cxClient and cyClient. This is necessary in case the user resizes the window. I'll be talking about that in a moment. For now, I need to explain the functions MoveToEx and LineTo:

If you have a line that goes from A to B, MoveToEx is used to move the point of the pen to point A, and LineTo then uses the pen to draw a line to point B. Here's the prototype for MoveToEx:

```cpp
BOOL MoveToEx(
    HDC      hdc,          // handle to device context
    int      X,            // x-coordinate of new current position
    int      Y,            // y-coordinate of new current position
    LPPOINT  lpPoint       // pointer to old current position
);
```

Give this function a handle to a device context and an X and Y position, and it moves the pen to that point without drawing. lpPoint may be used to retrieve the position of the pen before you started drawing, just in case you have to replace the pen back to its original position for some reason. I'm sure this is useful in some situations, but I've never used it. You can just set it to NULL for now and forget all about it.

Once you have positioned the pen at the beginning of the line, use LineTo to draw the line:

```
BOOL LineTo(
  HDC hdc,     // device context handle
  int nXEnd,   // x-coordinate of line's ending point
  int nYEnd    // y-coordinate of line's ending point
);
```

Again, you need to give LineTo an HDC so it knows into which device it's supposed to draw, and two points telling it the coordinates of what location to draw the line to.

And that's how you draw lines! Simple, huh? I just need to explain one more part of the WindowProc.

```
    case WM_SIZE:
    {
       cxClient = LOWORD(lParam);
       cyClient = HIWORD(lParam);
    }
    break;
```

It would be a good idea for you to compile the GDI_Lines_1 example without this WM_SIZE handler and then try resizing the window. Nasty, eh? That's why you need to keep track of the client area if you allow your user to resize.

When a user changes the dimensions of a window, a WM_SIZE message is dispatched. The dimensions of the new window are passed to the WindowProc in the high and low bytes of the 32-bit integer, lParam. Figure 2.3 shows how this information is arranged in lParam. HIWORD and LOWORD are Windows macros that you can use to extract this

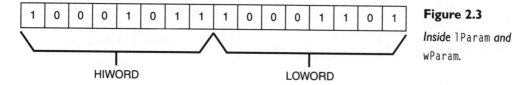

Figure 2.3

Inside lParam *and* wParam.

information. Then update cxClient and cyClient with the new window dimensions, and because you used these two variables as the basis for all the drawing calculations, the drawing is scaled accordingly.

Creating Custom Pens

The preceding example drew lines using the default black brush, but what if you want to draw in different colors and use different pen thicknesses? To do this, you must create your own custom pen, and you do that by using the CreatePen function. Let's take a look at this function:

```
HPEN CreatePen(
    int      fnPenStyle,   // pen style
    int      nWidth,       // pen width
    COLORREF crColor       // pen color
);
```

fnPenStyle is a flag that defines how the pen draws its lines. Take a look at Table 2.1 to see the most common styles.

> **TIP**
>
> You can prevent the user from resizing your window a number of ways, but the simplest is by removing the WS_THICKFRAME flag when you call CreateWindowEx. If you look up WS_OVERLAPPEDWINDOW in your documentation, you will find that it's a timesaver—a combination of several flags, one of which is WS_THICKFRAME. To achieve the same results as before, but without WS_THICKFRAME, use the flags:
>
> WS_OVERLAPPED | WS_VISIBLE | WS_CAPTION | WS_SYSMENU
>
> Try it and see what happens when you attempt to resize your window.

Table 2.1 Pen Drawing Styles

Style	Description
PS_SOLID	The pen draws a solid line.
PS_DASH	The pen draws a dashed line.
PS_DOT	You guessed right—the pen draws a dotted line.
PS_DASHDOT	The pen alternates between dashes and dots.
PS_DASHDOTDOT	The pen alternates between one dash and two dots.

`nWidth` sets the width of the pen in logical units. For our purposes, you can simply think of this as the width of the pen in pixels. If you set this value to zero, the pen will assume a thickness of one.

`crColor` is a `COLORREF` that defines the color you want the pen to be. Every color you see on your monitor is made up of just three colors: red, green, and blue. It is the varying combinations of the intensities of these three base colors that combine to create the spectrum of available colors. Each color is represented by one byte in a `COLORREF`, which means that you can assign intensities of between 0 and 255, with 255 being the brightest.

When defining a color, it is normal to set the intensities in red, green, and blue order. For example, the color (255, 255, 255) is white, (0, 0, 0) is black, (255, 0, 0) is bright red, and so on. Windows helps to create a `COLORREF` by providing a helpful little macro called RGB. So, to create the `COLORREF` for red, you write RGB(255, 0, 0).

`CreatePen` returns a handle to the pen you've just created. Let's create a solid red pen with a width of two pixels:

```
HPEN RedPen = CreatePen(PS_SOLID, 2, RGB(255, 0, 0);
```

And that's it. `RedPen` now contains a handle to the custom-defined pen. To use the pen, you must first select it into the device context so that the device knows which pen to draw with. You do this by using the `SelectObject` function.

```
HGDIOBJ SelectObject(
    HDC     hdc,        // handle to device context
    HGDIOBJ hgdiobj     // handle to object
);
```

This is a multi-purpose function that is used to select not only pens into the device context, but also bitmaps, brushes, fonts, and regions. That is why you pass it an `HGDIOBJ` (handle to a GDI object) and not an `HPEN`. `SelectObject` returns a handle to the object selected in the DC when the function is called. This is so you can keep a copy of the state of the DC before you start drawing and restore it later when you have finished.

> **NOTE**
> You can only have one pen selected into the device context at a time. To change pens, you must use `SelectObject` again to select another pen into the DC.

Because the function uses `HGDIOBJ`s, you have to cast appropriately—in this case to `HPEN`. So, to select the red pen into the device context, do this:

```
HPEN OldPen = (HPEN)SelectObject(hdc, RedPen);
```

After you finish your drawing, select the old pen back into the DC to tidy up.

```
SelectObject(hdc, OldPen);
```

Before your program terminates, you must make sure any pens you have created (or other objects, such as brushes and bitmaps) are deleted. To delete a pen use the DeleteObject function.

```
BOOL DeleteObject(
  HGDIOBJ hObject    // handle to graphic object
);
```

If you don't remember to delete your GDI objects, you will get resource leaks. This, as you may imagine, is a *bad* thing. Also, make sure you don't try to delete a GDI object that is already selected into the DC.

And that's all there is to creating pens. I've altered the code from GDI_Lines1 to use custom pens. Be warned—the colors I use are pretty nasty so you may feel a little nauseous! Now would be a good time for you to look at the source (GDI_Lines2) and play around with creating your own pen styles.

TIP

You can draw individual pixels onto the screen using the SetPixel **function. It looks like this:**

```
COLORREF SetPixel(
  HDC      hdc,         // handle to device context
  int      X,           // x-coordinate of pixel
  int      Y,           // y-coordinate of pixel
  COLORREF crColor      // pixel color
);
```

And you can grab the color of a pixel at any coordinate on your display by using the GetPixel **function:**

```
COLORREF GetPixel(
  HDC hdc,        // handle to device context
  int nXPos,      // x-coordinate of pixel
  int nYPos       // y-coordinate of pixel
);
```

Brushes

Brushes are used to *fill in* or *paint* shapes. Let's say you want to draw a rectangle, and you want the region it encloses to be painted in orange. You first create an orange brush, and then you draw the rectangle with that brush.

Creating brushes is very similar to creating pens: you create your brush, then you select it into the device context, and when you are done using it, you delete it. There are also the Windows stock brushes to use, but they are all black, white, or shades of gray (with one exception—the NULL_BRUSH, which is invisible). The default brush is white.

Unlike creating pens, there are several ways you can create a brush. Let's quickly go through them.

CreateSolidBrush

This function is the simplest to use. It creates a brush that will fill in a region with a block of solid color.

```
HBRUSH CreateSolidBrush(
  COLORREF crColor   // brush color value
);
```

All you do here is give the function a COLORREF, and it will return a handle to the custom brush.

CreateHatchBrush

This brush paints using hatch marks defined by the flag fnStyle. The available styles are shown in Figure 2.4.

```
HBRUSH CreateHatchBrush(
  int      fnStyle,   // hatch style
  COLORREF clrref     // color value
);
```

CreatePatternBrush

You can even define brushes that paint with bitmaps! All you need is a handle to a bitmap, and the brush will fill in the specified region with it. The function prototype looks like this.

```
HBRUSH CreatePatternBrush(
  HBITMAP hbmp   // handle to bitmap
);
```

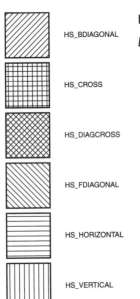

HS_BDIAGONAL

HS_CROSS

HS_DIAGCROSS

HS_FDIAGONAL

HS_HORIZONTAL

HS_VERTICAL

Figure 2.4

Brush pattern style flags.

There are a couple of other ways to create brushes—CreateBrushIndirect and CreateDIBPatternBrushPt—but it's not necessary to go into the details of them in this book. They are very infrequently used.

Now that you know what a brush is, let's have a look at some of the different shapes you can draw with the GDI.

Shapes

There are loads of shape types you can draw with the GDI. Each shape normally consists of a border drawn with the currently selected pen and an enclosed region that is painted with the current brush. Figure 2.5 illustrates most of the shape types you can draw.

Let me take a moment to go through some of the more useful shape drawing functions with you.

Rectangle

Rectangle is the simplest of the shape-drawing functions. Here's what the prototype looks like:

```
BOOL Rectangle(
    HDC hdc,          // handle to device context
```

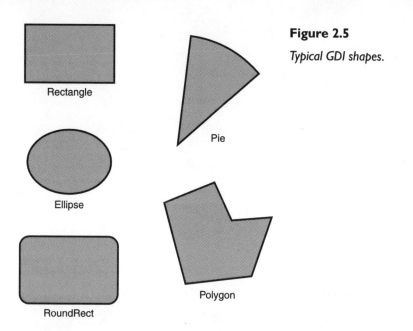

Figure 2.5

Typical GDI shapes.

```
   int nLeftRect,     // x-coord of bounding rectangle's upper-left corner
   int nTopRect,      // y-coord of bounding rectangle's upper-left corner
   int nRightRect,    // x-coord of bounding rectangle's lower-right corner
   int nBottomRect    // y-coord of bounding rectangle's lower-right corner
);
```

All you do is pass this function a handle to your device context and the coordinates for the upper-left and bottom-right corner of the rectangle, as shown in Figure 2.6.

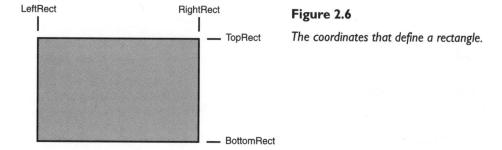

Figure 2.6

The coordinates that define a rectangle.

There are also two other rectangle functions you may find useful: FrameRect and FillRect.

FrameRect draws a border around the specified rectangle and with the specified brush.

```
int FrameRect(
  HDC          hDC,    // handle to device context
  CONST RECT *lprc,    // pointer to rectangle coordinates
  HBRUSH       hbr     // handle to brush
);
```

And FillRect simply fills the area you specify with the current brush.

```
int FillRect(
  HDC          hDC,    // handle to device context
  CONST RECT *lprc,    // pointer to structure with rectangle
  HBRUSH       hbr     // handle to brush
);
```

Ellipse

The Ellipse function is almost the same as the Rectangle function.

```
BOOL Ellipse(
  HDC hdc,           // handle to device context
  int nLeftRect,     // x-coord of bounding rectangle's upper-left corner
  int nTopRect,      // y-coord of bounding rectangle's upper-left corner
  int nRightRect,    // x-coord of bounding rectangle's lower-right corner
  int nBottomRect    // y-coord of bounding rectangle's lower-right corner
);
```

To draw an ellipse, you just specify coordinates as if you were drawing a rectangle that encloses the ellipse shape you want. Figure 2.7 shows you how this works.

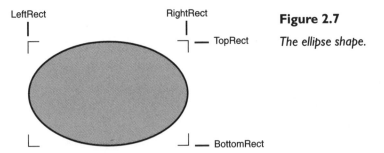

Figure 2.7

The ellipse shape.

So, if you want to draw a circle, all you have to do is pass the function coordinates that describe a square bounding box. It's as easy as that.

Polygon

A *polygon* is defined by a series of connected points that enclose an area. The last point is always connected to the first point. Figure 2.8 shows you what I mean.

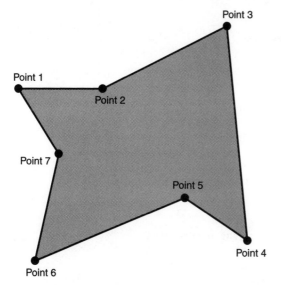

Figure 2.8

The polygon shape.

The points of a polygon are often referred to as *vertices*. Here's what the Polygon prototype looks like:

```
BOOL Polygon(
   HDC          hdc,          // handle to device context
   CONST POINT *lpPoints,     // pointer to polygon's vertices
   int          nCount        // count of polygon's vertices
);
```

This function takes a pointer to a list of POINT structures describing the coordinates of each vertex and also an integer that is the total number of vertices the shape contains. The POINT structure just defines a point in space; it looks like this:

```
typedef struct tagPOINT {
    LONG x;
    LONG y;
} POINT;
```

I've written a sample program that will draw a new polygon to the screen every time you press the spacebar. You'll find the source code in the Chapter2/GDI_Polygon folder on the CD. Here's a listing of the relevant parts of the WindowProc:

```
LRESULT CALLBACK WindowProc (HWND    hwnd,
                             UINT    msg,
                             WPARAM  wParam,
                             LPARAM  lParam)
{
    //create some pens to use for drawing
    static HPEN BluePen  = CreatePen(PS_SOLID, 1, RGB(0, 0, 255));
    static HPEN OldPen    = NULL;

    //create a solid brush
    static HBRUSH RedBrush = CreateSolidBrush(RGB(255, 0, 0));
    static HBRUSH OldBrush = NULL;

    //these hold the dimensions of the client window area
    static int cxClient, cyClient;

    //this will hold the vertices of the polygons we create
    static POINT verts[NUM_VERTS];

    //number of verts to draw
    static int iNumVerts = NUM_VERTS;
```

Here I've set up the variables used in the drawing. Notice that I created a pen to draw the outline and a brush to fill the interior. NUM_VERTS is #defined in defines.h.

```
    switch (msg)
    {
    case WM_CREATE:
      {
          RECT rect;
          GetClientRect(hwnd, &rect);
          cxClient = rect.right;
          cyClient = rect.bottom;

          //seed random number generator
```

```
        srand((unsigned) time(NULL));

        //now lets create some random vertices
        for (int v=0; v<iNumVerts; ++v)
        {
          verts[v].x = RandInt(0, cxClient);
          verts[v].y = RandInt(0, cyClient);
        }
    }
    break;
```

When the WM_CREATE message is dispatched, the random number generator is seeded,
and verts is filled with random coordinates. Each coordinate represents a vertex
of the polygon. RandInt is part of a group of random number functions defined in
the file utils.h. It simply returns a random integer between the two parameters
passed to it.

```
case WM_KEYUP:
    {
        switch(wParam)
        {
        case VK_SPACE:
          {
            //create some new points for our polygon
            //now lets create some random vertices
            for (int v=0; v<iNumVerts; ++v)
            {
              verts[v].x = RandInt(0, cxClient);
              verts[v].y = RandInt(0, cyClient);
            }

             //refresh the display so we can see our
             //new polygon
             InvalidateRect(hwnd, NULL, TRUE);
             UpdateWindow(hwnd);
          }
          break;
        }
    }
```

If the spacebar is pressed and released, a WM_KEYUP message is displayed. The program checks for this, and creates new random coordinates for the polygon. The important thing to notice here are the calls to InvalidateRect and UpdateWindow. InvalidateRect called with NULL as the second parameter tells Windows to add the entire client area to its update region. The update region represents the portion of the window's client area that must be redrawn the next time a WM_PAINT is performed. UpdateWindow simply sends a WM_PAINT message if there is a region that needs updating (hence our call to InvalidateRect first). It sends the WM_PAINT message directly to the WindowProc without putting it in the message queue first. This ensures that the window is updated immediately. The end result of these two little lines is that the client area gets redrawn, and you can see the newly created polygon.

```
case WM_PAINT:
  {
      PAINTSTRUCT ps;
      BeginPaint (hwnd, &ps);

      //first select a pen to draw with and store a copy
      //of the pen we are swapping it with
      OldPen = (HPEN)SelectObject(ps.hdc, BluePen);

      //do the same for our brush
      OldBrush = (HBRUSH)SelectObject(ps.hdc, RedBrush);

      //draw the polygon
      Polygon(ps.hdc, verts, iNumVerts);

      //replace the original pen
      SelectObject(ps.hdc, OldPen);
      //and brush
      SelectObject(ps.hdc, OldBrush);

      EndPaint (hwnd, &ps);
  }
  break;
```

The WM_PAINT section is pretty straightforward. You can see that the first thing I do is select the custom pen and brush into the DC. Then the call to Polygon is made using the vertices in verts.

And that's all there is to it. Play with the code for a while, and create some brushes and shapes of your own before you move on to the next section of this chapter.

Text

So far, you've learned how to draw and paint on your canvas, but you still haven't a clue how to sign your name on it! This section will rectify that.

As you can imagine, Windows has a lot of functions for displaying and manipulating text and fonts. I could write several chapters describing everything you could do with text with the windows API; however, for the purposes of this book (and my sanity), I'm just going to show you the basics.

TextOut

The easiest way to get text on your screen is the TextOut function. Let's take a look at it.

```
BOOL TextOut(
    HDC      hdc,          // handle to device context
    int      nXStart,      // x-coordinate of starting position
    int      nYStart,      // y-coordinate of starting position
    LPCTSTR  lpString,     // pointer to string
    int      cbString      // number of characters in string
);
```

As you can see, all the parameters are self-explanatory. You just give TextOut a handle to a DC, the coordinates of where you want your text to appear, a pointer to the text itself, and an integer describing the length of the text. The default color for the text is black (no surprises there), and the default background color is WHITE_BRUSH. I'll be describing how to change the defaults in a moment, but first I want to show you another way of displaying text.

DrawText

DrawText is slightly more complex than TextOut. Its prototype looks like this:

```
int DrawText(
    HDC      hDC,          // handle to device context
    LPCTSTR  lpString,     // pointer to string to draw
    int      nCount,       // string length, in characters
    LPRECT   lpRect,       // pointer to struct with formatting dimensions
```

```
   UINT    uFormat      // text-drawing flags
);
```

This function draws text within a text box defined by lpRect. The text is formatted within the box according to the flags set with uFormat. There are a whole load of flags; Table 2.2 illustrates a few of them.

Adding Color and Transparency

Fortunately, you can define your own background and foreground colors, and you can also set the transparency of the text. To set the color of the actual text, use SetTextColor

```
COLORREF SetTextColor(
   HDC      hdc,      // handle to device context
   COLORREF crColor   // text color
);
```

and to set the background color, use SetBkColor.

```
COLORREF SetBkColor(
   HDC      hdc,      // handle of device context
   COLORREF crColor   // background color value
);
```

Table 2.2   DrawText Formatting Flags

Flag	Description
DT_BOTTOM	The text gets justified to the bottom of the text box. If you include this flag, you must also include DT_SINGLELINE.
DT_CENTER	This flag centers the text horizontally with the text box.
DT_LEFT	Aligns text to the left.
DT_RIGHT	Aligns text to the right.
DT_SINGLELINE	Displays all text on a single line. Carriage returns do not break the line.
DT_TOP	Aligns text to the top.
DT_WORDBREAK	This flag acts like word wrap.

As you can see, they are very simple functions. Once set, the foreground and background colors will remain until you change them again. Both functions return the current color value so that you can keep a note of the original settings and restore them later if necessary.

As an example, to set the text color to red and the background to black, you do this:

```
//set text to red
SetTextColor(ps.hdc, RGB(255, 0, 0));


//background to black
SetBkColor(ps.hdc, RGB(0, 0, 0));
```

In addition to being able to set the background and foreground colors, you may also set the transparency. This sets the background pixels of the text output to display as transparent. (For example, if there were a pattern behind the text, it would look as though the text was printed directly onto the pattern.)

You can set the background transparency using the SetBkMode function:

```
int SetBkMode(
   HDC hdc,        // handle of device context
   int iBkMode     // flag specifying background mode
);
```

There are only two flags: OPAQUE and TRANSPARENT. So to draw text with a transparent background, you just set the mode accordingly before you do any text drawing.

The GDI_Text source code illustrates the use of all these different functions. Figure 2.9 shows a screenshot. Can you guess which films the quotes are from?

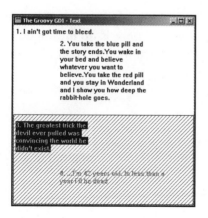

Figure 2.9

Different ways of rendering text.

A Real-Time Message Pump

In the GDI_Polygon example, pushing the spacebar every time to display a new polygon on the screen could get a little tedious. What if you wanted to hypnotize the user by rapidly flashing polygons in quick succession? With GetMessage, it's impossible. If there are no messages already in the queue, GetMessage just sits there and waits—like a patient fisherman—until a new message comes along. Because a lot of games happen to be of the action-packed, keyboard-bashing, temple-throbbing variety, the simple GetMessage message pump is usually not a good choice. You don't want your game to be motionless until the user does something—you want your aliens to be dashing about in the background, stalking you, hunting you down. To achieve this, you need a message pump that will only handle messages if there's a message to be handled, and the rest of the time lets your game code get on with the exciting stuff. To do this, you use the PeekMessage function. It looks like this:

```
BOOL PeekMessage(
    LPMSG lpMsg,            // pointer to structure for message
    HWND hWnd,              // handle to window
    UINT wMsgFilterMin,     // first message
    UINT wMsgFilterMax,     // last message
    UINT wRemoveMsg         // removal flags
);
```

As you can see, it's very similar to the GetMessage function. The only difference is the last parameter, wRemoveMsg. This can be set to either PM_NOREMOVE, which means the message is not removed from the queue after processing, or PM_REMOVE, which removes the message from the queue—usually you'll want the message removed. PeekMessage will return true if there is a message waiting, or false if there isn't.

Creating a real-time message pump is a little more complicated than before because if you just replace GetMessage with PeekMessage, as soon as there is no message in the queue, PeekMessage returns a zero and the application terminates. Try it and see; replace the message pump in the polygon example with this:

```
while (PeekMessage (&msg, NULL, 0, 0, PM_REMOVE))
{
    TranslateMessage (&msg);
    DispatchMessage (&msg);
}
```

All you get is an application window that flashes open and then immediately shuts down. What you need is something much more robust—and this is it:

```
// Enter the message loop
bool bDone = false;
MSG msg;

while(!bDone)
{
  while( PeekMessage( &msg, NULL, 0, 0, PM_REMOVE ) )
  {
    if( msg.message == WM_QUIT )
    {
      // Stop loop if it's a quit message
      bDone = true;
    }
    else
    {
      TranslateMessage( &msg );
      DispatchMessage( &msg );
    }
  }

  //this will call WM_PAINT that will render our scene
  InvalidateRect(hWnd, NULL, TRUE);
  UpdateWindow(hWnd);

}//end while
```

This message pump loops around the while(!bDone) loop until bDone becomes true. Each time through the loop, the PeekMessage function checks to see if there is a message waiting in the queue. If there is a message, it first checks to see if the message is a WM_QUIT message, in which case bDone is set to true and the application exits. If the message is not a WM_QUIT message, then it's processed and dispatched as you saw in earlier examples, and the message is removed from the queue. If there is no message to be processed, you can see that the loop then uses InvalidateRect and UpdateWindow to invoke WM_PAINT to redraw the window. When you are coding your game, this is the place you would also put your main game loop.

Take a look at the GDI_Polygons2 example to see this message pump in action. You will notice that the WM_PAINT section of the WindowProc now contains code to generate new polygons, and that I use the handy little function, Sleep to slow down the program a few milliseconds so you can actually see the polygons. To use Sleep, you just pass it a value representing the number of milliseconds you want the function to wait before it allows your program to continue.

How to Create a Back Buffer

When you're programming games, or any program in which the display gets updated many times a second, you quickly run into the flickering screen problem. I've written a little demo to show you what I mean. You will find the code in the GDI_Backbuffer folder. Please take a look at this program in action. You'll find that it just bounces some balls around the screen. Figure 2.10 is a screenshot of the program:

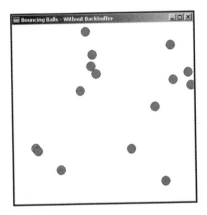

Figure 2.10

Balls!

What the screenshot can't show you is how the balls flicker as they are displayed. Nasty, isn't it? This happens because of the way your monitor works.

The inside surface of the display on your monitor is coated with three different kinds of phosphors that react when hit by a beam of electrons by emitting red, green or blue light. The relative brightness of each of these colors determines the color you eventually see on your screen. That's why earlier, when you learned about COLORREFS, you defined colors based on red, green, and blue (RGB). At the rear of your monitor is an electron gun. This is a device that emits high speed electrons. The electrons are aimed using an electromagnetic field. To draw an image, the gun starts off at the upper-left corner of the display and then moves horizontally to the right, shooting the phosphors a pixel at a time. When it reaches the end of a line, it moves back to the left and down a pixel and then starts all over again. It does this until it reaches the bottom-right corner of your display, and then it returns to its starting position, where the whole process is repeated again. Figure 2.11 shows the route the gun takes. The time it takes the electron gun to move back to the upper-left corner is called the *vertical refresh rate* and the number of times this process is repeated per second is called the *refresh rate*. (Bet a few of you always wondered what that was, eh?)

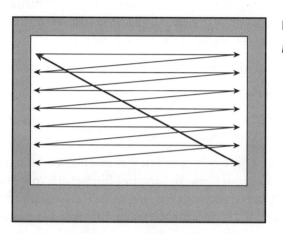

Figure 2.11

How your screen updates.

It's this process of updating the display that creates the flickering—basically, the program is drawing to the screen while the gun is still moving across it. So, your display ends up flashing, flickering, and tearing. Fortunately, there is a way to prevent this: by using a *back buffer*.

The front buffer is an area of memory that is mapped directly to your display. As soon as you draw something on it, whatever you have drawn will appear immediately on your screen. The front buffer is what you've been drawing to in all the code samples up until now. When you get your HDC from BeginPaint in the WM_PAINT section of your WindowProc, you are getting the HDC to the front buffer.

To prevent the flickering, you need to create another area in memory—in exactly the same format and size as the front buffer—and do all the drawing there. This will be the back buffer. Because you are drawing to an off-screen area of memory, you won't see anything at all. So, what you have to do (for every frame) is copy the contents of the back

> **TIP**
>
> Occasionally game coders require a third buffer to make the display even smoother. This is known as *triple buffering*. And nowadays, with the introduction of graphics accelerators, it's even possible to create whole chains of buffers, many levels deep.

buffer onto the front buffer. (This is often referred to as *blitting*.) Because this happens all at once, the screen update doesn't mess with the movement of the electron gun. And there you have it—flicker-free display. This technique is most often referred to as *double buffering* and occasionally as *page flipping*.

That Sounds Great, but How Do You Do It?

Because you are creating an area in memory to represent the front buffer (the display area), the first thing you need to do is create a *memory device context* that is compatible with the DC for the display. There are three stages to this.

First, you use the function CreateCompatibleDC to create a memory device context.

```
HDC hdcBackBuffer = CreateCompatibleDC(NULL);
```

When NULL is passed as a parameter, Windows defaults to creating a DC compatible with the current screen—and that's exactly what you want.

Unfortunately, when a memory device context is created, it is monochrome and only one pixel in height and width. Not much use to anyone! So, before you can use it to draw to, you have to create a bitmap that is exactly the same dimensions and format as the front buffer, and then select it into the memory DC, using the good ol' SelectObject function. This is the second stage.

You can create a bitmap by using the CreateCompatibleBitmap function. Its prototype looks like this:

```
HBITMAP CreateCompatibleBitmap(
   HDC hdc,        // handle to device context
   int nWidth,     // width of bitmap, in pixels
   int nHeight     // height of bitmap, in pixels
);
```

You pass this function the display's HDC and the height and width, and it will return a handle to a bitmap created in memory. So...

You first grab a handle to the device context using the GetDC function mentioned earlier in this chapter

```
HDC hdc = GetDC(hwnd);
```

And then you create the compatible bitmap

```
HBITMAP hBitmap = CreateCompatibleBitmap(hdc,
                            cxClient,
                            cyClient);
```

And that just leaves one last thing to do—select this bitmap into the memory device context you created in stage one. Once that is done, hdcBackBuffer will be set up exactly the same as the DC for the front buffer, and you can start drawing to it. This is done by using the SelectObject function:

```
HBITMAP hOldBitmap = (HBITMAP)SelectObject(hdcBackBuffer, hBitmap);
```

A copy of the existing 1×1 pixel mono bitmap is kept so you can select it back when you finish using the back buffer to tidy up. (The same way you have been doing with pens and brushes.)

All these stages in the new bouncing ball example are performed in WM_CREATE. This is what the relevant lines of the WindowProc look like. (I have omitted the ball setup stuff for clarity.)

```
LRESULT CALLBACK WindowProc (HWND    hwnd,
                             UINT    msg,
                             WPARAM  wParam,
                             LPARAM  lParam)
{
    //these hold the dimensions of the client window area
    static int cxClient, cyClient;

    //used to create the back buffer
    static HDC       hdcBackBuffer;
    static HBITMAP   hBitmap;
    static HBITMAP   hOldBitmap;

    switch (msg)
    {
    case WM_CREATE:
      {
          //get the client area
          RECT rect;
          GetClientRect(hwnd, &rect);

          cxClient = rect.right;
          cyClient = rect.bottom;

          //now to create the back buffer

          //create a memory device context
```

```
        hdcBackBuffer = CreateCompatibleDC(NULL);

        //get the DC for the front buffer
        HDC hdc = GetDC(hwnd);

        hBitmap = CreateCompatibleBitmap(hdc,
                                         cxClient,
                                         cyClient);



        //select the bitmap into the memory device context
        hOldBitmap = (HBITMAP)SelectObject(hdcBackBuffer, hBitmap);

        //don't forget to release the DC!
        ReleaseDC(hwnd, hdc);
    }
    break;
```

Okay, I Have My Back Buffer, Now How Do I Use It?

Once you've created your back buffer, it's easy sailing. To use it, all you have to do is this.

1. Clear the back buffer—this is usually done by filling it with the background color.
2. Draw your graphics, text, and so on by using the hdc you have for your back buffer.
3. Copy the contents of your back buffer to the front buffer.

Let's go through it, step by step.

To fill the back buffer with a solid color (usually your background color), use the BitBlt function. This function normally copies all the bits in one area of memory— your back buffer—to the bits in another area of memory—your display. Figure 2.12 shows an example. However, you can also use this function to fill an area with a block of color.

The BitBlt function is defined as:

```
BOOL BitBlt(
   HDC    hdcDest, // handle to destination device context
   int    nXDest,  // x-coordinate of destination rectangle's upper-left
```

Figure 2.12

The `BitBlt` *in action.*

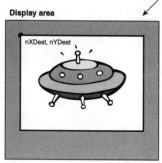

```
                    // corner
    int    nYDest,  // y-coordinate of destination rectangle's upper-left
                    // corner
    int    nWidth,  // width of destination rectangle
    int    nHeight, // height of destination rectangle
    HDC    hdcSrc,  // handle to source device context
    int    nXSrc,   // x-coordinate of source rectangle's upper-left
                    // corner
    int    nYSrc,   // y-coordinate of source rectangle's upper-left
                    // corner
    DWORD  dwRop    // raster operation code
);
```

You pass this function a handle to the source DC and a handle to the destination DC together with their respective upper-left corner coordinates and the width and height of the area you want copied. The final parameter is a flag that indicates how you want the color data in the source to be merged with the data in the destination. There are loads of these flags, and you can achieve all sorts of weird and wonderful effects with them, but for now, the only flags you are interested in are SRCCOPY, which will copy the bits exactly as they are into the destination area, and WHITENESS, which will fill the destination area with white—RGB(255, 255, 255)—pixels.

Here's the source code for WM_PAINT. For clarity, I've omitted the code that updates and draws the balls.

```
case WM_PAINT:
  {
    PAINTSTRUCT ps;
    BeginPaint (hwnd, &ps);

    //fill our backbuffer with white
    BitBlt(hdcBackBuffer,
            0,
            0,
            cxClient,
            cyClient,
            NULL,
            NULL,
            NULL,
            WHITENESS);
```

To fill the back buffer with white pixels, simply pass BitBlt the dimensions of the client area, set all the parameters for the source to NULL, and use the WHITENESS flag to set all the pixels to RGB(255, 255, 255).

```
    //------------------------------------------------------------------
    //This is where all the drawing is performed.
    //------------------------------------------------------------------
```

Remember, to draw, you now use the hdc for the back buffer you created in WM_PAINT: hdcBackBuffer.

```
    //now blit backbuffer to front
    BitBlt(ps.hdc,
            0,
            0,
            cxClient,
            cyClient,
            hdcBackBuffer,
            0,
            0,
            SRCCOPY);

        EndPaint (hwnd, &ps);

  }
```

This is where the contents of the back buffer are copied into the DC for the window. BitBlt is used again, but this time you give the function the relevant parameters for the memory DC and set the dwRop flag to SRCCOPY; that tells the function to copy the memory DC exactly as is. That way, whatever you have drawn to the back buffer gets displayed on the screens.

So, that's how you create and render to a back buffer. However, if you just insert the code as I have described, you will

still see a flickering display. The reason for this is that when you created the class for your window by filling in a WNDCLASSEX structure, you set the background color to white. So, even though you are using a back buffer to render to, when BeginPaint is called, the API fills your window with its background color, and this produces some flickering. To rid yourself of this problem, you can just set the appropriate member of your WNDCLASSEX structure to NULL.

```
winclass.hbrBackground = NULL;
```

Keeping It Tidy

Because you've created a bitmap and a memory DC, you have to make sure you delete them when your game terminates, or you will end up with resource leaks. This is very simple to do. First, you select back into the memory DC, hdcOldBitmap, which frees up your bitmap for deletion. Then you can safely delete the DC and the bitmap. Here's the code from WM_DESTROY to do that:

```
SelectObject(hdcBackBuffer, hOldBitmap);

DeleteDC(hdcBackBuffer);
DeleteObject(hBitmap);
```

Finally, you have to make sure the back buffer is resized if the user resizes the window. To do this, you must delete the existing compatible bitmap and create a new one of the appropriate size. All this is done inside WM_SIZE, like so:

```
case WM_SIZE:
  {
```

```
        //if so we need to update our variables so that any drawing
        //we do using cxClient and cyClient is scaled accordingly
        cxClient = LOWORD(lParam);
        cyClient = HIWORD(lParam);

        //now to resize the backbuffer accordingly. First select
        //the old bitmap back into the DC
        SelectObject(hdcBackBuffer, hOldBitmap);

        //don't forget to do this or you will get resource leaks
        DeleteObject(hBitmap);

        //get the DC for the application
        HDC hdc = GetDC(hwnd);

        //create another bitmap of the same size and mode
        //as the application
        hBitmap = CreateCompatibleBitmap(hdc,
                                         cxClient,
                                         cyClient);

        ReleaseDC(hwnd, hdc);

        //select the new bitmap into the DC
        SelectObject(hdcBackBuffer, hBitmap);
    }
    break;
```

Voilá! A flicker-free display.

Using Resources

A resource is any data your game may use that is combined with your compiled code to make just one executable file. This data may include bitmaps, sound files, icons, and cursors. See Figure 2.13. In fact, it may include anything your program needs to run. It can be useful to include your data files as resources because it keeps everything nice and tidy—you don't need many separate image and sound files—and also it prevents anyone from easily stealing your artwork or other files you've worked so hard to create.

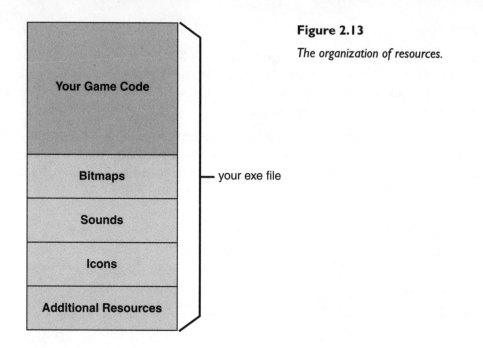

Figure 2.13

The organization of resources.

Although you can create custom-built resources, the predefined resource types will usually be enough for your requirements. The most common ones are

- **Icons.** The small icon you see in the upper-left corner of the application window, or the icon you see in Windows Explorer, or when you task switch using Alt+Tab.

- **Cursors.** You can use any of the default cursors, or you can create your own custom cursors to use.

- **Strings.** Although this might seem like a strange option for a resource, it can actually be a pretty good idea to keep all the character strings you use in one place. Why, you ask? Well, if you keep them all in one place, it makes it very easy to convert your game into different languages, or make small alterations without having to wade through thousands of lines of code listings.

- **Menus.** Most often you'll be using your own custom interface for games, but you'll also regularly require this type of menu for any tools you may need to code.

- **Bitmaps.** These are image files that consist of an array of pixels. Windows provides support for bitmaps with the BMP file extension.

- **Sound files.** You can include all your sound files (wav files) as resources.

- **Dialog boxes.** You can either use the predefined dialog boxes, such as MessageBox, or you can create your own custom-built ones and store them as a resource.

Now that you know what resources are, let me show you how to create them.

Icons

You can create two sizes of icons: a large icon that is 32×32 pixels or a small icon that is 16×16 pixels. The larger icon is displayed in the icon list you see when you Alt+Tab between applications, and the smaller icon is the one you see in Explorer and in the upper-left corner of your window.

You can either create your icons in your favorite paint program and save them with the .ico file extension, or if you use Microsoft Developer Studio, you can create them with the built-in icon editor. To do the latter, select Insert, Resource, Icon, New, and a simple editor window will appear, as shown in Figure 2.14.

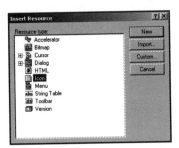

Figure 2.14

Insert resource options.

Now, just create your icons (one large and one small), give them meaningful names, such as IDI_ICON_SM and IDI_ICON_LRG, and then save them as a resource—a file with the .rc extension. You will find that Developer Studio will automatically generate a resource.h file that you *must* #include in your main source file.

All you have to do to make your icons appear is reference them when you register your windows class, like so:

```
WNDCLASSEX      winclass;

// first fill in the window class stucture
winclass.cbSize         = sizeof(WNDCLASSEX);
winclass.style          = CS_HREDRAW | CS_VREDRAW;
winclass.lpfnWndProc    = WindowProc;
winclass.cbClsExtra     = 0;
winclass.cbWndExtra     = 0;
winclass.hInstance      = hInstance;
winclass.hIcon          = LoadIcon(hInstance, MAKEINTRESOURCE(IDI_ICON_LRG));
winclass.hCursor        = LoadCursor(NULL, IDC_ARROW);
winclass.hbrBackground  = (HBRUSH)GetStockObject(WHITE_BRUSH);
winclass.lpszMenuName   = NULL;
```

```
winclass.lpszClassName = g_szWindowClassName;
winclass.hIconSm       = LoadIcon(hInstance, MAKEINTRESOURCE(IDI_ICON_SM));
```

MAKEINTRESOURCE is a Windows-defined macro that takes an integer and converts it into something meaningful to the windows resource management functions. If you take a peek at the resource.h file that Developer Studio generated when you created your resource script for the icons, you will see that IDI_ICON_LRG and IDI_ICON_SM are #defined as integers.

The sample project file Resources_Icons demonstrates how to use icons as resources.

Cursors

You create cursors the same way you create icons. They are usually 32×32, but can go as big as 64×64 and are saved with the .cur file extension. You will often use a custom cursor in your games to represent a crosshair, a hand, a spell, and so on.

In addition to drawing the cursor, you must specify a hotspot—the location of the cursor's active area. This is set relative to the upper-left corner (0, 0). In Developer Studio, you can set the hotspot by clicking on the hotspot button and then clicking on the area you want active.

The Resources_Cursors project file shows how to create and display a simple bulls-eye type cursor. It looks like Figure 2.15.

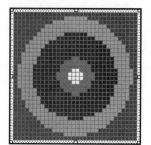

Figure 2.15

A simple custom cursor.

Menus

Adding a menu to your program window is almost as easy as adding a cursor or an icon. The menu you create is normally attached to the menu bar, which appears under the title bar of your window.

To create your menu using Developer Studio, select Insert, Resource, Menu, and you'll get something that looks like Figure 2.16.

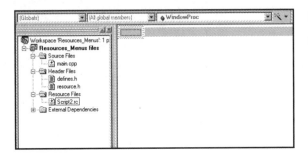

Figure 2.16

Menu creation screen.

Most menus consist of a row of captions, such as File, View, and Help, and a series of options under each header. To create a caption, double-click in the first gray rectangle and an option box will pop up. Type in the caption you require and close the box. You will notice that a second rectangle appeared below the first; this is where you put your menu options, such as Save or Load. Type in another caption and then give this caption a unique identifier—one that's easy to remember. If the caption is Save, then a good identifier would be IDSAVE. See Figure 2.17.

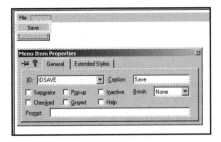

Figure 2.17

Menu properties.

Keep doing this—adding captions and identifiers—until you have created your desired menu, and then save it as a resource script just like you did when you created the icons and cursor. The menu will be assigned a default name, such as IDR_MENU1 but you can give it any name you like.

You then attach your menu to your window class by adding this line to your definition:

`winclass.lpszMenuName  = MAKEINTRESOURCE(IDR_MENU1);`

and Hey Presto! You get something that looks like Figure 2.18.

Figure 2.18

A simple menu.

Adding Functionality to Your Menu

Although you now have a visible menu, it's useless because—although it promises much—it doesn't actually *do* anything—a bit like a politician. What I need to show you now is how to link up the menu with your code so that it does what you want.

As you may have guessed, when a user clicks on one of your menu captions, a message is sent to the `WindowProc`. The message you need to intercept is `WM_COMMAND`, and for this message, the `lParam` contains the handle of the parent window sending the message, and the `wParam` contains the ID of the menu item clicked on. So, within the `WindowProc`, you need to create a case statement for `WM_COMMAND`, and then switch on the `wParam` and create case statements based around the menu selections you have created.

> **TIP**
>
> If you use Developer Studio and you have *Spy++* installed, you can use it to see all the messages being generated and put on the queue when your application is running. It's incredible just how many messages get generated, especially when you move your mouse! You can find it under Tools on the main Developer Studio menu bar. This can be an extremely useful tool at times so it's worth spending some time learning how to use it correctly.

Let's take a look at the relevant section of the WindowProc in the excitingly named example—Resources_Menus. All this example does is create a menu that allows you play one of two different sound files.

```
case WM_COMMAND:
    {
        switch(wParam)
        {
        case IDSAVE:
          {
            //do your saving here
          }
          break;

        case IDLOAD:
          {
            //do your loading here
          }
          break;

        case IDSOUND1:
          {
            PlaySound("wav1.wav", NULL, SND_FILENAME | SND_ASYNC);
          }
          break;

        case IDSOUND2:
          {
            PlaySound("wav2.wav", NULL, SND_FILENAME | SND_ASYNC);
          }
          break;
        }// end switch WM_COMMAND
    }
    break;
```

Easy, right? And that's all there is to creating a simple menu. Of course, there are myriads of options for creating all sorts of weird and wonderful menus, but I'll leave you to consult the documentation if you want to experiment further.

Dialog Boxes

There are two types of dialog boxes: *modal* and *modeless*.

Modal is the type you see most often—it requires the user to click on a button or give some input before it gives control back to its parent window. About dialog boxes are an example of the modal type, as is the Find and Replace dialog box in Developer Studio.

Modeless is a type of dialog box that can be present and yet still allow the user to interact with its parent window. You see this type of dialog box much less frequently. The Find and Replace option in WordPad is an example of this type.

I will not be using modeless dialog boxes in any of my code samples so I'm not going to cover them here, but I will give you an introduction to the modal variety.

A dialog box is another window without all the frills. They usually have no title bar, no client area, and no minimize/maximize button, but they do have a windows procedure just like the main window so they are able to process messages. To create a dialog box, you must make a *dialog template*. Although these can be created by hand, it's a laborious task and much better suited to using your IDE's resource editor.

To create a dialog template in Developer Studio, use the Insert, Resource, Dialog Box option, and you'll get the editor screen, as shown in Figure 2.19.

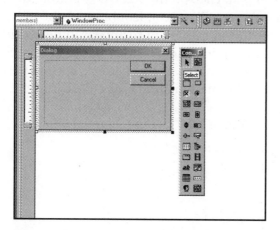

Figure 2.19

Creating a dialog box.

A Simple Dialog Box

First, I'm going to show you how to create a simple About dialog box to add to the previous code sample. The source for this sample can be found in the Resources_Dialog_Box1 folder.

All you need for this type of dialog box is a title, some informative text, and an OK button to click to return back to the application. The default dialog template that pops up in the editor has extraneous features, such as a Cancel button and a title bar that you don't want. To dispose of the Cancel button, click on the button, and when a frame appears around it, press delete. Now double-click on the title bar and a property box will appear, as shown in Figure 2.20.

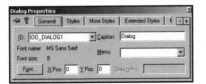

Figure 2.20

Dialog box properties.

Click on the Styles tab, and then uncheck the tick box for the title bar. Also note that the dialog box has been assigned a default ID, usually IDD_DIALOG1, and the ID for the OK button has been assigned IDOK. You can leave these as they are or change them to something you are more comfortable with. I tend to use the defaults.

All you have to do now is add some text and move the OK button to somewhere more pleasing. To move buttons around, click and drag. To add your text, there are three buttons on the tool bar that are associated with text controls. You just need the *static text* button for now. You are only adding text to be read by the user and not manipulated (like an edit box). To add text, click on the static text button, then click where you want the text, and a text box will appear. Double-click the text box and a properties box will appear. Enter the text you want to appear in here, and select how you want it displayed using the options in the Styles tab. I would recommend having a separate static text box for each line of text because it's much easier to manipulate. By now you have produced something that looks like Figure 2.21.

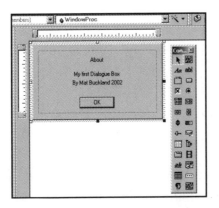

Figure 2.21

An About dialog box.

Once you have defined the dialog template, you need to create a dialog box procedure so it can process messages. This is what the dialog box procedure looks like for the Resources_Dialog_Box1 example:

```
BOOL CALLBACK DialogProc(HWND    hwnd,
                         UINT    msg,
                         WPARAM wParam,
                         LPARAM lParam)
{
  switch(msg)
  {
  case WM_INITDIALOG:
    {
      return true;
    }

    break;

  case WM_COMMAND:
    {
      switch(LOWORD(wParam))
      {
      case IDOK:
        {
          EndDialog(hwnd, 0);

          return true;
        }

        break;
      }
    }

    break;

  }//end switch

  return false;
}
```

As you can see, a dialog box procedure looks very similar to a windows procedure, but it has a few important differences. First, it returns a BOOL not an LRESULT. Second, it does not have a DefWindowProc to take care of unhandled messages. The DialogProc simply returns false for any unhandled messages sent to it. And third, there is no need to process WM_PAINT, WM_DESTROY, or WM_CREATE messages.

WM_INITDIALOG is the first message the DialogProc will receive when it is invoked. If the response to this message is true, Windows will put the focus on the first appropriate child control—in this example, the OK button.

The only other message you have to handle is WM_COMMAND. A WM_COMMAND message is sent to the DialogProc when the user pushes the OK button. The ID of the button, IDOK, is stored in the low word of wParam so test for this and call the function EndDialog if appropriate. EndDialog is a simple function that tells Windows to destroy the dialog box.

So… you've created a dialog template and a DialogProc, all you have to do now is add some code to invoke the dialog box if the user clicks About on the menu. If you examine the resource script with the sample code, you will see I've added an About menu box with an ID of IDABOUT. So, test for that message within the WM_COMMAND of your WindowProc as you have tested for all the other menu IDs, and invoke the dialog box appropriately. This is done by calling the function DialogBox.

```
int DialogBox(
    HINSTANCE hInstance,    // handle to application instance
    LPCTSTR   lpTemplate,   // dialog box template ID
    HWND      hWndParent,   // handle to owner window
    DLGPROC   lpDialogFunc  // pointer to dialog box procedure
);
```

As you can see, this is pretty straightforward. The only problem is you need an hInstance for your main window to pass to DialogBox as one of the parameters. To do that, I've just created a static HINSTANCE at the beginning of WindowProc and grabbed the hInstance in WM_CREATE using the line of code:

```
hInstance = ((LPCREATESTRUCT)lParam)->hInstance;
```

Now that you have the hInstance, the dialog box can be invoked using:

```
DialogBox(hInstance,
          MAKEINTRESOURCE(IDD_DIALOG1),
          hwnd,
          DialogProc);
```

And that's all there is to creating a simple dialog box.

Now for Something More Useful

Unfortunately, the dialog box in the preceding example is useless. What you most often require is a dialog box that enables the user to change your program's parameters in some way. So that's what I'm going to show you how to do now. The source code for the following can be found in the Resources_Dialog_box2 folder on the CD.

You are going to modify the bouncing ball program so the user may change the number and the radius of the balls. To do that, you need to create a simple dialog box with two edit boxes. One for the number of balls and the other for the ball radius. Something, in fact, that looks just like Figure 2.22. To make life easier, I've created three global variables at the beginning of main.h. Two store the ball radius and the number of balls—g_iNumBalls and g_iBallRadius—and the other keeps a global record of the main window handle, g_hwnd. You'll need all these global variables in your new dialog box procedure. Please note that these variables do not have to be global; it's just a quick fix for the purposes of this example.

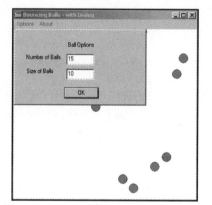

Figure 2.22

Dialog box with edit controls.

You create this dialog box just like you made the dialog box in the preceding example, only this time you add a couple of edit boxes with captions. The edit box identities are IDC_EDIT1 and IDC_EDIT2. Once the dialog box template is ready, you need to code a dialog box procedure. This will be different from the dialog box procedure you created previously because this time it has to display the value of the user-changeable parameters within the edit boxes. Also, when the OK button is pressed, it has to check to see if any of those parameters have been altered by the user, and update accordingly. Let's take a close look at the new dialog procedure and see what's changed.

```
BOOL CALLBACK OptionsDialogProc(HWND    hwnd,
                                UINT    msg,
```

```
                          WPARAM wParam,
                          LPARAM lParam)
{
  //get handles to edit controls
  HWND hwndNumBalls = GetDlgItem(hwnd, IDC_EDIT1);
  HWND hwndRadius   = GetDlgItem(hwnd, IDC_EDIT2);
```

The first thing to do is make a note of the handles of the edit controls so you can reference them later. GetDlgItem is a simple function, which given the handle to a dialog box and a control identifier will return a handle to that control.

```
  switch(msg)
  {
  case WM_INITDIALOG:
    {
      //we have to update the edit boxes with the current radius
      //and number of balls
      string s = itos(g_iNumBalls);
      SetWindowText(hwndNumBalls, s.c_str());

      s = itos(g_iBallRadius);
      SetWindowText(hwndRadius, s.c_str());

      return true;
    }
    break;
```

When the dialog box is invoked, you want the current values for the ball radius (g_iBallRadius) and number of balls (g_iNumBalls) to appear in the edit controls. To do this, you have to change the appropriate parameter into text and then use the SetWindowText function to position it in the correct edit box. The ints are changed into std::strings in this example using the handy itos function defined in utils.h.

```
  case WM_COMMAND:
    {
      switch(LOWORD(wParam))
      {
      case IDOK:
        {
          //for each edit box we collect the information and then change
          //the parameters accordingly
```

```
char  buffer[5];

//----------first the number of balls
GetWindowText(hwndNumBalls, buffer, 5);

//convert to an int
g_iNumBalls = atoi(buffer);

//----------Now the radius
GetWindowText(hwndRadius, buffer, 5);

//convert to an int
g_iBallRadius = atoi(buffer);
```

If the user clicks OK, you need to retrieve whatever is in the text boxes and update the parameters accordingly. Note that there is *no* error checking in this example. When you create your own dialog boxes, make sure you check for errors or you'll rapidly end up in trouble (although I'm sure I don't really need to tell you that!).

To retrieve the text from an edit control, use the function GetWindowText. Here's what the prototype of GetWindowText looks like:

```
int GetWindowText(
  HWND    hWnd,         // handle to window or control with text
  LPTSTR  lpString,     // pointer to buffer for text
  int     nMaxCount     // maximum number of characters to copy
);
```

As you can see, you just give this function the handle to the edit control, a buffer to store the text in, and the number of characters you want to retrieve. If the function succeeds, the return value is the length of the copied string, not including the terminating null character. Once you have retrieved the text, you just use atoi to convert the characters into an integer.

```
//send a custom message to the WindowProc so that
//new balls are spawned
PostMessage(g_hwnd, UM_SPAWN_NEW, NULL, NULL);

//kill the dialog box
EndDialog(hwnd, 0);

return true;
```

```
        }
      break;
    }
  }
  break;
}//end switch
return false;
}
```

Now you have your new values for g_iNumBalls and g_iBallRadius. Before you kill the dialog box, you need to let the program know the updated values so a new array of balls can be created. To do that, put a custom-defined message in the message queue and write a case statement in the WindowProc to handle it. To create user-defined messages, you just define them like so:

```
#define UM_CUSTOM_MESSAGE1 (WM_USER + 0)
#define UM_CUSTOM_MESSAGE2 (WM_USER + 1)
#define UM_CUSTOM_MESSAGE3 (WM_USER + 2)
```

For this example, you only need one custom message, which I've called UM_SPAWN_NEW. To send the message to the message queue, you can either use SendMessage or PostMessage. SendMessage sends the message straight to the windows procedure without going on the queue, and PostMessage simply puts it on the queue where it waits its turn to be processed. I've used PostMessage in this example. The prototype looks like this:

```
BOOL PostMessage(
    HWND    hWnd,    // handle of destination window
    UINT    Msg,     // message to post
    WPARAM  wParam,  // first message parameter
    LPARAM  lParam   // second message parameter
);
```

This is fairly straightforward. Just give the function the handle to the main window, g_hwnd, our custom message, UM_SPAWN_NEW, and set the last two parameters to NULL. The UM_SPAWN_NEW message will then be placed in the queue, and the dialog box procedure kills the dialog box and exits.

> **TIP**
>
> Although I've used global variables to keep track of the ball information, it is possible to use the wParam and lParam fields in PostMessage and SendMessage to pass information to the WindowProc.

For the sake of completeness, here's the UM_SPAWN_NEW case statement from the WindowProc:

```
case UM_SPAWN_NEW:
  {
    //create a new array of balls of the required size
    if (balls)
    {
      delete balls;
    }

    //create the array of balls
    balls = new SBall[g_iNumBalls];

    //set up the balls with random positions and velocities
    for (int i=0; i<g_iNumBalls; ++i)
    {
      balls[i].posX = RandInt(0, cxClient);
      balls[i].posY = RandInt(0, cyClient);
      balls[i].velX = RandInt(0, MAX_VELOCITY);
      balls[i].velY = RandInt(0, MAX_VELOCITY);
    }
  }
  break;
```

As you can see, this just deletes the old array of balls and creates a new one of the required size.

And that's it, mission accomplished. You should now be able to create a dialog box that enables the user to change your program's parameters.

Getting the Timing Right

I just want to cover one last thing with you before I move onto genetic algorithms: Timing.

When you code a game, you want it to work at the same speed on all different machines. Imagine if you code a Pac-Man game and the characters move around fine on your computer, but when you try it on your dad's old 486, the poor old Pac-Men jerk around the screen at three frames a second and then, even worse, when you upgrade to a new turbo charged AMD K15 TXL with a Geforce 9, the ghosts move so fast, they are just a blur! In effect, your game would be useless. What you need is a way of keeping the frame rate the same on any machine, and the way you do that is by making use of the Window's timer.

The timer class I use throughout this book is contained in the CTimer.h and CTimer.cpp files. I'm not going to go into the inner workings of this class because I don't think it's relevant—but I am going to show you how to use it. I've created a version of the Bouncing Balls program, which uses a timer, and you can find it in the Chapter2/Bouncing Balls with Timer folder on the CD.

If you examine the code in main.cpp, you'll see I've made it very easy to use a timer. Here is the relevant section of code:

```
//create a timer
CTimer timer(FRAMES_PER_SECOND);
```

First of all, you just create an instance of a timer and specify how many frames per second you want the timer to run at. I usually #define FRAMES_PER_SECOND in defines.h

```
//start the timer
timer.Start();
```

Then, just before you enter your main loop, you call Start to start the timer.

```
MSG msg;
while(!bDone)
{
    while( PeekMessage( &msg, NULL, 0, 0, PM_REMOVE ) )
    {
        if( msg.message == WM_QUIT )
        {
            // Stop loop if it's a quit message
            bDone = true;
        }
        else
        {
            TranslateMessage( &msg );
            DispatchMessage( &msg );
        }
    }

    if (timer.ReadyForNextFrame())
```

Now all you have to do is ask the timer if it's time to process the next frame or not. You do that by querying the ReadyForNextFrame method, which returns true if it is time to process the next frame and false if otherwise.

```
    {
        //**any game update code goes in here**

        //this will call WM_PAINT which will render our scene
        InvalidateRect(hWnd, NULL, TRUE);
        UpdateWindow(hWnd);
    }
}//end while
```

Creating and using a timer is as easy as that!

At Last!

Wow! Chapter complete! You've covered a lot of ground in this chapter, but by now you should be able to understand any of the Windows-relevant code that appears in the projects for the remainder of this book.

Now, go make yourself a strong cup of coffee, and let's get on with the AI.

Part Two

Genetic Algorithms

CHAPTER 3

AN INTRODUCTION TO GENETIC ALGORITHMS

One day a group of eminent scientists got together and decided that Man had come a long way and no longer needed God. So they picked one scientist to go and tell Him that they were done with Him.

The scientist walked up to God and said, "God, we've decided that we no longer need You. We're to the point that we can clone people and do many miraculous things, so why don't You just retire?"

God listened very patiently to the man and then said, "Very well, but first, how about this, let's have a Man-making contest."

To which the scientist replied, "Okay, great!"

But God added, "Now, we're going to do this just like I did back in the old days with Adam."

The scientist said, "Sure, no problem" and bent down and grabbed himself a handful of dirt.

God just looked at him and said, "No, no, no—You go get your own dirt!"

The Birds and the Bees

In the same way that creatures evolve over many generations to become more successful at the tasks of survival and reproduction, genetic algorithms grow and evolve over time to converge upon a solution, or solutions, to particular types of problems. Therefore, to understand how a genetic algorithm works, it helps to know a little about how living organisms evolve. I'll be spending the first few pages outlining the mechanisms of nature (what evolutionary algorithm people like to call "wet" evolution) and the terminology that goes with it. Don't worry if you were never comfortable with biology in school; I will not be going into a great amount of detail—just enough to help you understand the basic mechanisms. And besides, by the time you've finished a chapter or two, I reckon you'll be finding Mother Nature just as fascinating as I do!

All living organisms are essentially a large collection of cells. Each cell contains the same set of strings of DNA, called *chromosomes*. The DNA a chromosome contains is double–stranded, and the strands are connected to each other in a spiraling braid, which is the familiar DNA helix shape shown in Figure 3.1.

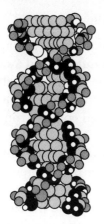

Figure 3.1

The amazing double helix of life.

Individual chromosomes are built from smaller building blocks, called *genes*, which in turn are comprised of substances called *nucleotides*. There are only four types of nucleotides: thymine, adenine, cytosine, and guanine. They are often shortened to T, A, C, and G (I wonder why… <smile>). These nucleotides are linked together into long chains of genes, and each gene encodes a certain trait of the organism, such as hair color or ear shape. The different settings a gene may possess—for example, brown, blonde, or black hair color—are called *alleles*, and their physical position along the length of the chromosome is called their *locus*.

Interesting Note

The alleles needn't just be the settings for physical characteristics; some will give rise to behavior patterns, such as the homing behavior of birds or salmon and the instinct of a mother's young to suckle.

The collection of chromosomes within a cell holds all the information necessary to reproduce that organism. This is how cloning works—you can copy an organism, such as a sheep, from the information contained in just one blood cell of a donor sheep. The new sheep will be identical in every respect to the donor sheep. This collection of chromosomes is known as the organism's *genome*. The state of the alleles in a particular genome is known as that organism's *genotype*. These are the hard-coded instructions that give rise to the actual organism itself, which is called the *phenotype*. You and I are phenotypes. Our DNA carries our genotype. To put it another way, the blueprint and specifications for a car design is a genotype, whereas the finished car rumbling off the production line is a phenotype. Just the plain old design, before the car specifications have been finalized, could be loosely called a genome.

Okay, that's enough jargon for the moment. Now let's talk about how all this applies to evolution. If you're the type of person who occasionally gets outside and away from a computer screen (*I* only know there's an outside because my friends tell me so), you would have noticed that the world is home to a whole bunch of creatures and plants—millions of them—and all different sizes, shapes, and colors. From microscopic single-celled organisms to the Great Barrier Reef—the only life form on earth visible from space. An organism is considered successful if it mates and gives birth to child organisms, which, hopefully, will go on to reproduce themselves. To do this, the organism must be good at many tasks, such as finding food and water, defending itself against predators, and making itself attractive to potential mates. All these attributes are dependent in some way upon the genotype of the organism—the creature's blueprint. Some of the organism's genes will give rise to attributes that will aid it in becoming successful, and some of its genes may hinder it. The measure of success of an organism is called its *fitness*. The more fit the organism is, the more likely it is to produce offspring. Now for the magic part...

When two organisms mate and reproduce, their chromosomes are mixed together to create an entirely new set of chromosomes, which consists of genes from both parents. This process is called *recombination* or *crossover*. This could mean that the offspring inherits mainly the good genes, in which case it may go on to be even more successful than its parents (for example, it has better defense mechanisms against predators), or it may inherit mainly the bad genes, in which case it may not even be able to reproduce. The important thing to note is that the more fit the offspring are, the more likely they will go on to reproduce and pass on their own genes to their offspring. Each generation, therefore, will show a tendency to be better at survival and mating than the last. As a quick and very simple example of this, imagine female creatures that are only attracted to males with large eyes. Basically, the larger the eyes, the greater the likelihood that a male creature is going to be successful at "wooing" the females. You could say that the fitness of a creature is proportional to the diameter of its eyes. So, if you start off with a population of these male creatures, all of whom display different eye sizes, you can see that the gene in the male creature that is set to build a larger eye when the animal is developing, is more likely to be copied to the next generation than when that gene's allele is set to develop a small eye. It follows, therefore, that after many generations, larger eyes are going to be dominant in the male population. You can say that, over time, the creatures are *converging* toward a particular genotype.

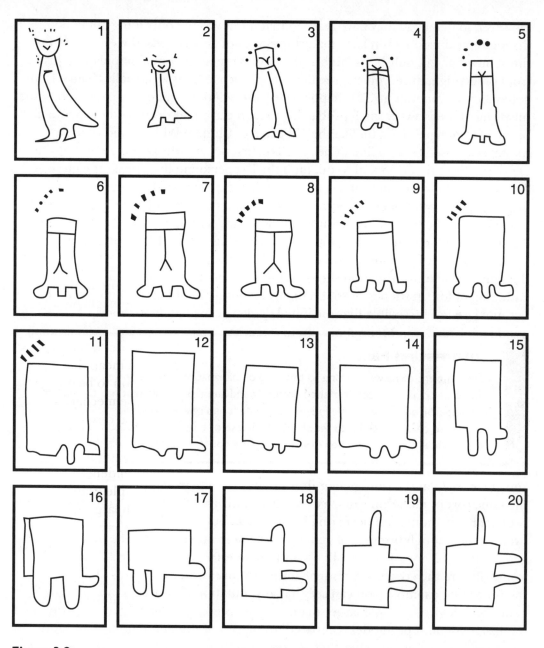

Figure 3.2

An experiment in information transference. (Figure from Illusions *by Thames and Hudson.)*

However, some of you may have realized that if this was the only thing going on during reproduction, even after many thousands of generations, the eye size of the fittest member can only be as large as the largest eye in the initial population. Just from observing nature, you can see that trends such as eye size actually change from generation to generation. This happens because when the genes are passed on to the offspring, there is a very small probability that an error may occur and the genes may be slightly changed. It's a bit like the old game of Chinese Whispers, in which a message is passed down a line of people. The first person whispers a phrase into the ear of the second person and so on, until the last person in line speaks the message he heard. Usually, to much amusement, the final message will be nothing like the original. These types of errors occur in just about any sort of information passed from one system to the next. An amazing example of this is the drawings shown in Figure 3.2. These are the results of a test in which a drawing of a bird (far left) was passed to the next person to be copied, and then that copy was passed to the next person, until the remarkable transformation shown at the end was reached. If you are ever in a gathering of fifteen friends or so, I'd highly recommend doing this little exercise, because it seems incredible that the initial drawing can change so much.

Interesting Fact

Even ancient coins were prone to this type of information loss. Early Celtic and Teutonic coins were counterfeited profusely, and an original coin that had the face of an emperor on it could be found—by the time it had reached outlaying towns and cities—to have changed into the shape of a horse or a bowl of fruit. You didn't need high-tech ultraviolet-detection devices to spot a counterfeit in those days!

You could say that the sentence or drawing has *mutated* from person to person, and the same sort of mutation can occur to genes during the reproduction process. The probability of a mutation occurring is very small, but nevertheless it is significant over a large enough number of generations. Some mutations will be disadvantageous (probably most), some will do nothing to effect the creature's fitness, but some will give the creature a distinct advantage over other creatures of its type. In the preceding example, you can see that any mutation that occurs in a creature's genes, which gives rise to a larger diameter eye, is going to make that creature stand out like a Vogue supermodel compared to the rest of the population. Therefore, the trend will be toward genes that are responsible for larger and larger eyes. After thousands of generations, this process of evolution may produce eyes as big as dinner plates! See Figure 3.3.

Figure 3.3

The evolution of an Adonis.

In addition to being able to alter an existing feature, the mechanisms of evolution can give birth to completely new features. Let's take the evolution of the eye as an example…

Imagine a time when the creatures didn't have eyes at all. In those days, the creatures navigated their environment and avoided their predators entirely by smell and touch. And they were pretty good at it too, because they had been doing just fine for thousands of generations—in those days, males with big noses and hands were popular with the girls. Then one day, when two of the creatures mated, a mutation occurred in the genes that provide the blueprint for skin cells. This mutation gave rise to offspring that developed a skin cell on their head, which was ever so slightly light-sensitive—just enough so that the offspring could tell whether it was light or dark in their environment. Now, this gave them a slight advantage, because if a predator—an eagle for example—got within a certain range, it would block out the light, and the creatures would know to run for cover. Also, the skin cell would indicate whether it was night or day, or whether they were overground or underground, which may give them an advantage in hunting and feeding. You can see that this new type of skin cell gave the creatures a slight advantage over the rest of the population and, therefore, a better probability of surviving and reproducing. Over time, because of the mechanisms of evolution, more creatures will possess chromosomes that include the gene for the light-sensitive skin cell.

Now, if you extrapolate this a little and imagine further advantageous mutations to the same skin cell gene, you can see how, over many generations, the area of light sensitivity may grow larger and obtain features that give better definition, such as a lens and additional cells to detect color. Imagine a mutation that would provide the creature with not just one of these areas of light sensitivity, but two, and therefore, gift the creature with stereo vision. Stereo vision is a *huge* step forward for an organism, because now it can tell exactly how far away objects are. Of course, you may also get mutations to those same genes, which give rise to features detrimental to the eye, but the important point here is that those creatures will not be as successful as their cousins with the new and improved eyes, and therefore, they will eventually die out. Only the more successful genes will be inherited. You can observe any feature in nature and see how it may have evolved using a myriad of tiny little mutations, all of which are advantageous to its owner. Incredible, isn't it?

So, these mechanisms of recombination and mutation illustrate how evolution works, and I hope you now understand how organisms can develop different types of features to help them be more successful within their environment.

A Quick Lesson in Binary Numbers

Before you go any further, I need to make sure you understand the binary number system. If you already know how binary numbers work, skip this little section. If you don't, let me enlighten you...

I think the easiest way to learn about binary numbers (or base 2) is to first examine how and why you count in decimal (base 10).

It's commonly accepted that humans count using base 10 because we have ten digits on our hands. Imagine one of our ancestors, let's call him Ug, hundreds of thousands of years ago counting the number of mammoths in a herd. Ug starts to count by making two fists, then for every mammoth he sees, he extends a digit. He continues doing this until all his fingers and thumbs have been used; then he knows he has counted ten mammoths. However, the herd contains far more than ten mammoths, so Ug has to think of a way to count higher. He scratches his head, has an idea, and calls his friend, Frak, over. Ug realized that by using Frak's thumb to represent the ten mammoths he just counted, frees up his fingers and thumbs to start the process all over again—to count eleven, twelve, thirteen, and so on, all the way up to twenty when another of Frak's digits is required. As you can see, Ug and Frak can count up to 110 mammoths using this process (that would be a terrific sight, don't you think?), but to count any higher, they would need to recruit yet another friend.

When humans eventually worked out how to write down numbers, they did it in a similar way. To represent base 10 numbers, you create a series of columns, each of which basically represents a person's pair of hands, just like this:

1000's	100's	10's	units

So, to count to 15, you increase the units column until you reach 9, and then because you cannot count any higher using this column, you increment the 10s column and start all over again from zero in the units column, until you end up with:

1000's	100's	10's	units
		1	5

The number fifteen is made up of one ten and five units. (I know this is probably sounding really obvious to you, but this detailed analysis is necessary.) You see, the binary number system (or any other number system for that matter) works in the same way. But instead of having ten digits to count with, you only have one! So, when you write down numbers in Base 2, the columns (in binary they are known as *bits*) represent numbers like this.

16's	8,s	4,s	2's	units

Now you will count to 15. First, you increment the units column.

16's	8,s	4,s	2's	units
				1

Now, because you cannot count any higher than this (you only have one digit, remember), you have to increment the column to the left to continue, so the number 2 looks like this:

16's	8,s	4,s	2's	units
			1	0

The number 3 looks like this:

16's	8,s	4,s	2's	units
			1	1

The number 4 looks like this:

16's	8,s	4,s	2's	units
		I	0	0

and so on until you reach 15.

16's	8,s	4,s	2's	units
	I	I	I	I

And that's all there is to it. By now, you should be able to convert from decimal to binary or vice versa. I should also point out that binary numbers are often a set number of bits, especially when you talk about them in relation to computers. That's why processors are described as being 8-, 16-, 32-, or 64-bit. This means that if you are representing the number 15 in 8-bit binary, you would write it like this:

0000I I I I

As an exercise, just to make sure you understand this concept, try to answer the following questions before you move on to the next section (the answers are at the end of this chapter):

1. Convert 27 from decimal to binary.

2. Convert the binary number 10101 into decimal.

3. Represent the decimal number 135 as an 8-bit binary number.

Easy, eh? Now that you have an elementary idea of binary numbers, let's get on with the more exciting stuff...

Evolution Inside Your Computer

The way genetic algorithms work is essentially mimicking evolution. First, you figure out a way of *encoding* any potential solution to your problem as a "digital" chromosome. Then, you create a start population of random chromosomes (each one representing a different candidate solution) and evolve them over time by "breeding" the fittest individuals and adding a little mutation here and there. With a bit of luck, over many generations, the genetic algorithm will converge upon a solution. Genetic algorithms do not guarantee a solution, nor do they guarantee to find the best solution, but if utilized the correct way, you will generally be able to code a genetic algorithm that will perform well. The best thing about genetic algorithms is that you *do not need to know how to solve a problem*; you only need to know how to encode it in a way the genetic algorithm mechanism can utilize.

Typically, the chromosomes are encoded as a series of binary bits. At the start of a run, you create a population of chromosomes, and each chromosome has its bits set at random. The length of the chromosome is usually fixed for the entire population. As an example, this is what a chromosome of length twenty may look like:

0I0I00I0I00I0I00I I I I

The important thing is that each chromosome is encoded in such a way that the string of bits may be *decoded* to represent a solution to the problem at hand. It may be a very poor solution, or it may be a perfect solution, but every single chromosome represents a possible solution (more on the encoding in a moment). Usually the starting population is *terrible*, a little like the English cricket team or an American playing football (sorry, soccer). Anyway, like I said, an initial population of random bits is created (let's say one hundred for this example), and then you do this (don't worry about the italicized phrases. I'll be explaining each one in just a moment):

Loop until a solution is found:

1. Test each chromosome to see how good it is at solving the problem and assign a fitness score accordingly.

2. Select two members from the current population. The probability of being selected is proportional to the chromosome's fitness—the higher the fitness, the better the probability of being selected. A common method for this is called *Roulette wheel selection.*

3. Dependent on the *Crossover Rate*, crossover the bits from each chosen chromosome at a randomly chosen point.

4. Step through the chosen chromosome's bits and flip dependent on the *Mutation Rate.*

5. Repeat steps 2, 3, and 4 until a new population of one hundred members has been created.

End loop

Each loop through the algorithm is called a *generation* (steps 1 through 5). I call the entire loop an *epoch* and will be referring to it as such in my text and code.

What's Roulette Wheel Selection?

Roulette wheel selection is a method of choosing members from the population of chromosomes in a way that is proportional to their fitness—for example, the fitter the chromosome, the more probability it has of being selected. It does not guarantee that the fittest member goes through to the next generation, merely that it has a very good probability of doing so. It works like this:

Imagine that the population's total fitness score is represented by a pie chart, or roulette wheel (see Figure 3.4). Now, you assign a slice of the wheel to each member of the population. The size of the slice is proportional to that chromosome's fitness score—the fitter a member is, the bigger the slice of pie it gets. Now, to choose a chromosome, all you have to do is spin the wheel, toss in the ball, and grab the chromosome that the ball stops on. I'll be showing you the exact algorithm for coding this a little later in the chapter.

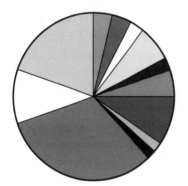

Figure 3.4

Roulette wheel selection of chromosomes.

What's the Crossover Rate?

The *crossover rate* is simply the probability that two chosen chromosomes will swap their bits to produce two new offspring. Experimentation has shown that a good value for this is typically around 0.7, although some problem domains may require much higher or lower values.

Every time you choose two chromosomes from the population, you test to see if they will crossover bits by generating a random number between 0 and 1. If the number is lower than the crossover rate (0.7), then you choose a random position along the length of the chromosome and swap all the bits after that point.

For example, given two chromosomes:

1000100111|0010010

0101000100|000011

you choose a random position along the length, say 10, and swap all the bits to the right of that point accordingly.

So the chromosomes become (I've left a space at the crossover point):

$$1000 1001 1 \ 0100001 1$$

$$0101000 10 \ 1001 0010$$

What's the Mutation Rate?

The *mutation rate* is the probability that a bit within a chromosome will be flipped (a 0 becomes 1, and a 1 becomes 0). This is usually a very low value for binary encoded genes, for example 0.001.

So, whenever you choose chromosomes from the population, you first check for crossover, and then you move through each bit of the offspring's chromosomes and test to see if it needs to be mutated.

Phew!

Don't worry if some of that was meaningless! Most of what you read from now until the end of the chapter is designed for you to read through twice. There are so many new concepts for you to understand, and they are all intermingled with each other. I believe this is the best way for you to learn. The first time you read through, you'll hopefully get a feel for the basic concepts, but the second time (if I've done my job correctly), you'll begin to see how the different ideas link together. When you finally start to play with the code, everything should slot into place nicely, and then it's only a matter of refining your knowledge and skills (that's the easy part).

And the best way for you to understand these new concepts is to throw yourself in at the deep end and start coding a simple genetic algorithm. Sound good? Okay, here's what you are going to do:

Helping Bob Home

Because path-finding seems to be one of the Holy Grails of game AI, you are going to create a genetic algorithm to

> **NOTE**
>
> You can find the source code for the pathfinder project in the Chapter3/ Pathfinder folder on the accompanying CD-ROM.
>
> If you feel like taking a quick peek before you read any further, there is a ready-made executable, 'pathfinder.exe', in the Chapter3/ Executable folder.
>
> (All the code and executables for each chapter are stored under their relevant folders on the CD in this way).

solve a very simple path-finding scenario. You will set up a maze that has an entrance at one end, an exit at the other, and some obstacles scattered about. Then you are going to position a virtual man, let's call him Bob, at the start and *evolve* a path for him that takes him to the exit and manages to avoid all the obstacles. I'll show you how to encode Bob's chromosomes in a second, but first I need to tell you how you are going to represent the maze…

The maze is a 2D array of integers; a 0 will represent open space, a 1 will represent a wall or an obstacle, a 5 will be the start point, and an 8 will be the exit. So, the integer array

{1, 1, 1, 1, 1, 1, 1, 1, 1, 1, 1, 1, 1, 1, 1,

1, 0, 1, 0, 0, 0, 0, 0, 1, 1, 1, 0, 0, 0, 1,

8, 0, 0, 0, 0, 0, 0, 0, 1, 1, 1, 0, 0, 0, 1,

1, 0, 0, 0, 1, 1, 1, 0, 0, 1, 0, 0, 0, 0, 1,

1, 0, 0, 0, 1, 1, 1, 0, 0, 0, 0, 0, 1, 0, 1,

1, 1, 0, 0, 1, 1, 1, 0, 0, 0, 0, 0, 1, 0, 1,

1, 0, 0, 0, 0, 1, 0, 0, 0, 0, 1, 1, 1, 0, 1,

1, 0, 1, 1, 0, 0, 0, 1, 0, 0, 0, 0, 0, 0, 5,

1, 0, 1, 1, 0, 0, 0, 1, 0, 0, 0, 0, 0, 0, 1,

1, 1, 1, 1, 1, 1, 1, 1, 1, 1, 1, 1, 1, 1, 1}

will look a little like Figure 3.5 when on the screen:

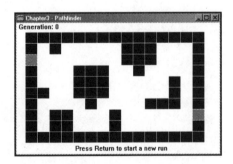

Figure 3.5

Bob's Maze. The entrance and exit are clearly marked in red. Eat your heart out, Carmack!

I've encapsulated this map concept in a class called CBobsMap. It is defined as:

```
class CBobsMap
{
private:
```

```
    //storage for the map
    static const int  map[MAP_HEIGHT][MAP_WIDTH];

    static const int  m_iMapWidth;
    static const int  m_iMapHeight;

    //index into the array which is the start point
    static const int  m_iStartX;
    static const int  m_iStartY;

    //and the finish point
    static const int  m_iEndX;
    static const int  m_iEndY;


public:

  //you can use this array as Bobs memory if rqd
  int  memory[MAP_HEIGHT][MAP_WIDTH];

  CBobsMap()
  {
    ResetMemory();
  }

  //takes a string of directions and see's how far Bob
  //can get. Returns a fitness score proportional to the
  //distance reached from the exit.
  double TestRoute(const vector<int> &vecPath, CBobsMap &memory);

  //given a surface to draw on this function uses the windows GDI
  //to display the map.
  void Render(const int cxClient, const int cyClient, HDC surface);

  //draws whatever path may be stored in the memory
  void MemoryRender(const int cxClient, const int cyClient, HDC surface);

  void ResetMemory();
};
```

As you can see, you simply store the map array as a constant, along with the start and end points. These values are defined in CBobsMap.cpp, which you can find in the relevant folder on the CD. In addition to storing the maze, this map class is also used to record Bob's progress through the maze in the array: memory[][]. This is not essential for the genetic algorithm itself, but a record is required for display purposes, so you can see where Bob wanders. The important member function here is TestRoute(), which takes a series of directions and tests them to see how far Bob can travel. I'll not waste the planet's trees by listing the TestRoute() function here, because it's one of those functions that is very simple, but would probably be a couple of pages long to list. It is suffice to say that, given a vector of directions—representing North, South, East, and West—TestRoute calculates the farthest position in the map Bob can reach and then returns a fitness score proportional to Bob's final distance from the exit. The closer to the exit he gets, the higher the fitness score he is rewarded. If he actually reaches the exit, Bob gets a pat on the back and receives the maximum (in this example) fitness score of one, and the loop automatically exits because you have found a solution. Hurrah!

Again, do not worry about understanding every aspect of this class immediately. Everything will start to click shortly.

Encoding the Chromosome

Each chromosome must be encoded to represent the movement of our little man, Bob. Bob's movement is restricted to four directions: North, South, East, and West, so the encoded chromosomes should be strings of information representing these four directions. The traditional method of encoding is changing the directions into binary code. Only two bits are necessary to represent four directions, as denoted by

Code	Decoded	Direction
00	0	North
01	1	South
10	2	East
11	3	West

Therefore, if you take a random string of bits, you can decode them into a series of directions for Bob to follow. For example the chromosome:

11111001101110111010010101

represents the genes

$$11, 11, 10, 01, 10, 11, 10, 11, 10, 01, 01, 01$$

that when decoded from binary to decimal become

$$3, 3, 2, 1, 2, 3, 2, 3, 2, 1, 1, 1$$

And again, in table form, just to make sure you are at one with this idea:

Code	Decoded	Direction
11	3	West
11	3	West
10	2	East
01	1	South
10	2	East
11	3	West
10	2	East
11	3	West
10	2	East
01	1	South
01	1	South
01	1	South

Now, all you have to do is place Bob at the start and tell him to follow those directions. If a direction makes Bob bump into a wall, that instruction is simply ignored and the program moves on to the next instruction. This continues until either the vector of directions is exhausted or Bob reaches the exit. If you imagine a collection of hundreds of these random chromosomes, you can see how some of them may decode to give a set of directions which would allow Bob to reach the exit (a solution), but most of them will fail. The genetic algorithm takes an initial population of random bit strings (the chromosomes), tests each one to see how close it lets Bob get to the exit, then breeds the better ones in hopes of creating offspring that will let Bob get a little bit closer to the exit. This continues until a solution is found or until Bob becomes hopelessly stuck in a corner (which can and will happen, as you will see).

So, a structure must be defined that holds a string of bits (the chromosome) and a fitness score associated with that chromosome. I call this the SGenome structure, and it's defined like this:

```
struct SGenome
{
```

```
vector<int> vecBits;
double       dFitness;
SGenome():dFitness(0){}
SGenome(const int num_bits):dFitness(0)
{
  //create a random bit string
  for (int i=0; i<num_bits; ++i)
  {
    vecBits.push_back(RandInt(0, 1));
  }
}
};
```

As you can see, if you create a SGenome object by passing the constructor an int as a parameter, it automatically creates a random bit string of that length, initializes the fitness to zero, and the genome is all primed to go.

Programming Note

std::vector is part of the STL (standard template library) and is a ready-made class for handling dynamic arrays. Elements are added to it by using the method push_back(). Here is a simple example:

```
#include<vector>

std::vector<int> MyFirstVector;

for (int i=0; i< 10; i++)
{
  MyFirstVector.push_back(i);
  cout << endl << MyFirstVector[i];
}
```

To empty a vector, use the clear() method.

```
MyFirstVector.clear();
```

You can get the number of elements in a vector using the size() method.

```
MyFirstVector.size()
```

That's it. No need to worry about memory management—std::vector does it all for you! I will be using it throughout the program, when appropriate.

The SGenome structure has no knowledge of how the chromosome (vecBits) should be decoded; that is a task for the genetic algorithm class itself. Let's take a quick peek at the definition of that class now. I've named it CgaBob (sometimes I surprise myself with my originality, I really do).

```cpp
class CgaBob
{
private:

  //the population of genomes
  vector<SGenome> m_vecGenomes;

  //size of population
  int             m_iPopSize;

  double          m_dCrossoverRate;

  double          m_dMutationRate;

  //how many bits per chromosome
  int             m_iChromoLength;

  //how many bits per gene
  int             m_iGeneLength;

  int             m_iFittestGenome;

  double          m_dBestFitnessScore;

  double          m_dTotalFitnessScore;

  int             m_iGeneration;

  //create an instance of the map class
  CBobsMap        m_BobsMap;

  // another CBobsMap object is used to keep a record of
  //the best route each generation as an array of visited
  //cells. This is only used for display purposes.
```

```
  CBobsMap        m_BobsBrain;

  //lets you know if the current run is in progress.
  bool            m_bBusy;


  void            Mutate(vector<int> &vecBits);

  void            Crossover(const vector<int> &mum,
                            const vector<int> &dad,
                            vector<int>       &baby1,
                            vector<int>       &baby2);

  SGenome&        RouletteWheelSelection();

  //updates the genomes fitness with the new fitness scores and calculates
  //the highest fitness and the fittest member of the population.
  void            UpdateFitnessScores();

  //decodes a vector of bits into a vector of directions (ints)
  vector<int> Decode(const vector<int> &bits);

  //converts a vector of bits into decimal. Used by Decode.
  int             BinToInt(const vector<int> &v);

  //creates a start population of random bit strings
  void            CreateStartPopulation();

public:

  CgaBob(double cross_rat,
         double mut_rat,
         int    pop_size,
         int    num_bits,
         int    gene_len):m_dCrossoverRate(cross_rat),
                          m_dMutationRate(mut_rat),
                          m_iPopSize(pop_size),
                          m_iChromoLength(num_bits),
                          m_dTotalFitnessScore(0.0),
```

```
                          m_iGeneration(0),
                          m_iGeneLength(gene_len),
                          m_bBusy(false)
  {
    CreateStartPopulation();
  }

  void   Run(HWND hwnd);

  void   Epoch();

  void   Render(int cxClient, int cyClient, HDC surface);

  //accessor methods
  int    Generation(){return m_iGeneration;}
  int    GetFittest(){return m_iFittestGenome;}
  bool   Started(){return m_bBusy;}
  void   Stop(){m_bBusy = false;}
};
```

As you can see, when an instance of this class is created, the constructor initializes all the variables and calls CreateStartPopulation(). This little function sets up a population of the required amount of genomes. Each genome, don't forget, initially starts off containing a chromosome comprised of random bits and a fitness score set to zero.

Epoch

The meat and bones of your genetic algorithm class is the Epoch() method. This is the genetic algorithm loop that I described earlier in the chapter and is the workhorse of the class. This one method more or less ties everything together. Let's take a close look at it then...

```
void CgaBob::Epoch()
{
  UpdateFitnessScores();
```

The first thing done each epoch is to test the fitness scores of each member of the population. UpdateFitnessScores is a function that decodes the binary chromosome of each genome and sends the decoded series of directions (comprised of integers representing north, south, east, and west) to CBobsMap::TestRoute. This, in turn, checks how far Bob traverses through the map and returns a fitness score proportional to his finished distance from the exit. Let me quickly talk you through the few lines of source that calculate Bob's fitness:

```
Int DiffX = abs(posX - m_iEndX);
int DiffY = abs(posY - m_iEndY);
```

DiffX and DiffY simply hold the number of cells Bob is offset horizontally and vertically from the exit. Take a look at Figure 3.6. The gray cells represent Bob's route through the maze, and the cell with **B** on it is where he finally ends up. At this position DiffX =3 and DiffY = 0.

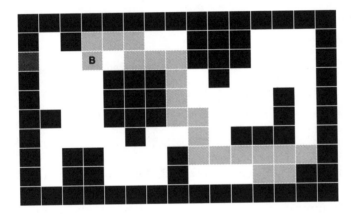

Figure 3.6

Bob attempts to find the exit.

```
return 1/(double)(DiffX+DiffY+1);
```

This next line calculates the fitness score by adding these two figures together and calculating the inverse. One is added to the sum of DiffX and DiffY to make sure we don't get a divide by zero error if Bob reaches the exit when DiffX + DiffY = 0.

UpdateFitnessScores also keeps track of the fittest genome of each generation and the total combined fitness of all the genomes. These values are used when performing Roulette Wheel Selection. Now that you've learned what UpdateFitnessScores() does, let's get back to the Epoch function...

Because a new population of genomes is created each epoch, we need to find somewhere to put them as they are created (two at a time).

```
//Now to create a new population
int NewBabies = 0;

//create some storage for the baby genomes
vector<SGenome> vecBabyGenomes;
```

Now to move on to the business of the genetic algorithm loop.

```
while (NewBabies < m_iPopSize)
{
  //select 2 parents
  SGenome mum = RouletteWheelSelection();
  SGenome dad = RouletteWheelSelection();
```

Each iteration, two genomes are selected to be the parents of two new baby chromosomes. I like to call them mum and dad (because that's what they will be). If you recall, the fitter a genome is, the better probability it will have of being selected to become a parent by the Roulette Wheel Selection method.

```
  //operator - crossover
  SGenome baby1, baby2;
  Crossover(mum.vecBits, dad.vecBits, baby1.vecBits, baby2.vecBits);
```

Two blank genomes are created—these are the babies—and are passed, along with the selected parents, to the Crossover function. This function performs crossover (dependent on the m_dCrossoverRate variable) and stores the new chromosome bit strings in baby1 and baby2.

```
  //operator - mutate
  Mutate(baby1.vecBits);
  Mutate(baby2.vecBits);
```

Next, the babies are mutated! Sounds horrible, but it's good for them. The probability that a baby's bits are mutated is dependent on the m_dMutationRate variable.

```
  //add to new population
  vecBabyGenomes.push_back(baby1);
  vecBabyGenomes.push_back(baby2);

  NewBabies += 2;
}
```

These two new offspring are finally added to the new population, and that's one completed iteration of the loop. This process is repeated until an amount of offspring has been created that is equal to the size of the start population.

```
  //copy babies back into starter population
  m_vecGenomes = vecBabyGenomes;

  //increment the generation counter
```

```
    ++m_iGeneration;
}
```

Here the old population is replaced with the new offspring and a counter is incremented to keep track of the current generation. And that's it. Easy, eh?

This Epoch function is repeated endlessly, until the chromosomes converge upon a solution or until the user decides to stop. I'll show you the code for each of the operators in a moment, but first let's have a chat about determining what parameters you should use.

Choosing the Parameter Values

I put all the parameters used in the code in the file defines.h. Most of these will be self–explanatory, but there are a few I'd like to discuss, namely

```
#define CROSSOVER_RATE    0.7
#define MUTATION_RATE    0.001
#define POP_SIZE          140
#define CHROMO_LENGTH      70
```

You may wonder how I know what variables to use. And that's the million dollar question, because there are no hard and fast rules for determining these values, only guidelines. In the end, choosing these values comes down to obtaining a "feel" for genetic algorithms, and you'll only get that by coding your own and playing around with the parameters to see what happens. Different problems need different values, but generally speaking, if you are using a binary-encoded chromosome, the values of 0.7 for the crossover rate and 0.001 for the mutation rate are good defaults with which to start. A useful rule for your population size is to have roughly twice as many genomes as the length of your chromosome.

I have chosen the chromosome length of 70 here because 70 represents a possible maximum of 35 moves, which is more than adequate for Bob to traverse the map and find the exit. As you learn techniques in later chapters to make your genetic algorithms more efficient, you will be able to reduce that length.

Historical Note

Genetic algorithms are the brain child of John Holland, who came up with the idea in the early 60s. Incredibly, he didn't feel the need to actually try them out on a computer and instead preferred to tinker about with a pen and paper! It was only when a student of his wrote a program that ran on a home personal computer that the world finally saw what could be achieved by implementing his ideas in software.

The Operator Functions

I'll now go through the code for each of the genetic operator functions—selection, crossover, and mutation. Although simple, going through the code with you gives you the opportunity to review these functions. You will be getting to know them intimately as you progress with your knowledge of genetic algorithms.

Roulette Wheel Selection Revisited

Let's start with Roulette wheel selection. Remember, this function chooses a genome from the population using a probability proportional to its fitness.

```
SGenome& CgaBob::RouletteWheelSelection()
{
  double fSlice = RandFloat() * m_dTotalFitnessScore;
```

First, a random number is chosen between zero and the total fitness score. I like to think that this number represents a slice in the pie of all the fitness scores, as shown earlier in Figure 3.4.

```
  double cfTotal       = 0;
  int    SelectedGenome = 0;

  for (int i=0; i<m_iPopSize; ++i)
  {
    cfTotal += m_vecGenomes[i].dFitness;

    if (cfTotal > fSlice)
    {
      SelectedGenome = i;
      break;
    }
  }

  return m_vecGenomes[SelectedGenome];
}
```

Now, the code iterates through the genomes adding up the fitness scores as it goes. When this subtotal is greater than the fSlice value, it returns the genome at that point. It's as simple as that.

Crossover Revisited

Here a function is required that splits the chromosomes at a random point and then swaps all the bits after that point to create two new chromosomes (the offspring).

```
void CgaBob::Crossover( const vector<int> &mum,
                        const vector<int> &dad,
                        vector<int>       &baby1,
                        vector<int>       &baby2)
{
```

This function is passed references to two parent chromosomes (don't forget a chromosome is just a std::vector of integers) and two empty vectors into which the offspring are copied.

```
  if ( (RandFloat() > m_dCrossoverRate) || (mum == dad))
  {
    baby1 = mum;
    baby2 = dad;

    return;
  }
```

First, a check is made to see if crossover is going to be performed on the two parents, mum and dad. The probability of crossover occurring is based on the parameter m_dCrossoverRate. If no crossover is to occur, the parents' chromosomes are copied straight into the offspring without alteration and the function returns.

```
  int cp = RandInt(0, m_iChromoLength - 1);
```

A random point is chosen along the length of the chromosome to split the chromosomes.

```
  for (int i=0; i<cp; i++)
  {
    baby1.push_back(mum[i]);
    baby2.push_back(dad[i]);
  }

  for (i=cp; i<mum.size(); i++)
  {
    baby1.push_back(dad[i]);
    baby2.push_back(mum[i]);
  }
}
```

These two little loops swap the bits of each parent after the crossover point (cp) and assign the new chromosomes to the children: baby1 and baby2.

Mutation Revisited

This function simply travels down the length of a chromosome and flips its bits with a probability dependent on m_dMutationRate.

```
void CgaBob::Mutate(vector<int> &vecBits)
{
  for (int curBit=0; curBit<vecBits.size(); curBit++)
  {
    //flip this bit?
    if (RandFloat() < m_dMutationRate)
    {
      //flip the bit
      vecBits[curBit] = !vecBits[curBit];
    }
  }//next bit
}
```

And that's it. Your first genetic algorithm is complete! Now let me take a moment to explain what you will see when you run the Pathfinder program.

Running the Pathfinder Program

When you run the Pathfinder program, you will see that the program does not find a path to the exit every time. Sometimes Bob gets stuck, wobbling about uncertainly like a drunken man trying to find his way home. This is mainly due to the population converging upon one particular type of chromosome too quickly. Therefore, because the population becomes so similar, the beneficial effects of the crossover operator are practically erased, and all that is happening is a small amount of mutation every now and then. Because the mutation rate is set so low, mutation itself is not enough to find a solution once the diversity of chromosome types is lost. Also, because of the way Roulette wheel selection works, the fittest chromosome in any given generation is not guaranteed to pass to the next generation. This means the genetic algorithm may find a population member that is almost a perfect solution, only to kill it off more or less instantly, and in doing so, lose all the good genes it possesses! In later chapters, I'll be addressing these problems and describing techniques that will help maintain diversity while retaining the fitter genomes. First, though, I want to spend some time looking at different encoding techniques and how they relate to different types of problems you may encounter. That's what we'll be doing in the next chapter.

ANSWERS TO BINARY NUMBER QUESTIONS (from page 98)

1. 11011
2. 21
3. 10000111

Stuff to Try

At the end of every chapter from this point on, I'm going to give you some ideas to play around with. I cannot stress how important it is to tinker with code. It's the only way you will develop that magical "feel" for these algorithms. And, when you start to do complicated stuff, that "feel" gets mighty important.

1. Experiment with different parameters for crossover rate, mutation rate, population size, and chromosome length. Observe how they affect the efficiency of the algorithm.

2. Try turning off the crossover operator and increasing the mutation rate. What happens? What happens if you just use crossover with no mutation?

3. Alter the fitness function so that chromosomes that step into the same cell more than once are penalized. This should result in more efficient paths to the exit.

4. What else could you do to make the path more efficient?

CHAPTER 4

PERMUTATION ENCODING AND THE TRAVELING SALESMAN PROBLEM

A traveling salesman came upon an old farmer sitting on his porch. Next to the farmer was a pig with only one leg. The salesman was about to give his sales pitch when his curiosity got the best of him.

"Excuse me sir, but why does your pig only have one leg?" asked the salesman.

"Well, sonny, I'll tell ya. One day I was out plowing the back 40 when my tractor overturned, pinning me underneath. I was losing blood and thought I would die when that pig came running. He dug and rooted around with his nose till he got me out and he dragged me back to the house—md]saved my life that pig did."

"Wow, that's really amazing," said the salesman," but I still don't know why the pig only has one leg."

"Well, sonny, when you get a pig that smart, you don't want to eat him all at once!"

Now that you understand the basics of genetic algorithms, I'll spend this chapter looking at a completely different way of encoding genetic algorithms that solve problems involving permutations. A good example of this is a famous problem called "The Traveling Salesman Problem."

The Traveling Salesman Problem

Given a collection of cities, the traveling salesman must determine the shortest route that will enable him to visit each city precisely once and then return back to his starting point. See Figure 4.1.

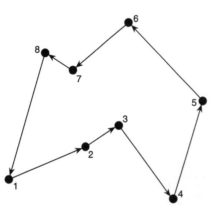

Figure 4.1

A simple eight-city Traveling Salesman Problem (TSP).

This problem is usually abbreviated to the TSP, which saves a lot of typing! It is a deceptively simple problem and is part of the set of what mathematicians call NP-Complete problems. It's not necessary to go into exactly what NP-Complete means here (it would involve a lot of mathematics for a start!), but basically, the difficulty is that as more cities are added, the computational power required to solve the problem increases exponentially. This means that an algorithm implemented on a computer that solves the TSP for fifty cities would require an increase in computer power of a thousand fold just to add an additional ten cities! You can see how the same algorithm would quickly reach the limits of any available hardware.

This type of problem frequently occurs when coding the AI for strategy games. Often it's necessary to create the shortest path for a unit that will start at one waypoint, end at another, and pass through several predefined areas along the way, to pick up resources, food, energy, and so on. It can also be used as part of the route planning AI for a Quake-like FPS bot. Obviously, a genetic algorithm cannot easily (on today's PCs) be run in real time to solve this type of problem, but it can be an invaluable tool to use either offline in the development phases of your AI, or if you have some sort of random map/level generation, it may even be used between levels in the map-creation code.

One of the great things about tackling the TSP during your learning curve—and the main reason I'm devoting over a chapter to it—is that it's a fantastic way of witnessing how making changes to your code can affect the results. Often, when coding genetic algorithms, it's not easy to visualize what effect a different mutation or crossover operator is having on your algorithm, or how a particular optimization technique is performing, but the TSP provides you with great visual feedback, as you shall see.

Table 4.1 shows some of the landmarks in TSP solving, starting from the 1950s.

As you'll discover when you start tinkering with your own genetic algorithms, finding a solution for over 15,000 cities is quite an achievement! You will be starting modestly, though. Twenty or so cities should be plenty for your first outing and is typically the amount of waypoints you would be using for a unit in a game. Although, trying to get your algorithm to perform well on larger numbers of cities can get addictive!

Traps to Avoid

At this point, it may be a good idea for you to make coffee, sit back, close your eyes, and spend a few minutes thinking about how you might tackle this problem...

Table 4.1   Landmarks in TSP Problem Solving

Year	Researcher/s	Number of cities
1954	Dantzig, Fulkerson, and Johnson	49
1971	Held and Karp	64
1975	Camerini, Fratta, and Maffioli	100
1977	Grötschel	120
1980	Crowder and Padberg	318
1987	Padberg and Rinaldi	532
1987	Grötschel and Holland	666
1987	Padberg and Rinaldi	2392
1994	Applegate, Bixby, Cook, and Chvátal	7397
1998	Applegate, Bixby, Cook, and Chvátal	13509
2001	Applegate, Bixby, Cook, and Chvátal	15112

As you may have realized, you can't take the same approach that you did in Chapter 3, "An Introduction to Genetic Algorithms." The main difference with the TSP is that solutions rely on permutations, and therefore, you have to make sure that all your genomes represent a valid permutation of the problem—a valid tour of all the cities. If you were to represent possible solutions using the binary encoding and crossover operator from the Pathfinder problem presented in Chapter 3, you can see how you would run into difficulties very quickly. Take the eight city example, shown in Figure 4.1. You could encode each city as a 3-bit binary number, numbering the cities from 0 to 7. So, if you had two possible tours, you could encode them like this:

Possible Tour	Binary Encoded Tour
3, 4, 0, 7, 2, 5, 1, 6	011 100 000 111 010 101 001 110
2, 5, 0, 3, 6, 1, 4, 7	010 101 000 011 110 001 100 111

Now, choose a crossover point (represented by an x) after the fourth city, and see what offspring you get.

Before Crossover

	Binary Encoded Tour	**Decoded Tour**
Parent 1	011 100 000 111 x 010 101 001 110	3, 4, 0, 7, 2, 5, 1, 6
Parent 2	010 101 000 011 x 110 001 100 111	2, 5, 0, 3, 6, 1, 4, 7

After Crossover

	Binary Encoded Tour	**Decoded Tour**
Child 1	011 100 000 111 x 110 001 100 111	3, 4, 0, 7, 6, 1, 4, 7
Child 2	010 101 000 011 x 110 001 100 111	2, 5, 0, 3, 2, 5, 1, 6

You can see the results of this crossover operation in Figure 4.2. You can see that there is a major problem! Both of the offspring have produced tours that contain duplicate cities, which of course means they are invalid.

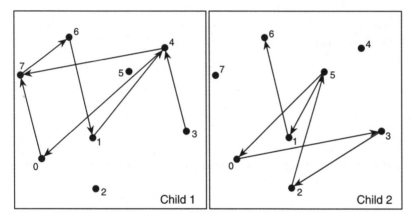

Figure 4.2

Invalid offspring.

To get this to work, you would have to code some hideous error-checking function to remove all the duplicates, which would probably lead to the destruction of any improvement gained up to that point in the tour. So, in the quest for a solution, a different type of crossover operator needs to be invented that only spawns valid offspring. Also, can you imagine what the previous mutation operator would do with this type of encoding? That's right, duplicate tours again. So, you also need to think about how you might implement a new type of mutation operator. Before you go any further though, doesn't binary encoding seem rather inelegant to you in the context of this problem? A better idea would be to use integers to represent each city. This, as you will see, will make life a lot easier all around. So, to clarify, the tour for parent one, shown in the preceding table, would be simply represented as a vector of integers:

3, 4, 0, 7, 6, 1, 4, 7

You will save a lot of computer time if you do it this way, because you don't have to waste processor cycles decoding and encoding the solutions back and forth from binary notation.

The CmapTSP, SGenome, and CgaTSP Declarations

Before I go on to describe the operators in detail, let's take a quick look at the header files for the TSP genetic algorithm program. The source code for this example is found in the appropriate folder on the accompanying CD. (I guess you've already figured that out though, eh?)

CmapTSP

To encapsulate the map data, the city coordinates, and the fitness calculations, I've created a class, CmapTSP, which is defined as follows (I shall comment further where necessary, but most of the definitions are self explanatory):

```
class CmapTSP
{
private:

  vector<CoOrd>  m_vecCityCoOrds;
```

A CoOrd is a simple structure defined to hold the x and y coordinates of each city. It looks like this:

```
struct CoOrd
{
  float x, y;

  CoOrd(){}
  CoOrd(float a, float b):x(a),y(b){}
};
```

Continuing with CmapTSP:

```
  //number of cities in our map
  int     m_NumCities;

  //client window dimensions
  int     m_MapWidth;
```

```
int     m_MapHeight;

//holds the length of the solution, if one is calculable.
double m_dBestPossibleRoute;

void        CreateCitiesCircular();
```

CreateCitiesCircular is a function that creates m_NumCities amount of cities in a circular pattern. I've coded it this way because it's easy to determine the best path (to check the genetic algorithm solution against) as well as being a great way of visualizing the genetic algorithm in progress. See Figure 4.3.

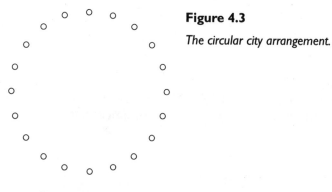

Figure 4.3

The circular city arrangement.

Cities are arranged in a circle

```
double      CalculateA_to_B(const CoOrd &city1, const CoOrd &city2);
```

This method simply calculates the distance between two cities using Pythagoras's famous equation "*Given a right-angled triangle, the square of the hypotenuse is equal to the sum of the squares of the other two sides.*" See Figure 4.4.

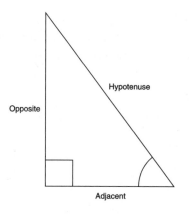

Figure 4.4

The sides of a right-angled triangle.

Hypotenuse

Opposite

Adjacent

```
void       CalculateBestPossibleRoute();
```

This function calculates the best possible route for a circular arrangement of cities. Because they are arranged in a circle, this is trivial to calculate. The shortest route is the one that connects all the cities together in a circular chain, as shown in Figure 4.5.

Figure 4.5

A last! A task where running around in circles is to be desired!

So, `CalculateBestPossibleRoute` simply calls `CMapTSP::CalculateA_to_B` for each pair of cities as it steps around the circle and returns the sum of all the distances between them.

```
public:

  CmapTSP(int w, int h, int nc):m_MapWidth(w),
                                 m_MapHeight(h),
                                 m_NumCities(nc)
  {
     //calculate the co-ordinates for the cities
     CreateCitiesCircular();

     CalculateBestPossibleRoute();
  }
```

When an instance of this class is created, the coordinates of the required number of cities are created and the best possible tour is calculated. The city coordinates are stored in `m_vecCityCoOrds`.

```
  //used if user changes the client window dimensions
  void    Refresh(const int new_width, const int new_height);

  double GetTourLength(const vector<int> &route);
```

Given a valid tour of cities, `GetTourLength` returns the total distance traveled. This is the workhorse of the fitness function.

```
//accessor methods
double        BestPossibleRoute(){return m_dBestPossibleRoute;}
vector<CoOrd> CityCoOrds(){return m_vecCityCoOrds;}
};
```

Figure 4.6 shows a screenshot of the program after the genetic algorithm has completed a successful run and found the optimum route between the cities. If you would like to run the program before you go any further, you can find a pre-compiled executable under the relevant chapter heading on the CD.

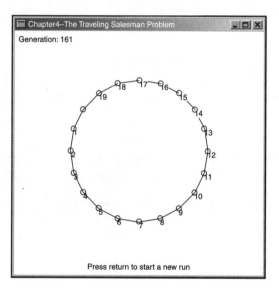

Figure 4.6

Success!

SGenome

The genome structure is defined as:

```
struct SGenome
{
  //the city tour (the chromosome)
  vector<int>    vecCities;
  double         dFitness;

  //ctor
```

```
SGenome():dFitness(0){}

SGenome(int nc): dFitness(0)
{
    vecCities = GrabPermutation(nc);
}

//creates a random tour of the cities
vector<int>   GrabPermutation( int &limit);

//used in GrabPermutation
bool          TestNumber(const vector<int> &vec, const int &number);

//overload '<' used for sorting
friend bool operator<(const SGenome& lhs, const SGenome& rhs)
{
    return (lhs.dFitness < rhs.dFitness);
}
};
```

The genome will consist of a candidate tour stored in a std::vector of integers, vecCities, and a fitness score, dFitness.

When an SGenome object is created by passing the constructor an integer (n) representing the number of cities in the tour, the method GrabPermutation is called. This creates a random permutation of the series 0,1, ...n and stores it in vecCities. The genome is then ready and primed to add to the population. The GrabPermutation function code looks like this:

```
vector<int> SGenome::GrabPermutation(int &limit)
{
  vector<int> vecPerm;

  for (int i=0; i<limit; i++)
  {
    //we use limit-1 because we want ints numbered from zero
    int NextPossibleNumber = RandInt(0, limit-1);

    while(TestNumber(vecPerm, NextPossibleNumber))
    {
      NextPossibleNumber = RandInt(0, limit-1);
```

```
    }

    vecPerm.push_back(NextPossibleNumber);
  }


  return vecPerm;
}
```

CgaTSP

This is the declaration of the genetic algorithm class. Most of the member variables should be self-explanatory. I'll describe the member functions in more detail in the next section.

```
class CgaTSP
{
private:

  //the population of genomes
  vector<SGenome>  m_vecPopulation;

  //instance of the map class
  CmapTSP*       m_Map;

  double         m_dMutationRate;

  double         m_dCrossoverRate;

  //total fitness of the entire population
  double         m_dTotalFitness;

  //the shortest tour found so far
  double         m_dShortestRoute;

  //the worst tour found so far
  double         m_dLongestRoute;

  //number of genomes in the population
  int            m_iPopSize;

  //length of chromosome
```

```cpp
    int           m_iChromoLength;

    //the fittest member of the most recent generation
    int           m_iFittestGenome;

    //keeps track of which generation we are in
    int           m_iGeneration;

    //lets us know if the current run is in progress
    //used in the rendering function
    bool          m_bStarted;

    //Exchange Mutation
    void          MutateEM(vector<int> &chromo);

    //Partially Matched Crossover
    void          CrossoverPMX(const vector<int> &mum,
                               const vector<int> &dad,
                               vector<int>       &baby1,
                               vector<int>       &baby2);

  SGenome&        RouletteWheelSelection();

  void            CalculatePopulationsFitness();

  void            Epoch();

  void            Reset();

  void            CreateStartingPopulation();

public:

  //ctor
  CgaTSP(double  mut_rat,
         double  cross_rat,
         int     pop_size,
         int     NumCities,
         int     map_width,
```

```
    int     map_height):m_dMutationRate(mut_rat),
                        m_dCrossoverRate(cross_rat),
                        m_iPopSize(pop_size),
                        m_iFittestGenome(0),
                        m_iGeneration(0),
                        m_dShortestRoute(999999999),
                        m_dLongestRoute(0),
                        m_iChromoLength(NumCities),
                        m_bBusy(false)
{
    //set up the map
    m_Map = new CmapTSP(map_width,
                        map_height,
                        NumCities);

    CreateStartingPopulation();
}


//dtor
~CgaTSP(){delete m_Map;}


void        Run(HWND hwnd);

//accessor methods
void        Stop(){m_bStarted = false;}
bool        Started(){return m_bStarted;} };
```

As before, a crossover operator, a mutation operator, and a fitness function need to be defined. The most complex of these for the TSP is the crossover operator, because, as discussed earlier, a crossover function must provide *valid* offspring. So, I'll wade in at the deep end and start with that...

The Permutation Crossover Operator (PMX)

There are many solutions that provide valid offspring for a permutation-encoded chromosome: Partially-Mapped Crossover, Order Crossover, Alternating-Position Crossover, Maximal-Preservation Crossover, Position-Based Crossover, Edge-Recombination Crossover, Subtour-Chunks Crossover, and Intersection Crossover to name just a few. In this chapter, I'll be discussing one of the more popular cross-over types: *Partially-Mapped Crossover*, or PMX as it's more widely known. In the next chapter, I'll begin by giving descriptions of some of the alternatives, because it will be good practice for you to experiment with different operators to see what effect they may have on the efficiency of your genetic algorithm. But for now, let's just use PMX.

So, assuming the eight city problem has been encoded using integers, two possible parents may be:

Parent1: 2 . 5 . 0 . 3 . 6 . 1 . 4 . 7

Parent2: 3 . 4 . 0 . 7 . 2 . 5 . 1 . 6

To implement PMX, you must first choose two random crossover points—let's say after cities 3 and 6. So, the split is made at the x's, like so:

Parent1: 2 . 5 . 0 . x **3 . 6 . 1** x . 4 . 7

Parent2: 3 . 4 . 0 . x **7 . 2 . 5** x . 1 . 6

Then you look at the two center sections and make a note of the mapping between parents. In this example:

3 is mapped to **7**

6 is mapped to **2**

1 is mapped to **5**

Now, iterate through each parent's genes and swap the genes wherever a gene is found that matches one of those listed. Step by step it goes like this:

Step I

Child1: 2 . 5 . 0 . 3 . 6 . 1 . 4 . 7

Child2: 3 . 4 . 0 . 7 . 2 . 5 . 1 . 6

*(here the children are just direct
copies of their parents)*

Step 2 [3 and 7]

Child1: 2 . 5 . 0 . **7** . 6 . 1 . 4 . **3**

Child2: **7** . 4 . 0 . **3** . 2 . 5 . 1 . 6

Interesting Fact

The first mention of the Traveling Salesman Problem came from a mathematician and economist named Karl Menger in the 1920s, but became popular when a man named Merill Flood started discussing it with colleagues at the RAND Corporation in the late 40s. This was a time when there was a lot of interest in combinatorial problems, and mathematicians loved the TSP because it was so simple to describe, yet extremely difficult to solve. Today it is still widely used as a test problem for new combinatorial optimization methods.

Step 2 [6 and 2]

Child1: **6** . 5 . 0 . 7 . **2** . 1 . 4 . 3

Child2: 7 . 4 . 0 . 3 . **6** . 5 . 1 . **2**

Step 3 [1 and 5]

Child1: 6 . **1** . 0 . 7 . 2 . **5** . 4 . 3

Child2: 7 . 4 . 0 . 3 . 6 . **1** . **5** . 2

Et Voilá! The genes have been crossed over and you have ended up with valid permutations with no duplicates. This operator can be a little difficult to understand at first, so it may be worth your while to read over the description again.

And then, when you *think* you've grasped the concept, try performing this crossover yourself with pen and paper. Make sure you understand it completely before you go on.

The implementation of the Partially Matched Crossover operator looks like this:

```
void CgaTSP::CrossoverPMX(const vector<int> &mum,
                          const vector<int> &dad,
                          vector<int>       &baby1,
                          vector<int>       &baby2)
{
```

```
baby1 = mum;
baby2 = dad;

//just return dependent on the crossover rate or if the
//chromosomes are the same.
if ( (RandFloat() > m_dCrossoverRate) || (mum == dad))
{
    return;
}

//first we choose a section of the chromosome
int beg = RandInt(0, mum.size()-2);

int end = beg;

//find an end
while (end <= beg)
{
    end = RandInt(0, mum.size()-1);
}

//now we iterate through the matched pairs of genes from beg
//to end swapping the places in each child
for (int pos = beg; pos < end+1; ++pos)
{
    //these are the genes we want to swap
    int gene1 = mum[pos];
    int gene2 = dad[pos];

    if (gene1 != gene2)
    {
        //find and swap them in baby1
        int posGene1 = *find(baby1.begin(), baby1.end(), gene1);
        int posGene2 = *find(baby1.begin(), baby1.end(), gene2);

        swap(posGene1, posGene2);

        //and in baby2
```

```
        posGene1 = *find(baby2.begin(), baby2.end(), gene1);
        posGene2 = *find(baby2.begin(), baby2.end(), gene2);

        swap(posGene1, posGene2);
    }
}//next pair
}
```

STL Note

find()

The find algorithm is defined in <algorithm> and may be used with any of the STL container classes to search for a value. Its definition is

```
InputIterator find (InputIterator beg, InputIterator end, const T& value)
```

What's an iterator you say? Well, simply put, you can think of an iterator as a pointer to an element. You can increment an iterator just as you would a pointer, using ++, and you can access the value of an iterator using *. An input iterator is a special type of iterator that can only step forward element by element with read access. Therefore, you pass the find algorithm two iterators defining the beginning and end of the search range and the value you are searching for. The find algorithm returns an iterator pointing to the first element it finds equal to the value. If no match is found, it returns end().

begin() and end() are member functions of container classes that return iterators, which represent the beginning and end of the elements in the container. end() returns a position that is one after the last element in the container.

For example, if you have a std::vector of random integers, vector<int> vecInts, and you want to search all its elements for the value 5, you must first create an iterator of the correct type and then use find to retrieve the information:

```
vector<int>::iterator it;
it = find(vecInts.begin, vecInts.end(), 5);
```

swap()

swap is also defined in <algorithm> and is used to swap the elements of a container. It is clearly defined as:

```
void swap(T& val1, T& val2);
```

The Exchange Mutation Operator (EM)

After PMX, this operator is a pushover! Remember, you have to provide an operator that will always produce valid tours. The *Exchange Mutation* operator does this by choosing two genes in a chromosome and swapping them. For example, given the following chromosome:

$$5 . 3 . 2 . 1 . 7 . 4 . 0 . 6$$

The mutation function chooses two genes at random, for example 4 and 3, and swaps them:

$$5 . 4 . 2 . 1 . 7 . 3 . 0 . 6$$

which results in another valid permutation. The code for the exchange mutation operator looks like this.

```
void CgaTSP::MutateEM(vector<int> &chromo)
{
  //return dependent upon mutation rate
  if (RandFloat() > m_dMutationRate) return;

  //choose first gene
  int pos1 = RandInt(0, chromo.size()-1);

  //choose second
  int pos2 = pos1;

  while (pos1 == pos2)
  {
    pos2 = RandInt(0, chromo.size()-1);
  }

  //swap their positions
  swap(chromo[pos1], chromo[pos2]);
}
```

Deciding on a Fitness Function

A fitness function, which gives an increasing score the lower the tour length, is required. You could use the reciprocal of the tour length, but that doesn't really give much of a spread between the best and worst chromosomes in the population. Therefore, when using fitness proportionate selection, it's almost pot luck as to whether the fitter genomes will be selected. See Table 4.2 for an example.

A better idea is to keep a record of the worst tour length each generation and then iterate through the population again subtracting each genome's tour distance from the worst. This gives a little more spread, which will make the roulette wheel selection much more effective. It also effectively removes the worst chromosome from the population, because it will have a fitness score of zero and, therefore, will never get selected during the selection procedure. See Table 4.3

Table 4.2   TSP Tour Lengths and Their Fitness Scores

Genome	Tour Length	Fitness
1	3080	0.000324588
2	3770	0.000263786
3	3790	0.000263786
4	3545	0.000282029
5	3386	0.000295272
6	3604	0.000277406
7	3630	0.000275417
8	3704	0.00026993
9	2840	0.000352108
10	3651	0.000273854

Table 4.3   Adjusted Fitness Scores

Genome	Tour Length	Fitness
1	3080	710
2	3770	20
3	3790	0
4	3545	245
5	3386	404
6	3604	186
7	3630	160
8	3704	86
9	2840	950
10	3651	139

This is what the final fitness function looks like:

```
void CgaTSP::CalculatePopulationsFitness()
{
  //for each chromo
  for (int i=0; i<m_iPopSize; ++i)
  {
    //calculate the tour length for each chromosome
    double TourLength =
    m_Map->GetTourLength(m_vecPopulation[i].vecCities);

    m_vecPopulation[i].dFitness = TourLength;

    //keep a track of the shortest route found each generation
    if (TourLength < m_dShortestRoute)
    {
      m_dShortestRoute = TourLength;
    }

    //keep a track of the worst tour each generation
```

```
  if (TourLength > m_dLongestRoute)
  {
    m_dLongestRoute = TourLength;
  }
}//next chromo


//Now we have calculated all the tour lengths we can assign
//the fitness scores
for (i=0; i<m_iPopSize; ++i)
{
  m_vecPopulation[i].dFitness =
  m_dLongestRoute - m_vecPopulation[i].dFitness;
}
}
```

Selection

Roulette wheel selection is going to be used again—but this time with a difference. To help the genetic algorithm converge more quickly, in each epoch before the selection loop you are going to guarantee that n instances of the fittest genome from the previous generation will be copied unchanged into the new population. This means that the fittest genome will never be lost to random chance. This technique is most often referred to as *elitism*.

Putting It All Together

This is the easy part. All you have to do now is define a function or two to step through the operators you have defined

TIP

Although elitism is a valuable tool to have in your GA toolkit and is generally a good idea to use— beware. You can run into difficulties when tackling some types of problems. Elitism may give your population of genomes a tendency to converge too quickly. In other words, the population will become too similar too soon and your GA will find a non-optimal solution. A non-optimal solution is usually referred to as a *local minima*. Ideally, you have to fine-tune a balancing act between retaining population diversity and cloning the best genomes from each generation. I'll be talking about this in more detail in the next chapter.

and keep track of the fittest members in the population. The main workhorse is our old friend Epoch. It should look familiar to you:

```
void CgaTSP::Epoch()
{
  //first reset variables and calculate the fitness of each genome
  Reset();

  CalculatePopulationsFitness();

  //if a solution is found exit
  if ((m_dShortestRoute <= m_Map->BestPossibleRoute()))
  {
    m_bBusy = false;
    return;
  }

  //create a vector to hold the offspring
  vector<SGenome> vecNewPop;

  //First add NUM_BEST_TO_ADD number of the last generation's
  //fittest genome(elitism)
  for (int i=0; i<NUM_BEST_TO_ADD; ++i)
  {
    vecNewPop.push_back(m_vecPopulation[m_iFittestGenome]);
  }

  //now create the remainder of the population
  while (vecNewPop.size() != m_iPopSize)
  {
    //grab two parents
    SGenome mum = RouletteWheelSelection();
    SGenome dad = RouletteWheelSelection();

    //create 2 children
    SGenome baby1, baby2;

    //Recombine them
    CrossoverPMX(mum.vecCities,
```

```
                    dad.vecCities,
                    baby1.vecCities,
                    baby2.vecCities);

    //and mutate them
    MutateEM(baby1.vecCities);
    MutateEM(baby2.vecCities);

    //add them to new population
    vecNewPop.push_back(baby1);
    vecNewPop.push_back(baby2);
  }

  //copy into next generation
  m_vecPopulation = vecNewPop;

  //increment generation counter
  ++m_iGeneration;
}
```

As you can see, this looks very similar to the Epoch function from the last chapter. The only real difference is that this time, elitism is being added to the selection procedure.

The #defines

As before, the main parameters for the genetic algorithm are defined in defines.h, like so:

```
#define WINDOW_WIDTH      500
#define WINDOW_HEIGHT     500

#define NUM_CITIES        20
#define CITY_SIZE         5

#define MUTATION_RATE     0.2
#define CROSSOVER_RATE    0.75
#define POP_SIZE          40

//must be a multiple of 2
#define NUM_BEST_TO_ADD   2
```

TIP

Because of the number of floating point calculations required to determine the tour distances, EPSILON needs to be defined as a way of correcting any precision errors incurred. For example, you perform a series of calculations on some floats, and you know the answer should be **X**. Often the answer will not be **X**; it will be slightly more or less. Therefore, if you have a condition like

```
if (some_number == X)
{
  do something
}
```

it will be missed more often than not. So instead, do this

```
if ( (some_number > X-EPSILON) && (some_number <
X+EPSILON))
{
  do something
}
```

and everything is hunky-dory. This is a useful technique to use whenever you deal with multiple floating point calculations.

This parameter is used to set the amount of elitism: the number of instances of the fittest genome that get copied into the new population each generation.

```
//used to rectify precision errors
#define EPSILON        0.000001
```

Summary

When you run the program, you will notice that the genetic algorithm does not converge on a solution every time; indeed, it gets "stuck" quite regularly. And this is only with a few cities! If you play around with the code (which I hope you do) and increase the number of cities, you will see just how poorly this example actually performs. Often you will end up with the program stuck in a rut and a route looking something like Figure 4.7.

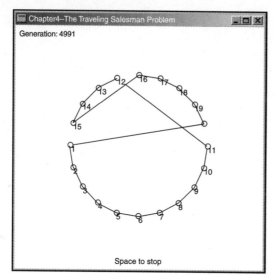

Space to stop

Figure 4.7

Doh! The genetic algorithm fails to find the solution.

Fortunately, there are a multitude of things you can do to improve the efficiency of a genetic algorithm, and I'll be addressing those in the next chapter as well as running through some of the other mutation and crossover operators that may be utilized. By the time you've finished Chapter 5, "Building a Better Genetic Algorithm," your GAs will be running with all cylinders firing.

Stuff to Try

1. Change the selection operator to use a type of elitism that will copy the four fittest genomes from the previous population directly into the new population before the rest are chosen by roulette wheel selection. Does this make the algorithm better or worse?

2. Change the fitness function to just use the reciprocal of the tour length and see if it makes a difference.

3. Take elitism off altogether and see what happens when you increase the number of cities from just a few (ten or so) to over 50.

CHAPTER 5

BUILDING A BETTER GENETIC ALGORITHM

Programming today is a race between software engineers striving to build bigger and better idiot-proof programs, and the Universe trying to produce bigger and better idiots.

So far, the Universe is winning.

Richard Cook

By now, I hope you are starting to get a feel for the mechanism of genetic algorithms. If not, review the last couple of chapters and play around with the code some more. I cannot stress enough how important it is to play around with code. It's a bit like when you learned how to program. Remember those days? Remember how much you learned through a hands-on approach, rather than just sitting down with a heavy programming book? Well genetic algorithms (and neural networks) are very much like that. You learn much faster by writing your own code and experimenting with all the different parameters because you develop a feel for what works and what doesn't. This "feel" is very important because, to date, there are few hard and fast rules about genetic algorithms—they are as much an art as they are science. It's only with time and experimentation that you will learn what the right population size should be for a problem, just how high the mutation rate should be set, and so on.

This chapter is all about experimentation. First, I want to get you used to looking at operators and thinking about what changes you can make to improve them, and then I'll discuss some additional techniques that may improve the performance of your genetic algorithm, such as various fitness scaling techniques. I say *may* improve the performance of your genetic algorithm because every problem is different and a technique that helps one problem may actually *hinder* another. After you've tackled a few problems of your own, though, you'll get to know pretty quickly which techniques are appropriate for which problems. It's all about that "feel" I mentioned earlier.

Just to see how much the techniques covered here are going to help solve the TSP from the last chapter, check out the executable for this chapter on the CD (Figure 5.1 shows a screenshot). Big improvement, huh? Anyway, now I've given you a taste for what's to come; let's get on with the theory.

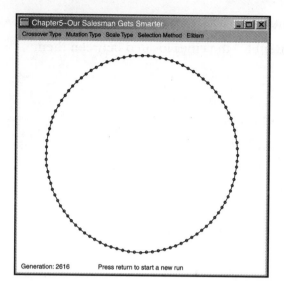

Figure 5.1

The salesman gets smart.

Alternative Operators for the TSP

The first topic I'm going to cover will be a discussion of those alternative mutation and crossover operators for the traveling salesman problem. Although none of them will improve the algorithm by a staggering amount, I feel I should spend a little time going over the more common ones because it's interesting to see how many different ways there are of approaching the problem of retaining valid permutations. Also, some of them give very interesting and thought provoking results when you watch the TSP algorithm in progress. More importantly, though, it will teach you that for every problem, there can be a multitude of ways to code the operators. Again—and I know I keep saying this—please make sure you play around with different operators to see how they perform. You will learn a lot. Hell, even go one step further and try to invent your own operators! That might prove a little tricky for the crossover operator for the TSP, but I bet you could think of a novel mutation operator, at the very least.

Alternative Permutation Mutation Operators

There have been many alternative mutation operators dreamed up by enthusiastic genetic algorithm researchers for the TSP. Here are descriptions of a few of the best followed by their code implementations.

Scramble Mutation (SM)

Choose two random points and "scramble" the cities located between them.

$$0.1.2.\mathbf{3.4.5.6}.7$$

becomes

$$0.1.2.\mathbf{5.6.3.4}.7$$

Here's what the code looks like.

```
void CgaTSP::MutateSM(vector<int> &chromo)
{
    //return dependent upon mutation rate
    if (RandFloat() > m_dMutationRate) return;

    //first we choose a section of the chromosome
    const int MinSpanSize = 3;

    //these will hold the beginning and end points of the span
    int beg, end;

    ChooseSection(beg, end, chromo.size()-1, MinSpanSize);
```

ChooseSection is a small function which determines a random start and end point to a span given a minimum span size and maximum span size. Please see the source code on the CD if further clarification is required.

```
    int span = end - beg;

    //now we just swap randomly chosen genes with the beg/end
    //range a few times to scramble them
    int NumberOfSwapsRqd = span;

    while(--NumberOfSwapsRqd)
    {
        vector<int>::iterator gene1 = chromo.begin();
        vector<int>::iterator gene2 = chromo.begin();

        //choose two loci within the range
        advance(gene1, beg + RandInt(0, span));
```

```
        advance(gene2, beg + RandInt(0, span));

        //exchange them
        swap(*gene1, *gene2);

    }//repeat
}
```

STL Note

erase()

erase() is a method for some STL containers that enables you to remove elements from a container. You can either just pass erase() a single element position (as an iterator)

```
//create an iterator pointing to the first element
vector<elements>::iterator beg = vecElements.begin();

//erase the first element
vecElements.erase(beg);
```

or you can pass erase() a range to remove. The range is defined by start and end iterators. So, to remove the first to the third element of an std::vector, you would do this:

```
vector<elements>::iterator beg = vecElements.begin();
vector<elements>::iterator end = beg + 3;
vecElements.erase(beg, end);
```

insert()

insert() is a method that enables you to insert elements into a container. As with erase(), you can choose to insert a single element at a position pointed to by an iterator or you can insert a range of elements. Here is a simple example, which inserts the first four elements in vecInt1 at position five in vecInt2.

```
vector<int> vecInt1, vecInt2;

for (int i=0; i<10; ++i)
{
  vecInt1.push_back(i);
  vecInt2.push_back(i);
}

vector<int>::iterator RangeStart = vecInt1.begin();
```

```
vector<int>::iterator InsertPos  = vecInt2.begin()+5;

vecInt2.insert(InsertPos, RangeStart, RangeStart+4);
```

assign()

assign() is a method that enables you to assign a range of elements in one container to another container. For example, if you had the std::vector of ints, vecInts, which contained all the integers from 0 to 9 and you wanted to create a new std::vector containing the range of integers from positions 3 to 6, you could do it like this:

```
vector<int>::iterator RangeStart = vecInt.begin() + 3;
vector<int>::iterator RangeEnd = vecInt.begin() + 6;

vector<int> newVec;
newVec.assign(RangeStart, RangeEnd);
```

You can also use it to add an element n number of times to an std::vector. The following example adds six copies of the integer 999 to the std::vector, vecInts.

```
vector<int> vecInt;
vecInt.assign(6, 999);
```

advance()

advance() is a handy method that enables you to advance an iterator by a required number of positions. To use it, you just pass advance() an iterator and the number of element positions it's to be advanced.

```
vector<int>::iterator RangeStart = vecInt.begin();
advance(RangeStart, 3);
```

sort()

To sort all the elements in a container, you can use sort, which will sort all the elements in a given range, like so:

```
sort(vecGenomes.begin(), vecGenomes.end());
```

This will only work provided some sorting criteria has been defined for the elements to be sorted. In the TSP program, I have provided a < overload for the SGenome struct, so SGenomes will be sorted by the member variable dFitness. It looks like this:

```
friend bool operator<(const SGenome& lhs, const SGenome& rhs)
{
    return (lhs.dFitness < rhs.dFitness);
}
```

Displacement Mutation (DM)

Select two random points, grab the chunk of chromosome between them, and then reinsert at a random position displaced from the original.

$$0.1.2.3.4.5.6.7$$

becomes

$$0.3.4.5.1.2.6.7$$

This is particularly interesting to watch because it helps the genetic algorithm converge to a short path very quickly, but then takes a while to actually go that few steps further to get to the solution.

```
void CgaTSP::MutateDM(vector<int> &chromo)
{
    //return dependent upon mutation rate
    if (RandFloat() > m_dMutationRate) return;

    //declare a minimum span size
    const int MinSpanSize = 3;

    //these will hold the beginning and end points of the span
    int beg, end;

    //choose a section of the chromosome.
    ChooseSection(beg, end, chromo.size()-1, MinSpanSize);

    //setup iterators for the beg/end points
    vector<int>::iterator SectionStart = chromo.begin() + beg;
    vector<int>::iterator SectionEnd   = chromo.begin() + end;

    //hold on to the section we are moving
    vector<int> TheSection;
    TheSection.assign(SectionStart, SectionEnd);

    //erase from current position
    chromo.erase(SectionStart, SectionEnd);

    //move an iterator to a random insertion location
```

```
vector<int>::iterator curPos;
curPos = chromo.begin() + RandInt(0, chromo.size()-1);

//re-insert the section
chromo.insert(curPos, TheSection.begin(), TheSection.end());
}
```

Insertion Mutation (IM)

This is a very effective mutation and is almost the same as the DM operator, except
here only one gene is selected to be displaced and inserted back into the chromosome. In tests, this mutation operator has been shown to be consistently better than
any of the alternatives mentioned here.

$$0 . 1 . \mathbf{2} . 3 . 4 . 5 . 6 . 7$$

becomes

$$0 . 1 . 3 . 4 . 5 . \mathbf{2} . 6 . 7$$

I use insertion mutation as the default mutation operator in the code project for
this chapter.

```
void CgaTSP::MutateIM(vector<int> &chromo)
{
    //return dependent upon mutation rate
    if (RandFloat() > m_dMutationRate) return;

    //create an iterator for us to work with
    vector<int>::iterator curPos;

    //choose a gene to move
    curPos = chromo.begin() + RandInt(0, chromo.size()-1);

    //keep a note of the genes value
    int CityNumber = *curPos;

    //remove from the chromosome
    chromo.erase(curPos);

    //move the iterator to the insertion location
```

```
    curPos = chromo.begin() + RandInt(0, chromo.size()-1);

    chromo.insert(curPos, CityNumber);
}
```

Inversion Mutation (IVM)

This is a very simple mutation operator. Select two random points and reverse the cities between them.

$$0 . 1 . 2 . 3 . 4 . 5 . 6 . 7$$

becomes

$$0 . 4 . 3 . 2 . 1 . 5 . 6 . 7$$

Displaced Inversion Mutation (DIVM)

Select two random points, reverse the city order between the two points, and then displace them somewhere along the length of the original chromosome. This is similar to performing IVM and then DM using the same start and end points.

$$0 . 1 . 2 . 3 . 4 . 5 . 6 . 7$$

becomes

$$0 . 6 . 5 . 4 . 1 . 2 . 3 . 7$$

I'll leave the implementation of these last two mutation operators as an exercise for you to code. (That's my crafty way of getting you to play around with the source!)

Alternative Permutation Crossover Operators

As with mutation operators, inventing crossover operators that spawn valid permutations has been a popular sport amongst genetic algorithm enthusiasts. Here are the descriptions and code for a couple of the better ones.

Order-Based Crossover (OBX)

To perform order-based crossover, several cities are chosen at random from one parent and then the *order* of those cities is imposed on the respective cities in the other parent. Let's take the example...

Parent1: 2 . **5** . **0** . 3 . 6 . **1** . 4 . 7

Parent2: 3 . 4 . 0 . 7 . 2 . 5 . 1 . 6

The cities in bold are the cities which have been chosen at random. Now, impose the order—5, 0, then 1—on the same cities in Parent2 to give Offspring1 like so:

Offspring1: 3 . 4 . **5** . 7 . 2 . **0** . **1** . 6

City one stayed in the same place because it was already positioned in the correct order. Now the same sequence of actions is performed on the other parent. Using the same positions as the first,

Parent1: 2 . **5** . **0** . 3 . 6 . **1** . 4 . 7

Parent2: 3 . **4** . **0** . 7 . 2 . **5** . 1 . 6

Parent1 becomes:

Offspring2: 2 . **4** . **0** . 3 . 6 . 1 . **5** . 7

Here is order-based crossover implemented in code:

```
void CgaTSP::CrossoverOBX(const vector<int>    &mum,
                          const vector<int>    &dad,
                          vector<int>          &baby1,
                          vector<int>          &baby2)
{
    baby1 = mum;
```

```cpp
baby2 = dad;

//just return dependent on the crossover rate or if the
//chromosomes are the same.
if ( (RandFloat() > m_dCrossoverRate) || (mum == dad))
{
  return;
}


//holds the chosen cities
vector<int> tempCities;

//holds the positions of the chosen cities
vector<int> positions;

//first chosen city position
int Pos = RandInt(0, mum.size()-2);

//keep adding random cities until we can add no more
//record the positions as we go
while (Pos < mum.size())
{
  positions.push_back(Pos);

  tempCities.push_back(mum[Pos]);

  //next city
  Pos += RandInt(1, mum.size()-Pos);
}


//so now we have n amount of cities from mum in the tempCities
//vector we can impose their order in dad.
int cPos = 0;

for (int cit=0; cit<baby2.size(); ++cit)
{
  for (int i=0; i<tempCities.size(); ++i)
  {
    if (baby2[cit]==tempCities[i])
```

```
                {
                    baby2[cit] = tempCities[cPos];

                    ++cPos;

                    break;
                }
            }
        }

        //now vice versa. Choose the same positioned cities from dad and impose
        //their order in mum
        tempCities.clear();
        cPos = 0;

        //first grab the cities from the same positions in dad
        for(int i=0; i<positions.size(); ++i)
        {
            tempCities.push_back(dad[positions[i]]);
        }

        //and impose their order in mum
        for (cit=0; cit<baby1.size(); ++cit)
        {
            for (int i=0; i<tempCities.size(); ++i)
            {
                if (baby1[cit]==tempCities[i])
                {
                    baby1[cit] = tempCities[cPos];

                    ++cPos;

                    break;
                }
            }
        }
    }
```

TIP

Often, when you want to find the optimum route for a unit in a game, it's not desirable to just take into account the distances involved. For example, say your game is based around a 3D terrain engine. You will probably want to consider such factors as the gradients encountered during the route (because units moving uphill usually travel slower and use more fuel) and also the surfaces the unit will be traveling over. (Moving through mud is a lot slower than moving across asphalt.)

To find the optimal route, a fitness function, which takes into account all these factors, must be defined. This way, you get the best trade off between distance covered and the surfaces and gradients traveled over. For example, create a sliding scale of penalties for all the different surfaces in your game. The slower the surface is to travel over, the higher the score your unit gets when you calculate distances between waypoints (remember, high values when calculating the distances convert to poor fitness scores). And similarly with the gradients, penalize for ascents and reward for descents. It may take a little fiddling to get the balance right, but eventually you will end up with a genetic algorithm that finds the *optimum* path for each different kind of unit, rather than just the *shortest* path.

Position-Based Crossover (PBX)

This is similar to Order-Based Crossover, but instead of imposing the order of the cities, this operator imposes the *position*. So, using the same example parents and random positions, here's how to do it.

Parent1: 2 . **5** . **0** . 3 . 6 . **1** . 4 . 7
Parent2: 3 . **4** . **0** . 7 . 2 . **5** . 1 . 6

First, move over the selected cities from Parent1 to Offspring1, keeping them in the same position.

$$\text{OffSpring1: } * . 5 . 0 . * . * . 1 . * . *$$

Now, iterate through Parent2's cities and fill in the blanks if that city number has not already appeared. In this example, filling in the blanks results in:

$$\text{Offspring1: } 3 . 5 . 0 . 4 . 7 . 1 . 2 . 6$$

Get it? Let's run through the derivation of Offspring2, just to be sure. First, copy over the selected cities into the same positions.

$$\text{Offspring2: } * . 4 . 0 . * . * . 5 . * . *$$

Now, fill in the blanks.

$$\text{Offspring2: } 2 . 4 . 0 . 3 . 6 . 5 . 1 . 7$$

And here's how it looks in code:

```
void CgaTSP::CrossoverPBX(const vector<int>    &mum,
                          const vector<int>    &dad,
                          vector<int>          &baby1,
                          vector<int>          &baby2)
{
  //Return dependent on the crossover rate or if the
  //chromosomes are the same.
  if ( (RandFloat() > m_dCrossoverRate) || (mum == dad))
  {
    //make sure baby1 and baby2 are assigned some cities first!
    baby1 = mum;
```

```
  baby2 = dad;

  return;
}


//initialize the babies with minus values so we can tell which positions
//have been filled later in the algorithm
baby1.assign(mum.size(), -1);
baby2.assign(mum.size(), -1);

int l = baby2.size();

//holds the positions of the chosen cities
vector<int> positions;

//first city position
int Pos = RandInt(0, mum.size()-2);

//keep adding random cities until we can add no more
//record the positions as we go
while (Pos < mum.size())
{
  positions.push_back(Pos);

  //next city
  Pos += RandInt(1, mum.size()-Pos);
}

//now we have chosen some cities it's time to copy the selected cities
//over into the offspring in the same position.
for (int pos=0; pos<positions.size(); ++pos)
{
  //baby1 receives from mum
  baby1[positions[pos]] = mum[positions[pos]];

  //baby2 receives from dad
  baby2[positions[pos]] = dad[positions[pos]];
}

//fill in the blanks. First create two position markers so we know
```

```
//whereabouts we are in baby1 and baby2
int c1 = 0, c2 = 0;

for (pos=0; pos<mum.size(); ++pos)
{
  //advance position marker until we reach a free position
  //in baby2
  while( (baby2[c2] > -1) && (c2 < mum.size()))
  {
    ++c2;
  }

  //baby2 gets the next city from mum which is not already
  //present
  if ( (!TestNumber(baby2, mum[pos])) )
  {
    baby2[c2] = mum[pos];
  }

  //now do the same for baby1
  while((baby1[c1] > -1) && (c1 < mum.size()))
  {
    ++c1;
  }

  //baby1 gets the next city from dad which is not already
  //present
  if ( (!TestNumber(baby1, dad[pos])) )
  {
    baby1[c1] = dad[pos];
  }
}
}
```

Now that you've seen how others have tackled the crossover operator, can you dream up one of your own? This is not an easy task, so congratulations if you can actually invent one!

I hope running through a few of the alternative operators for the traveling salesman problem has given you an indication of the scope you can have with genetic algorithm operators. For the remainder of this chapter, though, I'm going to talk about various tools and techniques you can apply to just about any kind of genetic algorithm to improve its performance.

The Tools of the Trade

Envision the complete set of possible solutions to a problem as a kind of landscape that dips and rises as you travel across it. The lower the ground, the more "fit" is the solution represented at that point. Conversely, the high ground represents extremely poor solutions. Imagine the genetic algorithm as a ball that rolls around on that landscape until it falls into a trough. As I've explained, this would represent a solution, but, it may not be the *best* solution. Only now, the ball is stuck and cannot roll any further. This is what is known as a *local minima*. Figure 5.2 shows you what I mean.

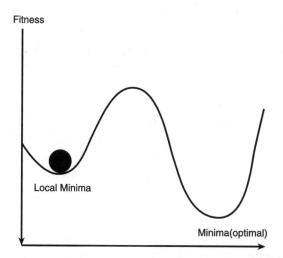

Figure 5.2

A GA stuck in a local minima.

Ideally, you want the ball to roll over as much landscape as possible, until it finds the deepest trough to fall into. This represents the best solution. Or, failing that, at least provide some way of "kicking" the ball out of the shallow troughs so it can continue its journey across the landscape.

NOTE

In some texts, you will find the fitness landscape inverted and, therefore, the author may refer to an algorithm getting stuck at a local *maxima*. Either way, the concept is the same.

Figure 5.2 shows the fitness landscape for a problem with just one parameter that needs solving. A two-parameter fitness landscape would be in 3D, as shown in Figure 5.3.

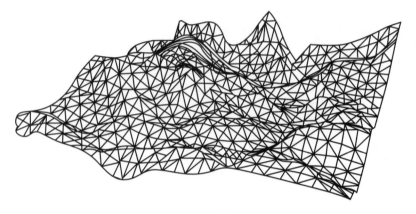

Figure 5.3

A two-parameter fitness landscape.

The x- and z-axis represent the parameters, and the y-axis represents the fitness. Now, there are all sorts of hills, troughs, ridges, and other features for the genetic algorithm to negotiate before it can settle at the optimum. And that's just with two parameters! When you go above two parameters, you have to let your imagination go wild because you've entered the incredible domain of mathematical hyper-spaces. However, the concept is just the same and there will be hills and troughs in the landscape, just the same. (If Dali had still been alive, I would have asked Pre-mier Press to hire him to draw you a diagram of hyperspace, but unfortunately, you'll have to make do with your imagination.)

To keep the ball rolling, you need to equip yourself with tools you can use to cajole your genetic algorithms into doing what you want. In this section, I'm going to spend some time discussing various techniques and additional operators you can use to help your genetic algorithms converge on a solution more efficiently.

Selection Techniques

In junior high, I was useless at most sports, particularly team sports, and for ages, I had to suffer the daily playground humiliation of being the last to be chosen for a game of soccer. Remember how all the kids would stand in a line and the two most athletic boys in the school would, as captains, take turns selecting their team? Well, I was the boy who was always chosen last and put safely out of the way in the goalie position. Imagine my relief when after a couple of years of this, an even geekier kid moved into town. Oh what joy!

Selection is how you choose individuals from the population to provide a gene base from which the next generation of individuals is created. This might mean individuals are selected and placed into the new generation without modification ala elitism, as we discussed in the last chapter, but usually it means the chosen genomes are selected to be parents of offspring which are created through the processes of mutation and recombination. How you go about choosing the parents can play a very important role in how efficient your genetic algorithm is. Unlike choosing a soccer team, if you choose the fittest individuals all the time, the population may converge too rapidly at a local minima and get stuck there. But, if you select individuals at random, then your genetic algorithm will probably take a while to converge (if it ever does at all). So, the art of selection is choosing a strategy which gives you the best of both worlds—something that converges fairly quickly yet enables the population to retain its diversity.

Elitism

As previously discussed, elitism is a way of guaranteeing that the fittest members of a population are retained for the next generation. In the last chapter, the code example used a little bit of elitism to select two copies of the best individual to go through to the next generation. To expand on this, it can be better to select n copies of the top m individuals of the population to be retained. I often find that retaining about 2-5% of the population size gives me good results. The function name I give for this expanded version of elitism is called GrabNBest. Its prototype looks like this:

```
void    GrabNBest(int             NBest,
                  const int       NumCopies,
                  vector<SGenome> &vecNewPop);
```

So, to retain two copies each of the fittest three members of the population, you would call

```
GrabNBest(3, 2, vecNewPop);
```

When you play around with the example program, you will discover that using elitism works well with just about every other technique described in this chapter (except stochastic universal sampling, which will be discussed soon).

Steady State Selection

Steady state selection works a little like elitism, except that instead of choosing a small amount of the best individuals to go through to the new generation, steady state selection retains all but a few of the worst performers from the current population. The remainder are then selected using mutation and crossover in the usual way. Steady state selection can prove useful when tackling some problems, but most of the time it's inadvisable to use it.

Fitness Proportionate Selection

Selection techniques of this type choose offspring using methods which give individuals a better chance of being selected the better their fitness score. Another way of describing it is that each individual has an expected number of times it will be chosen to reproduce. This expected value equates to the individual's fitness divided by the average fitness of the entire population. So, if you have an individual with a fitness of 6 and the average fitness of the overall population is 4, then the expected number of times the individual should be chosen is 1.5.

Roulette Wheel Selection

A common way of implementing fitness proportionate selection is roulette wheel selection, as I have already discussed. This technique does have its drawbacks, however. Because roulette wheel selection is based on using random numbers and because the population sizes of genetic algorithms are typically small (sizes between 50 and 200 are common), the number of children allocated to each individual can be far from its expected value. Even worse, it's probable that roulette wheel selection could miss the best individuals altogether! This is one of the reasons elitism is a good idea when utilizing roulette wheel selection—it ensures you never lose the best individuals to chance.

Stochastic Universal Sampling

Stochastic Universal Sampling (SUS for short) is an attempt to minimize the problems of using fitness proportionate selection on small populations. Basically, instead of having one wheel which is spun several times to obtain the new population, SUS uses n evenly spaced hands, which are only spun *once* as shown in Figure 5.4. The amount of pointers is equal to the amount of offspring required.

Here is the code which implements this type of sampling:

```
void CgaTSP::SUSSelection(vector<SGenome> &NewPop)
{
  //this algorithm relies on all the fitness scores to be positive so
  //these few lines check and adjust accordingly (in this example
```

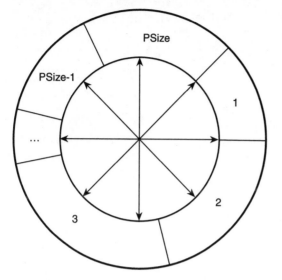

Figure 5.4

The SUS wheel of probability.

```
//Sigma scaling can give negative fitness scores
if (m_dWorstFitness < 0)
{
  //recalculate
  for (int gen=0; gen<m_vecPopulation.size(); ++gen)
  {
    m_vecPopulation[gen].dFitness += fabs(m_dWorstFitness);
  }

  CalculateBestWorstAvTot();
}
```

Some of the scaling techniques discussed in this chapter can result in negative fitness scores for some of the population. The preceding lines of code check for this possibility and readjust the scores accordingly. If you know for sure your fitness scores will never be negative, you can omit this.

```
int curGen = 0;
double sum = 0;

//NumToAdd is the amount of individuals we need to select using SUS.
//Remember, some may have already been selected through elitism
int NumToAdd = m_iPopSize - NewPop.size();

//calculate the hand spacing
```

```
    double PointerGap = m_dTotalFitness/(double)NumToAdd;

    //choose a random start point for the wheel
    float ptr = RandFloat() * PointerGap;

    while (NewPop.size() < NumToAdd)
    {
      for(sum+=m_vecPopulation[curGen].dFitness; sum > ptr; ptr+=PointerGap)
      {
        NewPop.push_back(m_vecPopulation[curGen]);

        if( NewPop.size() == NumToAdd)
        {
          return;
        }
      }

      ++curGen;
    }
}
```

If you use SUS in your own genetic algorithms, it is inadvisable to use elitism with it because this tends to mess up the algorithm. You will clearly see the effect that switching elitism on or off has on SUS selection when you run this chapter's executable.

Tournament Selection

To use tournament selection, n individuals are selected at random from the population, and then the fittest of these genomes is chosen to add to the new population. This process is repeated as many times as is required to create a new population of genomes. Any individuals selected are *not* removed from the population and therefore can be chosen any number of times. Here's what this algorithm looks like in code.

```
SGenome& CgaTSP::TournamentSelection(int N)
{
  double BestFitnessSoFar = 0;

  int ChosenOne = 0;

  //Select N members from the population at random testing against
```

```
  //the best found so far
  for (int i=0; i<N; ++i)
  {
    int ThisTry = RandInt(0, m_iPopSize-1);

    if (m_vecPopulation[ThisTry].dFitness > BestFitnessSoFar)
    {
      ChosenOne = ThisTry;

      BestFitnessSoFar = m_vecPopulation[ThisTry].dFitness;
    }
  }
  //return the champion
  return m_vecPopulation[ChosenOne];
}
```

This technique is very efficient to implement because it doesn't require any of the preprocessing or fitness scaling sometimes required for roulette wheel selection and other fitness proportionate techniques (discussed later in the chapter). Because of this, and because it's a darn good technique anyway, you should always try this method of selection with your own genetic algorithms. The only drawback I've found is that tournament selection can lead to too quick convergence with some types of problems.

I've also seen an alternative description of this technique, which goes like this: A random number is generated between 0 and 1. If the random number is less than a pre-determined constant, for example cT (a typical value would be 0.75), then the fittest individual is chosen to be a parent. If the random number is greater than cT, then the weaker individual is chosen. As before, this is repeated until a new population of the correct size has been spawned.

Interesting Fact

NASA has used genetic algorithms to successfully calculate low altitude satellite orbits and more recently to calculate the positioning of the Hubble space telescope.

Scaling Techniques

Although using selection on the raw (unprocessed) fitness scores can give you a genetic algorithm that works (it solves the task you've designed it for), often your genetic algorithm can be made to perform better if the fitness scores are *scaled* in some way before any selection takes place. There are various ways of doing this and I'm going to spend the next few pages describing the best of the bunch.

Rank Scaling

Rank scaling can be a great way to prevent too quick convergence, particularly at the start of a run when it's common to see a very small percentage of individuals outperforming all the rest.

The individuals in the population are simply ranked according to fitness, and then a new fitness score is assigned based on their rank. So, for example, if you had a population of five individuals with the fitness scores shown in Table 5.1, all you do is sort them and assign a new fitness based on their rank within the sorted population. See Table 5.2

Once the new ranked fitness scores have been applied, you select individuals for the next generation using roulette wheel selection or a similar fitness proportionate selection method. (Please note you would never, in practice, have a population of just five, I'm just using five to demonstrate the principle).

This technique avoids the possibility that a large percentage of each new generation is being produced from a very small number of highly fit individuals, which can quickly lead to premature convergence. In effect, rank scaling ensures your population remains diverse. The other side of the coin is that the population may take a lot longer to converge, but often you will find that the greater diversity provided by this technique leads to a more successful result for your genetic algorithm.

Table 5.1   Fitness Scores Before Ranking

Individual	Score
1	3.4
2	6.1
3	1.2
4	26.8
5	0.7

Table 5.2   Fitness Scores After Ranking

Individual	Old Fitness	New Fitness
4	26.8	5
2	6.1	4
1	3.4	3
3	1.2	2
5	0.7	1

Sigma Scaling

If you use raw fitness scores as a basis for selection, the population may converge too quickly, and if they are scaled as in rank selection, the population may converge too slowly. Sigma scaling is an attempt to keep the selection pressure constant over many generations. At the beginning of the genetic algorithm, when fitness scores can vary wildly, the fitter individuals will be allocated less expected offspring. Toward the end of the algorithm, when the fitness scores are becoming similar, the fitter individuals will be allocated more expected offspring.

The formula for calculating each new fitness score using sigma scaling is:

if $\sigma = 0$ then the fitness = 1

else

$$\text{NewFitness} = \frac{\text{OldFitness} - \text{AverageFitness}}{2\sigma}$$

where the Greek letter sigma, σ, represents the *standard deviation* of the population.

A few of you will probably be wondering what the standard deviation is and how it's calculated. Well, the standard deviation is the square root of the population's *variance*. The variance is a measure of spread within the fitness scores. Figure 5.5 shows an example of a population with a low variance.

The hump in the middle of the graph represents the mean (the average) fitness score. Most of the population's scores are clustered around this hump. The spread, or variance, is the width of the hump at the base. Figure 5.6 shows a population with a high variance, and as you can see, the hump is lower and more spread out.

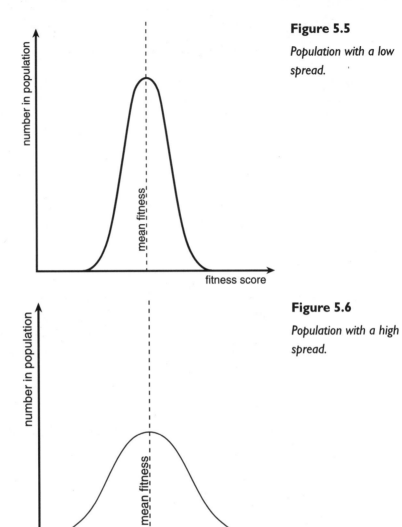

Figure 5.5

Population with a low spread.

Figure 5.6

Population with a high spread.

Now that you know what variance is, let me show you how to calculate it. Imagine we are only dealing with a population of three, and the fitness scores are 1, 2, and 3. To calculate the variance, first calculate the mean of all the fitness scores.

$$\text{mean} = \frac{1 + 2 + 3}{3} = 2$$

Then the variance is calculated like this

$$\text{variance} = \frac{(1-2)^2 + (2-2)^2 + (3-2)^2}{3} = 0.667$$

A more mathematical way of writing this is

$$\text{variance} = \frac{\sum (f - mf)^2}{N}$$

Where f is the fitness of the current individual, fm is the average fitness of the population, and N is the population size. The weird Greek symbol Σ is also called sigma but it's the capital of σ, just like A is the capital of a. The Σ symbol is a summation symbol, and in this example it indicates that all the values of

$$(f - mf)^2$$

should be summed before being divided by N.

Once the variance has been calculated, it's a trivial matter to compute the square root to give the standard deviation:

$$\sigma = \sqrt{\text{variance}}$$

The code for applying sigma scaling to the traveling salesman problem looks like this:

```
void CgaTSP::FitnessScaleSigma(vector<SGenome> &pop)
{
  double RunningTotal = 0;

  //first iterate through the population to calculate the standard
  //deviation
  for (int gen=0; gen<pop.size(); ++gen)
  {
    RunningTotal += (pop[gen].dFitness - m_dAverageFitness) *
                    (pop[gen].dFitness - m_dAverageFitness);
  }

  double variance = RunningTotal/(double)m_iPopSize;

  //standard deviation is the square root of the variance
  m_dSigma = sqrt(variance);

  //now iterate through the population to reassign the fitness scores
```

```
for (gen=0; gen<pop.size(); ++gen)
{
   double OldFitness = pop[gen].dFitness;

   pop[gen].dFitness = (OldFitness - m_dAverageFitness) /
                       (2 * m_dSigma);
}


//recalculate values used in selection
CalculateBestWorstAvTot();
}
```

The last call to `CalculateBestWorstAvTot` is there to recalculate all the best, worst, and average values for the entire population, which some of the selection types use. `m_dSigma` is a member variable because it can be used to stop the run if the variance becomes zero (all the fitness scores are therefore identical and so there is not much point continuing). There are a few areas in which this function could be speeded up, but I've written it like this so that it follows the equations more literally.

Sigma scaling is interesting to watch in action because the population converges very quickly in the first few generations, but then takes a long time to finally reach a solution.

Interesting Fact

The bots created for the game Quake3 were developed using genetic algorithms. A genetic algorithm was used to optimize the fuzzy logic controllers for each bot. Briefly put, fuzzy logic is logic extended to encompass partial truths. So, instead of something having to be black or white, as in conventional logic, when using fuzzy logic, something can be shades of gray too. The Quake3 bot uses fuzzy logic to indicate *how much* it wants to do something. It doesn't just indicate that it wants to pick a certain item; using fuzzy logic it can determine that it is in 78% favor of picking up the railgun and 56% in favor of picking up the armor.

Boltzmann Scaling

You've learned how to keep the selection pressure constant over a run of your genetic algorithm by using sigma scaling, but sometimes you may want the selection pressure to vary. A common scenario is one in which you require the selection pressure to be low at the beginning so that diversity is retained, but as the genetic algorithm converges closer toward a solution, you want mainly the fitter individuals to produce offspring.

One way of achieving this is by using *Boltzmann scaling*. This method of scaling uses a continuously varying *temperature* to control the rate of selection. The formula is

$$\text{NewFitness} = \frac{\text{OldFitness} / \text{Temperature}}{\text{AverageFitness} / \text{Temperature}}$$

Each generation, the temperature is decreased by a small value, which has the effect of increasing the selection pressure toward the fitter individuals. This is the code implementation of Boltzmann scaling from the TSP project.

```
void CgaTSP::FitnessScaleBoltzmann(vector<SGenome> &pop)
{

  //reduce the temp a little each generation
  m_dBoltzmannTemp -= BOLTZMANN_DT;

  //make sure it doesn't fall below minimum value
  if (m_dBoltzmannTemp< BOLTZMANN_MIN_TEMP)
  {
    m_dBoltzmannTemp = BOLTZMANN_MIN_TEMP;
  }

  //first calculate the average fitness/Temp
  double divider = m_dAverageFitness/m_dBoltzmannTemp;

  //now iterate through the population and calculate the new expected
  //values
  for (int gen=0; gen<pop.size(); ++gen)
  {
    double OldFitness = pop[gen].dFitness;

    pop[gen].dFitness = (OldFitness/m_dBoltzmannTemp)/divider;
  }

  //recalculate values used in selection
  CalculateBestWorstAvTot();
}
```

In the TSP solver, the temperature is initially set to twice the number of cities. `BOLTZMANN_DT` is #defined as 0.05 and `BOLTZMANN_MIN_TEMP` is #defined as 1.

Alternative Crossover Operators

Utilizing different crossover and mutation operators for your genetic algorithms can often be a good idea. How you implement these operators depends very much on how your problem is encoded. As you've already seen, using a crossover operator that works well for one type of problem may have disastrous results when applied to another. The same goes for mutation operators. Although, for most genome encodings you are limited in what you can do with a mutation operator—it's typically such a simple operation—there are usually a few different ways of performing crossover. Here are explanations of the most popular types.

Single-Point Crossover

This is the first crossover operator I introduced you to in Chapter 3, "An Introduction To Genetic Algorithms." It simply cuts the genome at some random point and then switches the ends between parents. It is very easy and quick to implement and is generally effective to some degree with most types of problems.

Two-Point Crossover

Instead of cutting the genome at just one point, two-point crossover (you guessed it) cuts the genome at two random points and then swaps the block of genes between those two points. So, if you had two binary encoded parents like this,

> Parent1: 1010001010
>
> Parent2: 1101110101

and the chosen crossover points were after the third and seventh genes, two-point crossover would go like this.

> Parent1: 101 **0001** 010
>
> Parent2: 110 **1110** 101

Swap the "belly" block of genes giving offspring.

Child1: 101 **1110** 010

Child2: 110 **0001** 101

See Figure 5.7 for an illustration of this process.

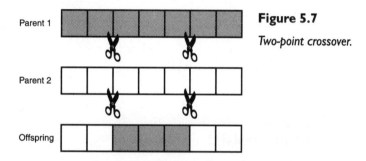

Figure 5.7

Two-point crossover.

Two-point crossover is sometimes beneficial because it can create combinations of genes that single-point crossover simply cannot provide. With single point, the end genes are *always* swapped over and this may not be favorable for the problem at hand. Two-point crossover eliminates this problem.

Multi-Point Crossover

Why stop at just two crossover points? There's no need to limit the amount of cross-over points you can have. Indeed, for some types of encoding, your genetic algorithm may perform better if you use multiple crossover points. The easiest way of achieving this is to move down the length of the parents, and for each position in the chromo-some, randomly swap the genes based on your crossover rate, as in Figure 5.8.

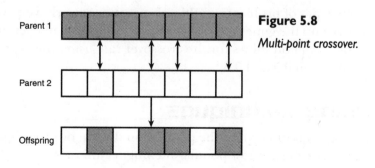

Figure 5.8

Multi-point crossover.

Here is what the code implementation of multi-point crossover looks like.

```cpp
void CGenAlg::CrossoverMultiPoint(const vector<gene_type> &mum,
                                  const vector<gene_type> &dad,
                                  vector<gene_type>       &baby1,
                                  vector<gene_type>       &baby2)

{

  //iterate down the length of the genomes swapping genes
  //depending on the crossover rate
  for (int gen=0; gen<mum.size(); ++gen)
  {
    if (RandFloat() < CrossoverRate))
    {
      //swap the genes
      baby2.push_back(mum[gen]);
      baby1.push_back(dad[gen]);
    }

    else
    {
      //don't swap the genes
      baby1.push_back(mum[gen]);
      baby2.push_back(dad[gen]);
    }
  }
}
```

Sometimes you will see this type of crossover described as *parameterized uniform crossover*. I tend to favor the name multi-point crossover because it says exactly what it does.

For some types of problems, multi-point crossover works very well, but on others it can jumble up the genes too much and act more like an over enthusiastic mutation operator. Common values for the crossover rate using this type of crossover operator are between 0.5 and 0.8.

Niching Techniques

Niching is a way of keeping the population diverse by grouping similar individuals together. One of the most popular niching techniques is called *explicit fitness sharing*.

This is a method in which the individuals in the population are grouped together according to how similar their genomes are, and then the fitness score of each individual is adjusted by "sharing" it amongst that group's members. This ensures similar individuals in the population are punished, thereby retaining diversity. To clarify, let's take the example of a population of binary encoded genomes. You can measure the difference between two genomes by counting all the bits in the genome that match. For example, the genomes

Genome1: **10**100**010100**
Genome2: **00**100**101010**

match at five places shown in bold. You can say their compatibility score is 5. To group the population into niches of similar genomes, you just test each genome against a sample genome to obtain a compatibility score for each. Genomes with similar compatibility scores are grouped together and then their fitness score is adjusted by dividing the raw fitness by the size of that genome's niche. Table 5.3 should help make this clearer for you.

Table 5.3 Fitness Sharing In Action

Genome ID	Niche ID	Raw Fitness	Adj Fitness
1	1	16	16/3 = 5.34
5	1	6	6/3 = 2
6	1	10	10/3 = 3.34
3	2	6	6/1 = 6
2	3	9	9/3 = 3
4	3	10	10/3 = 3.34
8	3	20	20/3 = 6.67
9	4	3	3/2 = 1.5
10	4	6	6/2 = 3

As you can see, fitness sharing is very effective at penalizing similarly constructed genomes and can be a terrific way of making sure your population remains diverse. I'll be discussing niching techniques in more detail later on in the book.

Summing Up

By the time you've experimented with a few of the techniques described in this chapter, you will have developed a pretty good feel for what genetic algorithms are all about.

In the next few chapters, I'll often be using the simplest combination of genetic algorithm techniques possible to achieve the desired result. This will give you the opportunity to try out, first hand, the techniques you've looked at so far to see how they may aid or hinder the evolution of different types of problems.

Stuff to Try

1. Go back and apply what you have learned in this chapter to the Pathfinder problem discussed in Chapter 3, "An Introduction to Genetic Algorithms."

2. Can you create a genetic algorithm for solving the 8-puzzle? (The 8-puzzle is that puzzle in which you have to slide numbered tiles around in a tray until all the numbers appear in order. See Figure 5.9)

3. Create a genetic algorithm to calculate the combination of letters that will give the highest score possible on a Boggle board.

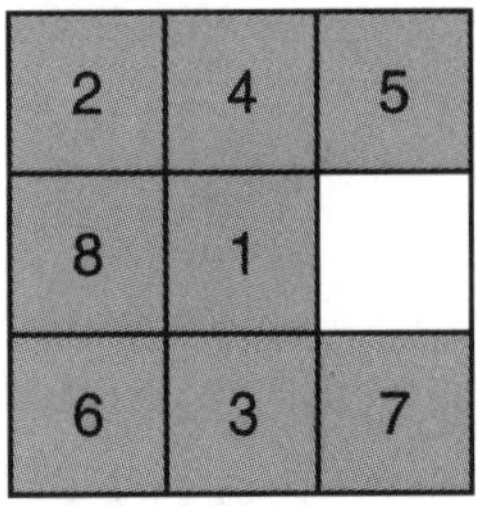

Figure 5.9

An unsolved 8-puzzle board.

CHAPTER 6

Moon Landings Made Easy

During the heat of the space race in the 1960s, NASA decided it needed a ballpoint pen to write in the zero gravity confines of its space capsules.

After considerable research and development, the Astronaut Pen was developed at a cost of $1 million.

The pen worked and also enjoyed some modest success as a novelty item back here on earth.

The Soviet Union, faced with the same problem, used a pencil.

In this chapter, you are going to learn how to encode and evolve *behavior patterns* with genetic algorithms. This type of encoding enables you to evolve behavior for a wide variety of game objects, from arcade-style aliens to racing lines for sports cars. When you think about it, the list of uses you could apply this type of genetic algorithm to is vast. What's more, behavior evolved using this method uses very little processor power in your actual game.

The example I'm going to use is that of evolving the sequence of control patterns required to gently guide and land a lunar module onto a small landing platform, as shown in Figure 6.1.

Figure 6.1

A luminous lunar lander landing.

Before I talk about the genetic algorithm though, I'm going to spend some time explaining all the graphics techniques used in this and later code examples and the physics and mathematics that goes with them. This way, I can be sure you understand every line of code.

If you already know about matrices, transformations, vectors, and Newtonian physics, be my guest and skip the next few pages. If not, then make like a sponge, read on, and absorb.

Creating and Manipulating Vector Graphics

I think the best way of teaching you graphics and math stuff is by talking you through the creation of a user-controlled lunar lander, step by step. This way, in addition to becoming familiar with the required techniques, you will also get the chance to see how difficult it is to land the lunar module before you learn how to code a genetic algorithm to do it!

The 2D graphics needed for the game will be very simple. You'll need a lunar lander object, a landing platform object, and a sprinkling of twinkling stars. So, I guess the first thing I need to show you is how to create a data structure for representing 2D shapes.

Points, Vertices, and Vertex Buffers

A shape is defined by a series of connected points in space. A point in 2D space is represented by its position on the x-axis and its position on the y–axis, as shown in Figure 6.2.

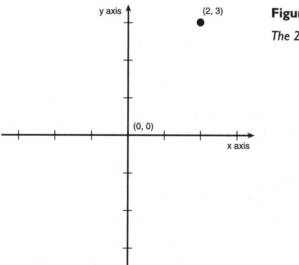

Figure 6.2

The 2D coordinate system.

A point, in computer graphics parlance, is most often referred to as a *vertex*. To create a shape, all you have to do is store all the vertices that make up that shape in some sort of data structure. Let's take the extremely simple shape shown in Figure 6.3 as an example. If my memory is correct, that's a similar type of shape to the gun in the original space invader games. What a long way graphics have come since those days, eh? Notice the shape is centered around the origin (0, 0).

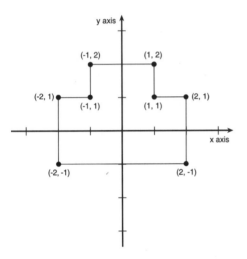

Figure 6.3

Defining a simple shape.

I'll be discussing why your shapes should be centered around the origin shortly, but for now, just take it from me that they should be. The data structure I use to store a vertex in my code is called an SPoint and its definition looks like this.

```
struct SPoint
{
  double x, y;

  SPoint(double a = 0, double b = 0):x(a),y(b){}
};
```

To store an entire shape, you just create an array of SPoints, which is a collection of all the vertices that make up that shape. I use std::vectors to store all the shapes used in the sample code. These vectors of vertices are called *vertex buffers*, and I suffix their names with "VB" to clarify this. For example, I would define and initialize a vertex buffer for the shape shown in Figure 6.3 like this:

```
vector<SPoint>  vecGunVB;
const int NumGunVerts = 8;
const SPoint gun[NumGunVerts] = {SPoint(2,1),
```

```
                              SPoint(2,-1),
                              SPoint(-2,-1),
                              SPoint(-2,1),
                              SPoint(-1,1)
                              SPoint(-1,2),
                              SPoint(1,2),
                              SPoint(1,1)};

for (int i=0; i<NumGunVerts; ++i)
{
  vecGunVB.push_back(gun[i]);
}
```

Then to draw the shape you simply write a function which connects all the vertices with lines in the correct order—just like those join the dots books you used to love as a kid!

It's common practice to load all the vertex coordinates required for your game objects from data files. However, because my examples do not use many objects, I simply defined all my vertices as const arrays at the beginning of the appropriate file and then initialized the vertex buffers from these arrays in the constructor of the class. If you take a quick peek at the CLander.cpp file found on the CD in the folder Chapter6/Lunar Lander - Manned, you will see how I initialized the vertex buffers for the lunar lander shape and the lunar lander jet shape.

Well, now you know how to define a shape, but you don't know how to draw it at the correct position and orientation on the screen. After all, if you were to draw the space invader gun shape to your screen as you have defined it, you'd get something that looks like Figure 6.4!

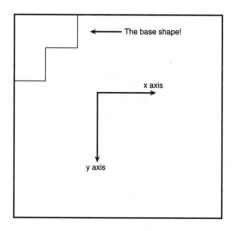

Figure 6.4

Uh-oh!

This is because the gun shape's vertices are centered around the origin. A lot of the vertices have negative coordinates, which the default Windows drawing mode does not support. Also, the direction of the windows y-axis is inverted to the normal coordinate system and therefore the shape appears upside down. What a mess!

Transforming Vertices

You need a way of adjusting the shape's vertices so they appear in the correct place and with the correct orientation and scale. This is where *transformations* come in. Before I rush ahead of myself though, first you need to know a few more details about your game object before you can calculate where to place it on your screen. You need to know its *position* in screen coordinates, its *rotation*, and its *scale*. Therefore, a very simple data structure for a game object might look like this:

```
struct GameObject
{
    double dPosX, dPosY;

    double dRotation;

    double dScale;

    //its vertices
    vector<SPoint> vecShapeVB;
};
```

Now that you know where the object should be, you have to figure out how to calculate the new positions of each vertex in the vertex buffer so the object is drawn in the correct place on the screen. You do this using a series of transformations, so let's spend some time taking a look at each type of transformation.

Translation

Translation is simply the process of moving a point or group of points from one place to another. Let's use the space invader gun shape as an example, and let's say that its present location in the game world is at coordinate (5, 6), meaning the gun's *center* should be positioned around (5, 6).

You need to find a way of adjusting the vertices in the gun's vertex buffer so that when drawn, the gun will appear on your screen at the correct location—centered around (5, 6) instead of centered around (0, 0). To do that, all you have to do is write a function which will add 5 to the x element of every vertex, and add 6 to every y element. This way, the vertices will be transformed accordingly and positioned on your screen, as shown in Figure 6.5 (note the shape still appears upside down because the y-axis is inverted).

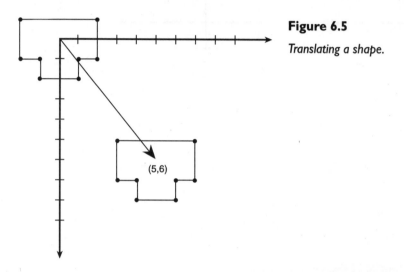

Figure 6.5

Translating a shape.

In other words, if the coordinates of each vertex in the vertex buffer are described by vertX and vertY, and the position in the game world of the object these vertices describe is posX and posY, then you can say:

```
ScreenX = vertX + posX;
ScreenY = vertY + posY;
```

So, to move a whole object, you just apply this to each vertex in the vertex buffer and bingo! It's positioned correctly.

NOTE

The untransformed coordinates of an object are known as the object's *Local Coordinates* and the coordinates of the transformed vertices— the coordinates in the game world— are known as the object's *World Coordinates.*

Scaling

Scaling is the process by which your object is increased or decreased in size. It's very simple to perform; all you need to do is multiply your object's local coordinates by the scaling factor. Figure 6.6 shows the gun object being scaled by a factor of two.

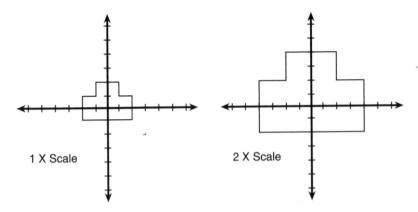

Figure 6.6

Scaling in action.

1 X Scale

2 X Scale

You can also extend this so you can scale independently in each direction. For example, if you want to scale by sx in the x direction and sy in the y direction, the formula becomes

$$newX = x \times sx$$

$$newY = y \times sy$$

Rotation

Rotation is the hardest transformation to understand because you need to use trigonometry. But once you get the hang of it, rotation becomes as easy as one, two, three; especially when you learn about rotation matrices in the next section. Well, maybe not *that* easy, but you know what I mean.

The first thing you need to understand is that the angles used in computer functions are almost always measured in *radians*, not degrees. As you probably already know, there are 360 degrees in a circle. That's the equivalent of 2 × pi radians, in which pi is 3.14159. It is very important that you remember this fact!

Now, assume you have a point, p1, at (5, 3) and you want to rotate that point by 30 degrees so it will end up giving you a new coordinate, p2. See Figure 6.7.

The equations you need to rotate a point around the origin by an angle *theta* are these:

$$newX = oldX \times \cos(theta) - oldY \times \sin(theta)$$

$$newY = oldX \times \sin(theta) + oldY \times \cos(theta)$$

For the given example, first convert 30 degrees into radians. Each degree is 2 × pi/360 radians—or 0.017453 radians, so

$$30 \text{ degrees} = 30 \times 0.017453 = 0.52359 \text{ radians}$$

Figure 6.7

Rotating a point.

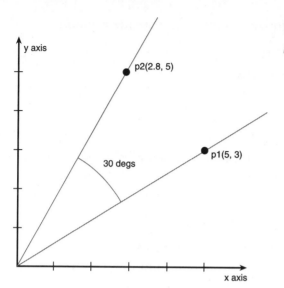

Plugging the numbers into the formula results in:

$$newX = 5 \times \cos(0.52359) - 3 \times \sin(0.52359) = 2.830$$
$$newY = 5 \times \sin(0.52359) + 3 \times \cos(0.52359) = 5.098$$

The result of the rotation is shown in Figure 6.7. As you can see, when you rotate a point by an angle, the point moves around the origin in an *anticlockwise* direction (the y-axis is pointing upwards and the x-axis is pointing to your right). This is because, although most of us think in a clockwise direction, mathematicians like to think in an anticlockwise direction!

When you use the same equation using a y-axis that points downward and an x-axis pointing to the right (as in a normal application window), the rotation will go clockwise. If you ever require the rotation to go in the opposite direction, you can simply reverse the signs of the sin parts of the equations, like so:

$$newX = oldX \times \cos(theta) + oldY \times \sin(theta)$$
$$newY = (-1) \times oldX \times \sin(theta) + oldY \times \cos(theta)$$

> **NOTE**
>
> In reality, converting degrees into radians and then back into degrees again is far too time-consuming for a game. It's much better to just get used to using radians all the time. Trust me, after a very short time you'll find radians to be just as easy to use as degrees. You'll even start to think in radians. (Although, if you skateboard, I doubt you'll ever say stuff like, "Wow! What an incredible *Five Pi that was, man!*")

Or even easier, you can use the original equation but just negate the rotation:

$$\text{newX} = \text{oldX} \times \cos(-theta) - \text{oldY} \times \sin(-theta)$$
$$\text{newY} = \text{oldX} \times \sin(-theta) + \text{oldY} \times \cos(-theta)$$

Putting It All Together

Now that you know how to transform vertices, all you need to do is put all three transforms together into one function, which is called just before you draw the shape to the screen. This function is usually referred to as the *World Transformation* function because it converts your shape's vertices from local coordinates into world coordinates. I've written some simple code that demonstrates all three transformations working on the space invader gun shape, which can be found in the Chapter6/ShapeManipulation folder on the CD. You can use the cursor keys to alter the gun's rotation and scale. The A, S, P, and L keys move it around the screen.

This is what the CGun class definition and the CGun::WorldTransform function look like from that code:

```
class CGun
{
public:

    //its position in the world
    double          m_dPosX,
                    m_dPosY;

    //its rotation
    double          m_dRotation;

    //its scale
    double          m_dScale;

    //its vertices
    vector<SPoint> m_vecGunVB;

    vector<SPoint> m_vecGunVBTrans;

    CGun(double x,
         double y,
         double scale,
```

```
                double rot);

    void WorldTransform();
    void Render(HDC &surface);
    void Update();
};

void CGun::WorldTransform()
{
    //copy the original vertices into the buffer about to be transformed
    m_vecGunVBTrans = m_vecGunVB;

    //first we rotate the vertices
    for (int vtx=0; vtx<m_vecGunVBTrans.size(); ++vtx)
    {
        m_vecGunVBTrans[vtx].x = m_vecGunVB[vtx].x * cos(m_dRotation) -
                                 m_vecGunVB[vtx].y * sin(m_dRotation);

        m_vecGunVBTrans[vtx].y = m_vecGunVB[vtx].x * sin(m_dRotation) +
                                 m_vecGunVB[vtx].y * cos(m_dRotation);
    }

    //now scale the vertices
    for (vtx=0; vtx<m_vecGunVBTrans.size(); ++vtx)
    {
        m_vecGunVBTrans[vtx].x *= m_dScale;
        m_vecGunVBTrans[vtx].y *= m_dScale;
    }

    //and finally translate the vertices
    for (vtx=0; vtx<m_vecGunVBTrans.size(); ++vtx)
    {
        m_vecGunVBTrans[vtx].x += m_dPosX;
        m_vecGunVBTrans[vtx].y += m_dPosY;
    }
}
```

The order in which the transformations take place is *very* important. If the shape is translated before it's rotated, the *translated* shape will be rotated around the origin. This is why you should always design your game objects with their vertices centered around the origin—so the rotations and scaling work out correctly. Actually, it's a good idea for you to try jumbling up the order of the transformations in the sample code just to see what sort of results you end up with.

The gun object uses two vertex buffers: one to keep a record of the original vertices before transformation and the other to store the transformed vertices ready for rendering to the screen. This way, you always have a copy of the original vertices to work from.

Matrix Magic

In the previous example, you saw how a shape is transformed by shoving each vertex in the shape through three different transformations: rotation, scaling, and translation. So, for every vertex, your program is doing *three* calculations. Matrices allow you to combine all the transformations into *one* matrix, and then you use that one matrix on all the vertices. That saves a *load* of processor time when you are transforming hundreds or even thousands of vertices each frame.

Matrices are fantastic things for computer graphics. You may have hated them in school, but I can assure you, if you program a lot of graphics, you'll grow to love them.

Okay, but What Exactly Is a Matrix?

A matrix is an array of numbers. It can be one-dimensional, two-dimensional, or many-dimensional—just like the arrays you create within your code. A *transformation matrix* is always two-dimensional. This is an example of a 2D matrix.

$$\begin{bmatrix} 4 & 15 & 0 \\ 3 & 3 & 1 \\ 0 & 8 & 12 \end{bmatrix}$$

The example matrix has three rows and three columns, so it is described as a 3 x 3 matrix. Each number in the matrix is referred to as an *element*. So, for example, the number 15 in the previous matrix is the element at position (1, 2).

NOTE

Although programmers number the elements in their arrays from zero, mathematicians number their matrices from 1. This can be very confusing when you first start reading mathematical texts!

You can add, subtract, divide, and multiply matrices just like you can real numbers, although the only operation you need to perform transformations is multiplication. So, that's what I'm going to show you.

How to Multiply Two Matrices Together

Yikes! I wasn't looking forward to explaining this! It's not that it's hard to do, it's just hard to explain. I think the best way is to show you.

First of all, let me explain how you multiply a row with a column. Here's an example.

$$[1 \quad 2 \quad 3] \times \begin{bmatrix} 7 \\ 8 \\ 9 \end{bmatrix} = (1 \times 7) + (2 \times 8) + (3 \times 9) = 7 + 16 + 27 = 50$$

The number of elements in the row and the number of elements in the column *must* be the same. If they are different, you cannot do this multiplication.

Now that you understand how to multiply a row and a column, you can multiply matrices. To multiply matrix A by matrix B, multiply every row of A with every column of B. Here is an example.

$$\begin{bmatrix} 1 & 2 \\ 3 & 4 \end{bmatrix} \times \begin{bmatrix} 6 & 7 \\ 8 & 9 \end{bmatrix} = \begin{Bmatrix} (1 \times 6) + (2 \times 8) & (1 \times 7) + (2 \times 9) \\ (3 \times 6) + (4 \times 8) & (3 \times 7) + (4 \times 9) \end{Bmatrix} = \begin{bmatrix} 22 & 25 \\ 50 & 57 \end{bmatrix}$$

Let me repeat: to multiply two matrices together, the size of the rows and columns *must be the same.* Therefore, you can multiply the following two matrices together.

$$[1 \quad 2 \quad 3 \quad 4] \times \begin{bmatrix} 5 & 9 \\ 6 & 10 \\ 7 & 11 \\ 8 & 12 \end{bmatrix}$$

But not these:

$$[1 \quad 2 \quad 3 \quad 4] \times \begin{bmatrix} 5 & 8 \\ 6 & 9 \\ 7 & 10 \end{bmatrix}$$

Try doing the multiplication for the first equation. The answer is given at the end of this chapter.

The Identity Matrix

In mathematics, the number 1 is very useful. This is because you can multiply any number by 1 and end up with the number you started with. I know that sounds like a really obvious thing to say, but take my word for it, mathematicians would be lost without the number 1.

Matrices have an equivalent of the number 1, and it is called the *identity matrix*. Because matrices can be any size, you need to define an identity matrix for the size you require. You'll be working with 3 x 3 matrices, so the identity matrix looks like this:

$$\begin{bmatrix} 1 & 0 & 0 \\ 0 & 1 & 0 \\ 0 & 0 & 1 \end{bmatrix}$$

As you can see, if you multiply this identity matrix with any other compatible matrix (remember the rows and columns rule?), you'll end up with the same matrix you started with.

$$\begin{bmatrix} 1 & 0 & 0 \\ 0 & 1 & 0 \\ 0 & 0 & 1 \end{bmatrix} \times [4 \ \ 5 \ \ 6] = [(1 \times 4) + (0 \times 4) + (0 \times 4) \ \ (0 \times 5) + (1 \times 5) + (0 \times 5) \ \ (0 \times 6) + (0 \times 6) + (1 \times 6)] = [4 \ \ 5 \ \ 6]$$

You need this type of matrix to use as a base to create other matrices.

Using Matrices to Transform Vertices

Now here's the great thing. A point in space (for example, x, y) can be represented as a matrix.

$$[x \ \ y \ \ 1]$$

Don't worry about the third element (the 1) for now. Just be assured it has to be there for this to work.

Because you can represent a point as a matrix, it's possible to multiply it with another matrix and perform transformations. Let's go through the three transformations and see exactly how it's done.

Translation

Remember how you translated a point in the last section? You added the distance dx, dy to its x and y coordinates to get the new point, like this:

$$newX = x + dx$$

$$newY = y + dy$$

So, to do the same thing with a matrix, you create a translation matrix, which looks like this

$$\begin{bmatrix} 1 & 0 & 0 \\ 0 & 1 & 0 \\ dx & dy & 1 \end{bmatrix}$$

and then multiply it with your point x, y. This is what the whole thing looks like:

$$[x \ y \ 1] \times \begin{bmatrix} 1 & 0 & 0 \\ 0 & 1 & 0 \\ dx & dy & 1 \end{bmatrix} = [(1 \times x) + (0 \times y) + (1 \times dx) \ \ (0 \times x) + (1 \times y) + (1 \times dy) \ \ (0 \times 0) + (0 \times 0) + (1 \times 1)] = [x + dx \ \ y + dy \ \ 1]$$

I hope you can see why the 1 needed to be added to the x and y coordinate to create the matrix which represents the point. This allows the translation factors to be part of the final sum.

Scaling

This is the transformation matrix, which performs scaling by sx in the x-axis and sy in the y-axis:

$$\begin{bmatrix} sx & 0 & 0 \\ 0 & sy & 0 \\ 0 & 0 & 1 \end{bmatrix}$$

To give you an example, do you remember how I showed you how to scale a point in the last section?

$$newX = x \times sx$$

$$newY = y \times sy$$

You end up with exactly the same equations by using the scale matrix on a point x, y:

$$[x \ y \ 1] \times \begin{bmatrix} sx & 0 & 0 \\ 0 & sy & 0 \\ 0 & 0 & 1 \end{bmatrix} = [x \times sx \ \ y \times sy \ \ 1]$$

Getting the hang of it? Great, let's move on to the most complicated transformation: rotation.

Rotation

To perform rotation using a matrix, you need to create a matrix that will re-create the rotation formula in the "Rotation" section dealing with vertices.

$$newX = oldX \times \cos(theta) - oldY \times \sin(theta)$$
$$newY = oldX \times \sin(theta) + oldY \times \cos(theta)$$

The matrix that does this job looks like this:

$$\begin{bmatrix} \cos(\theta) & \sin(\theta) & 0 \\ -\sin(\theta) & \cos(\theta) & 0 \\ 0 & 0 & 1 \end{bmatrix}$$

As you can see, when you multiply a point x, y by this matrix, you end up with a correctly rotated point.

$$[x \ y \ 1x] \begin{bmatrix} \cos(\theta) & \sin(\theta) & 0 \\ -\sin(\theta) & \cos(\theta) & 0 \\ 0 & 0 & 1 \end{bmatrix} = [x\cos(\theta) - y\sin(\theta) \ \ x\sin(\theta) + y\cos(\theta) \ \ 1]$$

Now for the Magic Part

Here's the great thing about matrices: If you have a series of transformations, you can create a matrix for each one and then combine all those matrices into one transformation matrix, which you can use on all your points. To combine matrices, you multiply them together. Just as before, the *order* in which you perform the multiplication is important. Here are the stages in creating and using a transformation matrix.

1. Create an identity matrix.
2. Create a scale matrix and combine it with the matrix created in Step 1.

3. Create a rotation matrix and combine it with the result from Step 2.

4. Create a translation matrix and combine it with the result from Step 3.

5. Use the matrix you ended up with in Step 4 on each vertex in your shape.

Actually, the steps for rotation and scaling may be interchanged, but the rest of the steps must be in that order or you'll end up getting some pretty weird results!

I've changed the code in the last example to use matrix transformations. You can find it in the Chapter6/Shape Manipulation with Matrices folder. If you load the project into your compiler, you'll notice I have defined a matrix class, C2DMatrix, to do all the matrix calculations. The CGun::WorldTransformation function now looks like this:

```
void CGun::WorldTransform()
{
  //copy the original vertices into the buffer about to be transformed
  m_vecGunVBTrans = m_vecGunVB;

  //create a transformation matrix
  C2DMatrix matTransform;
```

When you create an instance of a C2DMatrix, it's initially just an identity matrix that provides a base for creating the transformations required.

```
  //scale
  matTransform.Scale(m_dScale, m_dScale);
```

To scale an object use the Scale method, which requests x and y scaling factors. Because the gun object uses the same scaling factor for both axes, I've entered m_dScale for both.

```
  //rotate
  matTransform.Rotate(m_dRotation);

  //and translate
  matTransform.Translate(m_dPosX, m_dPosY);

  //now transform the ships vertices
  matTransform.TransformSPoints(m_vecGunVBTrans);
}
```

The last method, TransformSPoints, takes a reference to a vector of SPoints and multiplies them with the combined transformation matrix.

As you can see, in addition to being a piece of cake to use, the matrix class is much faster and more convenient than the transformation methods used in the previous Shape Manipulation code.

Now that you have matrices under your belt, I'm going to spend some time talking about another indispensable tool for game programmers: *vectors*.

What's a Vector?

Before I move on to vectors, let's take a quick look at what a point is again. Figure 6.8 shows a point, p, represented in 2D space at coordinate (3, 4).

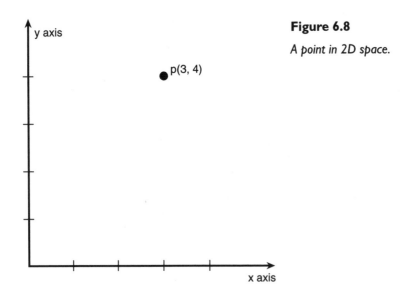

Figure 6.8

A point in 2D space.

And that's all a point is—just a place in space. No more, no less.

A *vector* (although its notation may look just like a point) gives you a lot more information. A vector represents a *magnitude* and a *direction*. So, for example, the same point, p (3, 4), represented as a vector looks like Figure 6.9.

Let's look at it another way to make absolutely sure you know what a vector represents. Say you are programming a Red Alert type game and there's a tank unit motoring around the map. Its velocity and direction can be represented by a vector. The direction the vector is pointing is the direction the tank is heading, and the magnitude (the length) of the vector represents its speed. The greater the magnitude, the faster the tank is traveling.

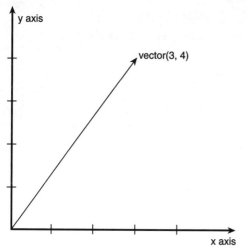

Figure 6.9

A vector in 2D space.

vector(3, 4)

y axis

x axis

In my code samples, I'll be using 2D vectors, which are given by two coordinates, x and y, just like a point in 2D space. The definition of the vector structure I use looks very similar to the SPoint structure discussed earlier:

```
struct SVector2D
{
  double x, y;

  SVector2D(double a = 0.0f, double b = 0.0f):x(a),y(b){}
};
```

If you're working in 3D however, you would add a third dimension—the z–dimension—just as if you were representing a point in 3D space. As you can see, you only need one point in space to define a vector, because the other end of the vector is always assumed to be at the origin (0, 0).

Okay, so now that you know what a vector is, let's look at some of the things you can do with them.

Adding and Subtracting Vectors

Imagine you found a treasure map (if only… <smile>), but instead of the usual …*from the palm tree walk three paces east, then walk six paces northeast, twelve paces northwest…* you have a list of instructions to follow, like this:

To find the treasure, from the palm tree follow the vectors (3, 1), (-2, 4), (6, -2), (-2, 4).

The map shown in Figure 6.10 shows the route you would take to find the treasure.

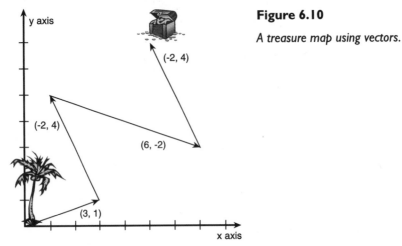

Figure 6.10

A treasure map using vectors.

The great thing about vectors is, instead of following four individual vectors, you can add them up and follow just one vector to the treasure. To add vectors, you add all the x components and then all the y components (and all the z components if you are working in 3D). Therefore, the new vector is found like so:

New x = 3 + (-2) + 6 + (-2) = 5

New y = 1 + 4 + (-2) + 4 = 7

So, all the vectors added together give you the new vector (5, 7), which takes you straight to the treasure, as shown in Figure 6.11, beating all the competition to the loot!

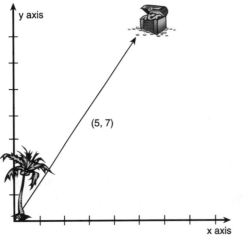

Figure 6.11

A smart use of vector addition.

To subtract vectors, you do exactly the same except, well... you subtract the components instead of adding them.

Interesting Fact

There is a species of ant that lives in a hole in the desert. These ants forage by randomly selecting a direction, walking in a straight line for a period of time, then selecting another direction and following that for a while. This continues until the ant finds food. By this time, it may be some distance (in ant terms) away from the protection of its hole—sometimes as far as many hundreds of feet.

The incredible thing about this ant is as soon as it discovers food, it returns to its hole in a *straight line*. So, what this clever little insect is doing is summing up the series of vectors it has walked and then inverting the summed total to calculate the way home. I bet you never knew ants could do math, eh?

Calculating the Magnitude of a Vector

Now that you've found the treasure, let's say you want to know how far away the chest is from the palm tree. To determine that, you need to calculate the magnitude (the length) of the vector.

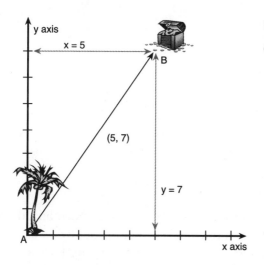

Figure 6.12

Calculating the magnitude of a vector.

The magnitude of a vector is easily calculated by using Pythagoras's famous equation. Therefore, the length AB in Figure 6.12 is determined by:

$$AB = \sqrt{x^2 + y^2}$$

Slotting in the numbers gives you:

$$AB = \sqrt{5^2 + 7^2} = 8.6023$$

So, you know the length from the palm tree to the treasure is 8.6023 units.

Multiplying Vectors

To multiply a vector by a number, you simply multiply each of the vector's components by that number. So, to multiply the vector (1, 2) by 4.

$$(1, 2) \times 4 = (4, 8)$$

You get a vector heading in the same direction, but it is four times longer than it was before the multiplication, as shown in Figure 6.13.

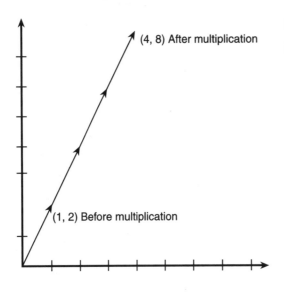

(4, 8) After multiplication

(1, 2) Before multiplication

Figure 6.13

Vector multiplication.

Normalizing Vectors

A *normalized* vector is a vector with a magnitude that is always 1.0. A normalized vector is also referred to as a *unit* vector. To create a normalized vector, you divide each component of the vector by the magnitude of the vector. That way you have a vector which is pointing in the same direction as the original but now has a length of 1.0.

For example, take the vector $\mathbf{V} = (3, 4)$. The length is calculated as:

$$Length = \sqrt{3^2 + 4^2} = \sqrt{25} = 5$$

Now that the length is known, divide each component of the vector by this to get the normalized vector:

$$3/25 = 0.12 \text{ and } 4/25 = 0.16$$

Therefore, the normalized vector, **N**, is determined by **N** = (0.12, 0.16).

Normalized vectors have some very useful properties, the first of which I'll be talking about in a moment.

Resolving Vectors

One really cool thing you can do with vectors is to *resolve* the magnitude into its respective x and y *components*. Let me show you what I mean. Imagine a car traveling at 50 kph in the direction shown in Figure 6.14.

TIP

Mathematicians usually denote a vector using boldface uppercase letters like so, **V**. The length of the vector is denoted by enclosing the vector within two vertical bars like this, |**V**|. Therefore, the normalized vector, **V**, may be written as:

$$N = \frac{V}{|V|}$$

Occasionally, you may see a normalized vector referred to in lowercase or with an asterisk by the side. So...

V normalized may be written as **v** or as **V***.

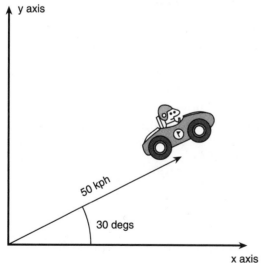

Figure 6.14

A velocity vector.

You can split the velocity vector into two separate vectors representing how fast the car is traveling in the x direction and how fast the car is traveling in the y direction. These are known as the x and y components of the vector. From trigonometry, you know that in a right-angled triangle:

$$\cos(angle) = \text{adjacent}/ \text{hypotenuse}$$
$$\sin(angle) = \text{opposite}/ \text{hypotenuse}$$

In this example, the angle is 30 degrees and the hypotenuse is represented by the magnitude of the vector (the speed of the car), 50 kph. The x and y components you are trying to find represent the adjacent and opposite sides. So, applying the preceding equations, you can say that:

$$\text{The x component} = 50 \times \cos(30) = 43.3 \text{ kph}$$
$$\text{The y component} = 50 \times \sin(30) = 25 \text{ kph}$$

And Bingo! You now know that in one hour the car will have traveled 25 klicks along the y-axis and 43.3 klicks along the x-axis. Being able to resolve vectors like this is incredibly useful for all sorts of stuff. Let me show you how you would use this technique in a game.

Imagine you are designing a tank battle game. A user controlled tank's position is represented by a SVector2D structure and its rotation by a double.

```
SVector2D vTankPos;
double    dTankRotation
```

When the user steps on the gas, you want to be able to apply a velocity of 10 kph in the direction the tank is facing. To do that, you resolve 10 kph into its x and y components and then add the respective component to the appropriate component of the tank's position to get the updated position for the next frame. The code would look like this:

```
double xComponent = 10*cos(dTankRotation);
double yComponent = 10*sin(dTankRotation);
vTankPos.x += xComponent;
cTankPos.y += yComponent;
```

I'll be using this technique quite a lot in the rest of the code projects, as you will see.

The Magical Marvelous Dot Product

The *dot product* of two vectors is a fantastic thing because it gives you the angle between two vectors—something you require often when programming games.

Given two vectors, **U** and **V,** the dot product can be calculated using either of the following two equations:

$$\mathbf{U} \cdot \mathbf{V} = \mathbf{U}_x\mathbf{V}_x + \mathbf{U}_y\mathbf{V}_y$$

or

$$\mathbf{U} \cdot \mathbf{V} = |\mathbf{U}||\mathbf{V}|\cos\theta$$

Wait a moment! You said the dot product is used to give me the angle between the vectors. Looks to me like in the second equation you need the angle to get the dot product! What's going on?

Ah well, that's a very good question. But here's the magic. Remember, |**V**| simply means the magnitude of the vector, **V**? Now, because you've just learned how to normalize the vector—in other words, to make its length 1—the second equation simply boils down to the following, if you normalize the vectors first.

$$\mathbf{U} \cdot \mathbf{V} = \cos\theta$$

So slotting equation 1 into equation 2, you get this lovely formula.

$$\mathbf{U}_x\mathbf{V}_x + \mathbf{U}_y\mathbf{V}_y = \cos\theta$$

And Hey Presto!! You now know how to calculate the angle between two vectors.

The SVector2D Helper Utilities

I have written some code to help with 2D vector operations. You can find the code in the SVector2D.h file, which is present in almost all code projects from here onward. If you examine the source, you'll find that I've overloaded the operators so that vectors can be easily multiplied, divided, added, or subtracted. There are also functions to perform the most useful vector operations, as follows:

```
inline double Vec2DLength(const SVector2D &v);
inline void Vec2DNormalize(SVector2D &v);
inline double Vec2DDot(SVector2D &v1, SVector2D &v2);
inline int Vec2DSign(SVector2D &v1, SVector2D &v2);
```

The last function, Vec2DSign returns 1 if v2 is clockwise from v1, and -1 if anticlockwise. As you will discover, this can be a useful little function at times.

The SPoint structure is also defined in the SVector2D file. In general, I use SPoints for vertices and SVector2Ds for things like velocities and object positions.

What a Clever Chap That Newton Fellow Was

As games become more sophisticated and the environments they take place in become more realistic, the more educated programmers have to become. Nowadays, not only do you have to know how to code, you also need to know a combination of artificial intelligence methods, mathematics, fast algorithms and data structures for 3D graphics, such as BSP (Binary Space Partition) trees, texture mapping and manipulation, and fast collision detection techniques. However, programming something that feels real is impossible, even with all the preceding techniques, if you don't use *physics*.

So what is physics? My dictionary defines it as

The science of matter and energy and of the interactions between the two.

The rules of physics are the rules that define the behavior of everything in our universe—the way the wind plays with fields of corn, the orbits of the planets around the sun, and the reason water spins like a tornado when it falls through the hole in your shower basin. To know physics is to know the world around you.

When you learn how to program physics into your game world, that world starts to *feel* real in addition to looking real. Objects move as they should, cars slide convincingly around corners, bullets and missiles make beautiful trajectories through the air, particle smoke rises and swirls just like real smoke, and objects can "feel" heavy or light.

Physics is a very large subject. In addition to other topics, physics is comprised of the following:

- Mechanics
- Kinematics
- Dynamics
- Optics
- Electricity and magnetism
- Acoustics
- Thermodynamics
- Atomic particles
- Quantum phenomena

Because the lunar lander in the project for this chapter is moving and because it is affected by gravity, I'll be limiting the physics I show you to just that—the physics of motion and gravity. First, a definition of the basic units scientists use to measure physical objects and actions is required.

Time

Time is abstract and hard to define. It has a slippery quality; sometimes it seems to go fast, sometimes slow. Some philosophers even think time doesn't really exist and is just a figment of our imagination. (Try that one with your boss the next time you're late for work!) Scientists have also shown that creatures with different metabolisms perceive time differently. If mice wore wristwatches, you would have a hard time synchronizing your own with it, because the tiny hands would be whipping around much faster than the ones on your own.

Physicists however, have to measure time accurately, and to do that, they must define exactly what a unit of time is. They require a *standard*. The name they gave to the unit of time is the *second* and it is defined as—get ready for it…

> *The duration of 9,192,631,770 periods of the radiation corresponding to the transition between the two hyperfine levels of the ground state of the cesium 133 atom.*

Wow! I bet that makes everything much clearer now! Seriously though, you don't have to worry about what a second actually *is* as long as everyone uses the same definition. When programming games, you are usually working in time units that are *fractions of a second* because your code will be doing calculations for each frame update and most games run at a minimum of 30 frames per second.

Interesting Fact

Not so long ago, before the invention of railways, not only did different countries operate on different timescales, but different towns and villages did too! You could set your watch in London, but by the time you reached Oxford in your rickety carriage, the time would be many minutes different. This must have been very strange—having to set your watch each time you traveled a few miles—but nevertheless, this is what the world was like back then.

Length

The standard unit of distance is the meter. Until fairly recently, it was defined as the distance between two etched lines on a metal bar kept in some research institute. Nowadays, physicists like a more accurate representation, so a meter is now defined as:

> *The distance traveled by light in a vacuum over a period of (1/299792458) seconds.*

When designing computer games, distance is usually measured in arbitrary units that are related to the resolution of the graphics display.

Mass

Mass is the measure of an *amount* of something. This is a tricky quality to measure correctly because you have to calculate the mass of an object by weighing it, and yet mass is not a unit of *weight*; it is a unit of *matter*. Weight is a measurement of how much force *gravity* is exerting upon something.

The force of gravity acting upon the paperweight sitting in front of me is different in different places. It would weigh a lot less on the moon, for example. And because the earth is not exactly spherical and because it contains mountain ranges and different densities of rock, it would weigh different amounts in different places on Earth. But wherever it's located, the paperweight would always have the same *mass*.

Again, scientists need a standard, and what they came up with was this: Somewhere in France, in Paris I believe, is a metal cylinder made out of an exotic platinum-iridium alloy. This cylinder has been agreed upon by physicists to be THE kilogram. That is, the kilogram by which everything else is measured. If you were a scientist and you wanted your own version of the kilogram, you would go to France and have a duplicate made which weighs (on incredibly accurate scales) exactly the same as THE kilogram. You would then enjoy the sights, have a few bottles of wine, and fly back home. Now, even if the gravity in your place of the world is different from that in Paris, you would know that your kilogram still has exactly the same mass as THE kilogram.

Once you have a definition of *force*, you can do away with any reference to gravity when measuring mass.

Force

Here is the definition of force, as Newton put it:

> *An impressed force is an action exerted upon a body in order to change its state, either of rest, or of uniform motion in a right line.*

So, a force is anything that can alter an object's speed or line of motion. Some forces are extremely obvious, such as the force a soccer player uses to kick a ball, the force your toaster makes to pop up the toast, and the force you feel when you use an elevator. Other forces are less obvious because they can cancel each other out, and therefore, although forces are being exerted, that object may not move.

For example, the force exerted by gravity upon an apple sitting on a table is canceled out by the force the table is exerting upon it in the opposite direction. See Figure 6.15.

Figure 6.15

Forces acting upon a stationary body.

This concept—of the table exerting an upward force—seems strange at first, but it's real nevertheless.

The unit of force is the *newton*, named after the great man himself. A newton is defined as:

The force required to make a one kilogram mass move from rest to a speed of one meter per second.

You can now use this definition of force to define mass, without having to resort to referring to gravity. For example, if it takes 3 newtons to get my paperweight moving at a speed of 1 m/s, then my paperweight *must* (by the definition of a newton) have a mass of 3 kilograms. Voilá! Everything is neat and tidy.

Motion—Velocity

Velocity is the *rate of change of position of an object with respect to time* and is normally measured in meters per second (m/s). If you are traveling in a car however, your velocity is measured in mph or kph. The velocities of game objects are normally calculated in pixels per second.

If you know how long a car has been moving, and you know its average speed, it's easy to calculate how much distance the car has covered in that time using the equation:

New Position = Old Position + Velocity × Time

For example, look at the car in Figure 6.16.

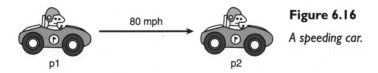

80 mph

p1   p2

Figure 6.16

A speeding car.

If the car has been traveling for two hours, the distance between p1 and p2 is calculated as:

$$distance = 0 + 80 \times 2 = 160 \text{ miles}$$

Motion—Acceleration

Velocity is the rate of change of distance, but acceleration is the *rate of change of velocity* and is measured in meters per second. (m/s^2).

To elaborate, if the car in Figure 6.16 starts at rest and then accelerates at a constant acceleration of 5 m/s^2, then every second an additional 5 m/s will be added to its velocity, as shown in Table 6.1.

Figure 6.17 shows this information plotted onto a graph.

NOTE

This brings me to another point: *where* exactly are the points p1 and p2? Are they at the front of the car, at the back, on the roof?

Well, when measuring the position of an object, it's usually measured at the *center of mass* of that object. The center of mass of an object can be thought of as the balance point of the object. If you could manage to balance a car on your finger, the center of mass would lay directly above your fingertip.

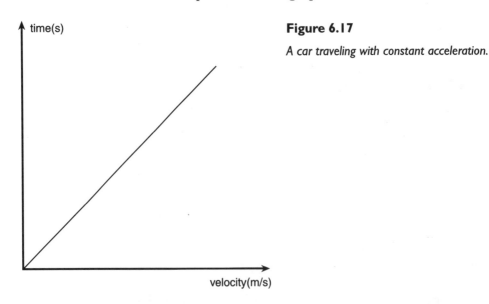

Figure 6.17

A car traveling with constant acceleration.

A good example of something traveling with constant acceleration is a falling rock, which travels at a constant acceleration because the only force acting upon it is the Earth's gravity.

Table 6.1 Velocity Due to Acceleration

Time(s)	Acceleration m/s²	Velocity(m/s)
1	5	5
2	5	10
3	5	15
4	5	20
5	5	25

Objects can also travel at a non-constant acceleration. For example, a drag racer might produce a graph which looks a little like Figure 6.18. This shows a rapid increase in speed at the beginning of the graph but then gradually trails off as the acceleration falls.

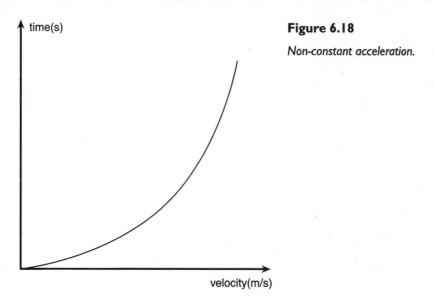

Figure 6.18

Non-constant acceleration.

To calculate the distance an object has traveled if it is moving with a constant acceleration, a, for a time, t, you use the following equation:

$$\text{Distance traveled} = ut + \frac{1}{2} at^2$$

where u is the starting velocity of the object.

So, to use the earlier example of a car traveling from rest with acceleration 5 m/s^2 for 5 seconds, you can now calculate how far it has traveled by slotting the numbers into the equation:

$$\text{Distance traveled} = 0 \times 5 + \_\, 5 \times 5 \times 5$$
$$= 62.5 \text{ meters}$$

> **NOTE**
>
> Although the letter *a* is normally used to represent acceleration, the acceleration due to gravity is represented using a "g". That's why you hear jet fighters saying stuff like *"Wow man, I pulled eight g's back there!"*
>
> g, on Earth, averages out to around 9.8 m/s^2.

Feel the Force, Luke

You learned earlier that force is an action exerted upon a body and that it's measured in newtons. Now I'm going to show you the relationship between force, mass, and acceleration.

$$\text{Force} = \text{Mass} \times \text{Acceleration}$$

As you can see, the force exerted on an object is in proportion to its mass and its acceleration. This is why you feel a force pushing you back into your seat when the airplane you're in takes off. This is a very important equation in physics and you'll find yourself using it a lot, especially when written in the following form:

$$\text{Acceleration} = \text{Force/Mass}$$

Because now, given a game object's mass and the force exerted upon it (like the thrust of a spacecraft, for example), it's easy to calculate the acceleration and update the object's velocity and position accordingly. In each frame of your game, you would do something like this:

NewAcceleration = OldAcceleration + (Force/Mass)

NewVelocity = OldVelocity + NewAcceleration × FrameTime

NewPosition = OldPosition + NewVelocity × FrameTime

The frame time is the time which has elapsed between the current frame and the preceding frame.

Gravity

Gravity is the force of attraction between two objects. It is the force which stops us from spinning off into space, the force which makes the planets orbit around the sun, and the force which creates the earth's tides. Gravity is everywhere; there is even a force exerted from your own body mass onto this book, albeit a very small one.

Although nobody really knows what gravity is, fortunately Newton figured out an equation for calculating it. Given two objects, as in Figure 6.19, one with mass m, the other with mass M, and a distance between them of r, the equation to calculate the gravitational force between them is this:

$$F = \frac{GMm}{r^2}$$

Where G is the gravitational constant 6.673×10^{-11}

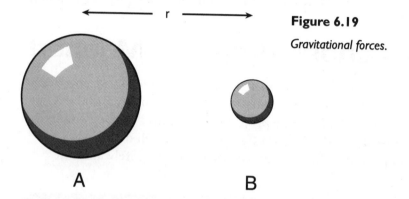

Figure 6.19

Gravitational forces.

So, how much force is exerted is proportional to the masses of the objects and is inversely proportional to the square of the distance between them. As an experiment, let's use this equation to calculate the mass of the earth. First, imagine a tennis ball with mass m sitting on the world (with a mass M).

Because you know force exerted on an object is equal to its mass times its acceleration (F = ma), you can replace the F in the preceding equation, like so:

$$ma = \frac{GMm}{r^2}$$

The small m's cancel each other out, resulting in:

$$a = \frac{GM}{r^2}$$

And using algebra, you can shuffle the equation around until you get an equation for the earth's mass:

$$M = \frac{ar^2}{G}$$

Now, all you need to do is pop in some numbers. You know what a is because that's the acceleration due to gravity, g (approximately 9.8 m/s^2). G is the gravitational constant (6.673 x 10^{-11}), and the value r is the same as the earth's radius (6378000 m), because the ball's radius is negligible in comparison. This gives you:

$$M = \frac{9.8 \times (6378000)^2}{6.67 \times 10^{-11}} = 5.974 \times 10^{24}$$

Tah Dah! If you look up the earth's mass in an encyclopedia, you'll see that the equation worked perfectly (given that you only used approximate figures, of course).

The Lunar Lander Project—Manned

Well, now that you've learned all the clever stuff required to understand how the objects in the game are created, displayed, and moved around in a realistic way, let me take you through the lunar lander code project. You can find all the code in the Chapter6/Lunar Lander—Manned folder on the CD. Take a well-deserved break before you move on and play with the executable; see if you can safely land the lander. It's not easy is it?

The two classes of interest in the project are CLander and CController. CLander is like a more complex version of the CGun class I described earlier. It holds all the information you need to know about a lunar lander object and its vertices. CController is a class that acts as an interface between windows and the

> **NOTE**
>
> To control the lander, use the cursor keys to rotate the ship left and right, and the spacebar to thrust. Good luck!

lander class. It also takes care of the landing pad shape and the stars.

Let's take a look at the header for CController first.

The CController Class Definition

A global pointer to a CController class instance is initialized in WM_CREATE and then called where appropriate (see comments in main.h) to render and update the scene.

```
class CController
{
```

```cpp
private:

  //this is the lander the user can control
  CLander*        m_pUserLander;

  //true if we have successfully landed
  bool            m_bSuccess;

  //vertex buffer for the stars
  vector<SPoint>  m_vecStarVB;

  //vertex buffer to store the landing pads vertices
  vector<SPoint>  m_vecPadVB;

  //position of the landing pad
  SVector2D       m_vPadPos;

  //keeps a record of the window size
  int             m_cxClient,
                  m_cyClient;

  void WorldTransform(vector<SPoint> &pad);

  void RenderLandingPad(HDC &surface);

public:

  CController(int cxClient, int cyClient);

  ~CController();

  //this is called from the windows message loop and calls
  //CLander::CheckForKeyPress() which tests for user input
  //and updates the lander's position accordingly
  bool  Update();

  //initialize a new run
  void  NewRun();

  //this is called from WM_PAINT to render all the objects
```

```
//in our scene
void  Render(HDC &surface);
};
```

Mapping Modes

The mapping mode is the way the GDI is configured to plot coordinates. Normally this means coordinates are plotted on a window which has a downward pointing y-axis. Because this sample project is all about the effects of gravity and flight, using the default Window's mapping mode is counter intuitive. What's needed is a y-axis that increases as it moves upward so that the lunar module's height is plotted correctly. If the default mapping mode is used, then as the lander's height is increased, the lower down in the window it would be drawn! Fortunately, Windows let's you define your own way of mapping coordinates to the screen. Here's how you change the mapping mode so that the y-axis points upward:

```
SetMapMode( surface, MM_ANISOTROPIC );
SetViewportExtEx( surface, 1, -1, NULL );
SetWindowExtEx( surface, 1, 1, NULL );
SetViewportOrgEx( surface, 0, m_cyClient, NULL );
```

I'm not going to go into the details of each of these functions, but if you're interested, look them up in your documentation. You will likely find, however, that having the choice of which way your y-axis points is adequate for most tasks, so you will probably never need to use any other mapping modes.

To restore the mapping mode, you use this sequence of function calls:

```
SetMapMode( surface, MM_ANISOTROPIC );
SetViewportExtEx( surface, 1, 1, NULL );
SetWindowExtEx( surface, 1, 1, NULL );
SetViewportOrgEx( surface, 0, 0, NULL );
```

The CLander Class Definition

The CLander class keeps a record of everything you need to know about the lander and has methods for rendering the lander shape, getting input from the user, and updating the physics. The header file for the CLander class is as follows. The comments included within the code should be enough to give you the gist of the class.

```
class CLander
{
```

```
private:

    //position in world
    SVector2D            m_vPos;

    //rotation in the world
    double               m_dRotation;

    //the ships mass.
    double               m_dMass;

    //and velocity
    SVector2D            m_vVelocity;

    //need to know where the landing pad is for collision detection
    SVector2D            m_vPadPos;

    //buffer to store the ships vertices
    vector<SPoint>       m_vecShipVB;

    //scaling factor for rendering the ship
    double               m_dScale;

    //buffer to hold our transformed vertices
    vector<SPoint>       m_vecShipVBTrans;

    //and the jets vertices
    vector<SPoint>       m_vecJetVB;
    vector<SPoint>       m_vecJetVBTrans;

    //we use this to determine whether to render the ship's jet or not
    //(if the user is pressing thrust then the jet is rendered)
    bool                 m_bJetOn;

    //local copy of client window size
    int                  m_cxClient;
    int                  m_cyClient;

    //used to flag whether or not we have already tested for success
```

```
        //or failure
        bool                m_bCheckedIfLanded;

        //returns true if the user has satisfied all the conditions for landing
        bool    LandedOK();

        //tests if any vertex of the ship is below the level of the landing
        //platform
        bool    TestForImpact(vector<SPoint> &ship);

        //this function transforms the ships vertices so we can display them
        void WorldTransform(vector<SPoint> &ship);


public:

    CLander(int       cxClient, //so we can keep a local record
            int       cyClient, //of the window dimensions
            double    rot,      //starting rotation of lander
            SVector2D pos,      //starting position of lander
            SVector2D pad);     //landing pad position

    void Render(HDC surface);

    //resets all relevant variables for the start of a new attempt
    void Reset(SVector2D &NewPadPos);

    //updates the ship from a user keypress
    void  UpdateShip();
};
```

The UpdateShip Function

You now know how to create a lunar lander and render it to the screen, but I haven't shown you how input is received from the user and how its position and velocity are updated. This is all done in the UpdateShip function. This is a summary of what the update function needs to do each frame:

- Test to see if the user is pressing a key
- Update the lander's velocity, acceleration, and rotation accordingly

- Update the lander's position
- Transform the lander's vertices
- Test to see if any of the lander's vertices are below "ground" level
- If the lander has reached ground level, test for success or failure

And now let me talk you through the code which does all that:

```
void CLander::UpdateShip(double TimeElapsed)
{
```

The first thing to notice is that this function is called with the *time elapsed* since the last frame. This is done because although you can set the timer for a fixed number of frames per second, as all the examples have done so far in this book, you can run into problems. For example, if the framerate is set at 60 fps and then the program is run on a machine much slower than your own overclocked-ninja-hardware-accelerated-monster of a machine, the slower machine may not be able to do 60 fps. It may only be able to do 40. If this was the case, then all the physics calculations would be messed up and the spaceship/racing car/tank would handle completely differently on machines incapable of the fixed framerate. Because this is undesirable, it's much safer to calculate the physics using the time elapsed from the last frame. This is easy to calculate because the CTimer class already has a method to do this for you—cunningly named GetTimeElapsed.

```
//just return if ship has crashed or landed
if (m_bCheckedIfLanded)
{
  return;
}
```

If the program has detected that the ship has landed (in the TestForImpact function), then m_bCheckedIfLanded is set to true and the update function simply returns without doing anything.

```
//switch the jet graphic off
m_bJetOn = false;
```

Whenever the user presses the thrust key (the spacebar), a little graphic of a thrust jet is drawn beneath the lander module. This flag is set on or off to indicate whether the graphic should be drawn in the render function.

```
//test for user input and update accordingly
if (KEYDOWN(VK_SPACE))
{
```

```
//the lander's acceleration per tick calculated from the force the
//thruster exerts, the lander's mass and the time elapsed since the
//last frame
double ShipAcceleration = (THRUST_PER_SECOND * TimeElapsed) / m_dMass;

//resolve the acceleration vector into its x, y components
//and add to the lander's velocity vector
m_vVelocity.x += ShipAcceleration * sin(m_dRotation);
m_vVelocity.y += ShipAcceleration * cos(m_dRotation);

//switch the jet graphic on
m_bJetOn = true;
}
```

When the spacebar is pressed, the correct amount of acceleration due to thrust must be calculated and applied to the lander. First, the acceleration is calculated from the force applied to the ship's mass during this time slice (Acceleration = Force / Mass). The acceleration vector is then resolved into its x and y components, as discussed earlier, and added to the relevant component of the ship's velocity.

> **NOTE**
>
> Rather than checking for key presses in the `WindowProc`, I'm using the alternative method I described in Chapter 1, "In the Beginning, There Was a Word, and the Word Was Windows." To make my life easier, I defined a macro you can find at the top of the CLander.cpp file like this:
>
> ```
> #define KEYDOWN(vk_code)
> ((GetAsyncKeyState(vk_code) &
> 0x8000) ? 1 : 0)
> ```

```
if (KEYDOWN(VK_LEFT))
{
  m_dRotation -= ROTATION_PER_SECOND * TimeElapsed;

  if (m_dRotation < -PI)
  {
    m_dRotation += TWO_PI;
  }
}

if (KEYDOWN(VK_RIGHT))
{
```

```
    m_dRotation += ROTATION_PER_SECOND * TimeElapsed;

    if (m_dRotation > TWO_PI)
    {
      m_dRotation -= TWO_PI;
    }
  }


  //now add in the gravity vector
  m_vVelocity.y += GRAVITY * TimeElapsed;

  //update the lander's position
  m_vPos += m_vVelocity * TimeElapsed * SCALING_FACTOR ;
```

Here, the lander module's velocity is updated according to the laws of physics. The important thing to notice here is the value SCALING_FACTOR. The reason that this constant is present is to make the game more fun. Let me show you what I mean...

As I mentioned earlier in the section on physics, when programming a game, units of distance are measured in pixels and not in meters. The lunar lander starts its descent approximately 300 pixels above the landing pad, so this represents 300 meters in the real world. Let's do the calculation to see how long it would take for the lander to reach the pad, falling 300 meters under the influence of the moon's gravity (1.63 m/s²).

From the equation

$$d = ut + \frac{1}{2} at^2$$

u (the start velocity) is zero, so you can simplify to

$$d = \frac{1}{2} at^2$$

and then shuffle using a bit of algebra.

$$t = \sqrt{\frac{2 \times d}{a}}$$

Putting in the numbers gives you

$$t = \sqrt{\frac{2 \times 300}{1.63}} = 19.18 \text{secs}$$

a time of over 19 seconds to reach the pad. In this case, 19 seconds is just too long. It would be boring (take the scaling off and try it to see just how tedious it is!). So, to compensate, a scaling factor is introduced. In effect, this is equivalent to the lander starting its descent from a lower altitude. The physics remain exactly the same, but now the lander is much more fun to control.

Moving back to the update function:

```
//bounds checking
if (m_vPos.x > WINDOW_WIDTH)
{
    m_vPos.x = 0;
}

if (m_vPos.x < 0)
{
    m_vPos.x = WINDOW_WIDTH;
}
```

These few lines of code make sure the lander module wraps around the screen if it flies too far left or right.

Now, the following tests if the lander has crashed or made a successful landing.

```
//create a copy of the lander's verts before we transform them
m_vecShipVBTrans = m_vecShipVB;

//transform the vertices
WorldTransform(m_vecShipVBTrans);
```

Before a test can be made to see if the ship has reached "ground" level or not, its vertices have to be transformed into world coordinates.

```
//if we are lower than the ground then we have finished this run
if (TestForImpact(m_vecShipVBTrans))
{
```

TestForImpact is a function which tests all the ship's vertices to find if any are below the ground plane. If a vertex is found to be below the ground, the program checks to see if the module has landed gracefully or crashed like an albatross.

```
//check if user has landed ship
if (!m_bCheckedIfLanded)
{
```

```
      if(LandedOK())
      {
        PlaySound("landed", NULL, SND_ASYNC|SND_FILENAME);;
      }

      else
      {
        PlaySound("explosion", NULL, SND_ASYNC|SND_FILENAME);
      }

      m_bCheckedIfLanded = true;
    }
  }
  return;
}
```

LandedOK is a function which tests if the lander module has satisfied all the requirements for a successful landing. The UpdateShip function then plays an appropriate wav file and returns.

This is what the LandedOK function looks like:

```
bool CLander::LandedOK()
{
  //calculate distance from pad
  double DistFromPad = fabs(m_vPadPos.x - m_vPos.x);

  //calculate speed of lander
  double speed = sqrt((m_vVelocity.x * m_vVelocity.x)
                    +(m_vVelocity.y * m_vVelocity.y));

  //check if we have a successful landing
  if( (DistFromPad        < DIST_TOLERANCE)      &&
      (speed              < SPEED_TOLERANCE)     &&
      (fabs(m_dRotation)  < ROTATION_TOLERANCE))
  {
    return true;
  }

  return false;
}
```

All the tolerances for a successful landing can be found in defines.h. As you can see, for a landing to be successful, the lander has to be flying below SPEED_TOLERANCE speed, be less than DIST_TOLERANCE away from the center of the pad, and have a rotation of less than ROTATION_TOLERANCE.

Now that you have learned how to fly a lunar lander (you did manage to land it, didn't you?), let's look at how a genetic algorithm can be programmed to control a spacecraft.

A Genetic Algorithm Controlled Lander

As with all genetic algorithms, the secret of solving the lunar lander control problem lies in correctly defining these three things:

- The encoding of candidate solutions
- Meaningful mutation and crossover operators
- A good fitness function

Once you have these steps sorted, you can leave the rest of the work to the magic of evolution. So, let's look at each step in turn. First, the encoding…

Encoding the Genome

You have already seen how candidate solutions may be encoded as binary bit strings or as permutations of integers, and you may have already guessed that you can just as easily encode some problems as a series of real numbers. What is not so obvious, though, is that it's possible to encode candidate solutions *anyway you like* as long as the genes are consistent and you can figure out mutation and crossover operators for them. You can even use complex data structures as genes, and I'll be showing you how to do that toward the end of the book. For now though, the important thing to note is that you must ensure that crossover and mutation operators can be applied in a way that is meaningful to the problem. So then, how do you encode the lander problem?

As you have seen, the lander may be controlled in four different ways:

- You can apply thrust.
- You can apply a rotational force to the left.
- You can apply a rotational force to the right.
- You can do nothing (drift).

Each of these four controls is applied for a certain period of time, which is measured in the fraction of a second it takes to update each frame. Therefore, an encoding has to be found that incorporates both an *action* and a *duration*. Figure 6.20 shows how the data is encoded. As you can see, each gene contains a data pair. The first half of the gene indicates the action the ship should take, and the second half indicates how long that action should be undertaken.

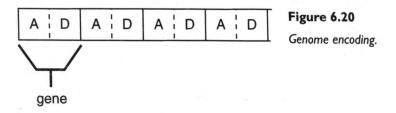

Figure 6.20

Genome encoding.

If you look in defines.h, you will find that the maximum duration an action can be undertaken per gene is #defined as 30 ticks (frames) in MAX_ACTION_DURATION.

Here's how the gene structure looks in code:

```
//first enumerate a type for each different action the Lander can perform
enum action_type{rotate_left,
                 rotate_right,
                 thrust,
                 non};

struct SGene
{
  action_type action;

  //duration the action is applied measured in ticks
  int         duration;

  SGene()
  {
    //create a random move
    action = (action_type)RandInt(0,3);

    duration = RandInt(1, MAX_ACTION_DURATION);
```

```
    }

    SGene(action_type a, int d):action(a), duration(d){}

    //need to overload the == operator so we can test if actions are
    //equal (used in the crossover process of the GA)
    bool operator==(const SGene &rhs) const
    {
        return (action == rhs.action) && (duration == rhs.duration);
    }
};
```

Now that you have a way of encoding the genes, it's a straightforward process to define the genome:

```
struct SGenome
{
    vector<SGene> vecActions;

    double        dFitness;

    SGenome():dFitness(0){}

    SGenome(const int num_actions):dFitness(0)
    {
        //create a random vector of actions
        for (int i=0; i<num_actions; ++i)
        {
            vecActions.push_back(SGene());
        }
    }

    //overload '<' used for sorting
    friend bool operator<(const SGenome& lhs, const SGenome& rhs)
    {
        return (lhs.dFitness < rhs.dFitness);
    }
};
```

Assuming the genetic algorithm commences with an initial population of random genomes—that is to say a random string of actions and durations—it's easy to see how each action can be applied in turn for the indicated amount of time, and therefore, control the spacecraft. It's almost certain that most of the genomes will perform terribly—a bit like sending up the space shuttle with a turnip at the controls—but a few will perform better than the rest. And as you know by now, that's all you need to get the ball rolling.

Crossover and Mutation Operators

Because you've not seen it in action yet, and because it appears to perform slightly better than single point crossover in this example, I've used multi-point crossover for this code project. Just in case you've forgotten, multi-point crossover works by stepping through each gene in the genome and swapping them at random. Refer to Figure 5.8 in Chapter 5, "Building a Better Genetic Algorithm," if your memory needs to be jogged.

The mutation operator runs down the length of a genome and alters the genes in two parts. First, depending on the mutation rate, the operator will change the action to another random action (this could mean the action remains the same). Second, the mutation operator may change the duration of the action by an amount not exceeding MAX_MUTATION_DURATION. The duration is also bounded between zero and MAX_ACTION_DURATION.

Here is the code for the mutation operator:

```
void CgaLander::Mutate(vector<SGene> &vecActions)
{
  for (int gene=0; gene<vecActions.size(); ++gene)
  {
    //do we mutate the action?
    if (RandFloat() < m_dMutationRate)
    {
      vecActions[gene].action = (action_type)RandInt(0,3);
    }

    //do we mutate the duration?
    if (RandFloat() < m_dMutationRate/2)
    {
      vecActions[gene].duration += RandomClamped()*MAX_MUTATION_DURATION;

      //clamp the duration
      Clamp(vecActions[gene].duration, 0, MAX_ACTION_DURATION);
```

```
    }
  }//next gene
}
```

The Fitness Function

The fitness function can often be the hardest part of a genetic algorithm to define because the problem often has multiple objectives. In this example, there are several objectives that need satisfying before the lunar lander can land successfully. These are

- The distance from the landing pad has to be within a certain limit.
- The lander's velocity has to be below a certain speed by the time it reaches the landing pad.
- The lander's rotation from the vertical has to be within predefined limits.

When I first implemented a fitness function based on just these three objectives, the lander was *too* good at landing. Basically, the algorithm came up with solutions that just dropped the lander straight out of the sky, rotating it perfectly and applying just the right amount of thrust to land flawlessly. In short, although technically perfect, this sort of behavior can look bad in games. Players want to see something more realistic—more human. So, to add that human touch, I incorporated one more objective. The fitness scores were boosted for ships that remained in the air longer than the others. This worked well and the algorithm now converges on realistic-looking solutions. Often the ship will weave around, hover uncertainly, and twitch before alighting on the landing platform, just as a human player does.

Let's take a look at the code for the fitness function.

```
void CLander::CalculateFitness(int generation)
{
  //calculate distance from pad
  double DistFromPad = fabs(m_vPadPos.x - m_vPos.x);

  double distFit = m_cxClient-DistFromPad;

  //calculate speed of lander
  double speed = sqrt((m_vVelocity.x*m_vVelocity.x)
                    +(m_vVelocity.y*m_vVelocity.y));

  //fitness due to rotation
```

```
double rotFit = 1/(fabs(m_dRotation)+1);

//fitness due to time in air
double fitAirTime = (double)m_cTick/(speed+1);
```

cTick is a counter which keeps track of how many frames have passed since the
beginning of the lunar lander's descent. This is divided by the lander's landing
speed to give a reward combining the air time and the lander's final speed.

```
//calculate fitness
m_dFitness = distFit + 400*rotFit + 4*fitAirTime;
```

As you can see, I had to use some multipliers to tweak the fitness function. This is
something you'll typically have to do when designing a genetic algorithm that has
multiple objectives. In my experience, a good starting point is to make the fitness
score from each objective contribute equally to the total fitness score. In this example, the maximum score the lander can receive from getting close to the landing
pad is 400 (the width of the window). The maximum score it can receive from its
rotation is 1, so I've used a multiplier of 400, and the score derived from the
lander's speed and airtime seemed to average around 100, so I have used a multiplier of 4. This way each of the objectives may contribute a maximum of 400 (approximately) to the overall fitness score.

```
//check if we have a successful landing
if( (DistFromPad        < DIST_TOLERANCE)        &&
    (speed              < SPEED_TOLERANCE)       &&
    (fabs(m_dRotation)  < ROTATION_TOLERANCE))
{
  m_dFitness = BIG_NUMBER;
}
}
```

Finally the fitness function checks to see if the lander has passed all the requirements for a safe landing and assigns a large number to the fitness score accordingly,
so that the program knows a solution has been found.

The Update Function

I want to take some time to describe the update function for the GA version of the
lander program because the physics have to be handled differently. The reason for
this is that when implementing a genetic algorithm, it is desirable (unless you are
very patient) to be able to run the code in accelerated time. What I mean by this is
that when evolving candidate solutions, you really want your computer to zip along

as fast as it can so that a solution is found quickly. Because the update function from the user controlled version used the time elapsed between each frame as the basis for its physics calculations, even if you ran it at 5000 frames a second, the lander would still move as though in real time.

To enable the code to be run in accelerated time—the acceleration due to gravity—the thrust of the lander and the rotation rate are all pre-calculated using the frame rate specified in defines.h.

```
#define GRAVITY_PER_TICK      GRAVITY/FRAMES_PER_SECOND
#define THRUST_PER_TICK       THRUST/FRAMES_PER_SECOND
#define ROTATION_PER_TICK     ROTATION/FRAMES_PER_SECOND
```

These values can then be used to update the physics. When the program is running at FRAMES_PER_SECOND frames per second, everything is as it should be, but now you can let rip and run the machine as fast as possible and the physics will be accelerated, along with everything else. This allows the genetic algorithm to find a solution as fast as possible.

There is an added bonus to using this method for your updates: the update function is much faster because there are less calculations to do. The drawback though, is that if you were to use this technique in the user-controlled version and the program was run on a slow computer (not able to hit your desired framerate), the physics would feel different at different framerates. This is usually undesirable behavior.

This is the first part of the code for the modified UpdateShip function:

```
bool CLander::UpdateShip()
{
  //just return if ship has crashed or landed
  if (m_bCheckedIfLanded)
  {
    return false;
  }

  //this will be the current action
  action_type action;

  //check that we still have an action to perform. If not then
  //just let the lander drift til it hits the ground
  if (m_cTick >= m_vecActions.size())
  {
```

```
  action = non;
}

else
{
  action = m_vecActions[m_cTick++];
}
```

Before each epoch, each individual's genome is converted into a vector of actions using the function Decode. This way, it's easy to use the tick counter as an index into the array of actions to find which action needs to be performed each frame. See Figure 6.21.

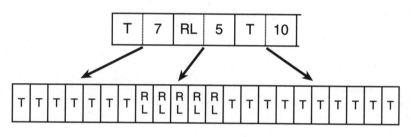

Figure 6.21

Decoding a genome to a vector of actions.

```
//switch the jet graphic off
m_bJetOn = false;

  switch (action)
  {
    case rotate_left:

      m_dRotation -= ROTATION_PER_TICK;

      if (m_dRotation < -PI)
      {
        m_dRotation += TWO_PI;
      }
      break;

    case rotate_right:

      m_dRotation += ROTATION_PER_TICK;

      if (m_dRotation > TWO_PI)
```

```
       {
         m_dRotation -= TWO_PI;
       }
       break;

   case thrust:

       //the lander's acceleration per tick calculated from
       //the force the thruster exerts and the lander's mass
       double ShipAcceleration = THRUST_PER_TICK/m_dMass;

       //resolve the acceleration vector into its x, y components
       //and add to the lander's velocity vector
       m_vVelocity.x += ShipAcceleration * sin(m_dRotation);
       m_vVelocity.y += ShipAcceleration * cos(m_dRotation);

       //switch the jet graphic on
       m_bJetOn = true;

       break;

   case non:

       break;

 }//end switch


//now add in the gravity vector
m_vVelocity.y += GRAVITY_PER_TICK;

//update the lander's position
m_vPos += m_vVelocity;
```

As you can see, all the physics calculations have been simplified loads. The observant among you might be wondering where SCALING_FACTOR is from the previous update function. Well, fortunately for the math, the scaling factor (60) is set the same as the framerate (60), so they cancel each other out $(60/60 = 1)$.

I've omitted the rest of the code because it's very similar to the last version. The last few lines just do some bounds checking—checks to see if the lander is below the ground plane and updates its fitness score.

Running the Program

When you run the executable for the GA controlled lunar lander, the entire population is displayed on the screen at once. Pressing the B key toggles between displaying the entire population and displaying the fittest individual from the last generation. The F key accelerates time and R resets everything for a new run. On average, the genetic algorithm takes between 100 and 300 generations to find a solution. If the number of generations reaches a predefined maximum number of generations (#defined as 500 here), the genetic algorithm resets and starts all over again.

The genetic algorithm in this project is set up very simply. It just uses roulette wheel selection with elitism and no fitness scaling. So there's lots of things you can experiment with to try and improve its performance.

Because it's possible to view all the individuals performing at the same time, you can see exactly how diverse the population is. You'll discover that this is great way of seeing what effect different selection, mutation, and crossover operators are having.

Summary

If I've done my job correctly, by now your head should be buzzing with your own ideas for genetic algorithms and you'll be impatient to try them out. You will also have developed a feel for them, which is going to help you greatly in your own projects.

However, if you think genetic algorithms are cool, wait until you get to the next chapter where I show you how neural networks work!

Stuff to Try

1. Try out the different methods you learned last chapter on the lunar lander code. See how different techniques alter the rate of convergence. Do any of them improve the genetic algorithm? (It's useful to accelerate the GA using the F key and then keep toggling with the B key to see how the population is diverging or converging.)

2. Add a fifth objective to the problem. For example, the lunar lander could start with a fixed amount of fuel, which is burned every time the thrust control is used. This means the ship now has to find a way of landing before all the fuel runs out.

3. Use a genetic algorithm to evolve the orbits of several planetary bodies around a star in a 2D universe. When you crack that problem, see if you can then evolve the planets' orbits *and* their moons' orbits. Found that easy? Then what about a binary star system?

   (This exercise will help reinforce everything you've learned so far in this book—genetic algorithm techniques, mathematics, and physics).

4. Create a space invader style game, whereby each different alien species' behavior has been evolved using a genetic algorithm.

Answer to matrix multiplication question:

$$[1 \quad 2 \quad 3 \quad 4] \times \begin{bmatrix} 5 & 9 \\ 6 & 10 \\ 7 & 11 \\ 8 & 12 \end{bmatrix} = [70 \quad 110]$$

Part Three

Neural
Networks

CHAPTER 7

NEURAL NETWORKS IN PLAIN ENGLISH

Because we do not understand the brain very well, we are constantly tempted to use the latest technology as a model for trying to understand it. In my childhood we were always assured that the brain was a telephone switchboard. (What else could it be?) I was amused to see that Sherrington, the great British neuroscientist, thought that the brain worked like a telegraph system. Freud often compared the brain to hydraulic and electromagnetic systems. Leibniz compared it to a mill, and I am told some of the ancient Greeks thought the brain functions like a catapult. At present, obviously, the metaphor is the digital computer.

John R. Searle

Introduction to Neural Networks

For a long time, artificial neural networks were a complete mystery to me. I'd read about them in literature, of course, and I was able to describe their architecture and mechanisms, but I just didn't get that "Ah Ha!" feeling you get when a difficult concept finally clicks in your mind. It was like hitting my head repeatedly with a sledgehammer, or like that character in the movie Animal House screaming in pain "Thank you Sir, I'll have another!" I couldn't make the transition from mathematical concepts to practical uses. Some days I wanted to hunt down the authors of all the books I'd read about artificial neural networks, tie them to a tree and scream, "Stop giving me all the jargon and mathematics and just show me something PRACTICAL!" Needless to say, this was never going to happen. I was going to have to bridge that gap myself… so I did the only reasonable thing one can do in that position. I gave up. <smile>

Then one beautiful day a few weeks later, I was on holiday gazing out across a misty Scottish Loch, when suddenly I was struck by an insight. All of a sudden I *knew* how artificial neural networks worked. I'd got that "Ah Ha!" feeling! But I had no computer to rush to and write some code to confirm my intuition—just a tent, a sleeping bag, and half a box of Kellog's Cornflakes. Arghhhhh! That was the moment I knew I should have bought that laptop. Anyway, some days later I arrived back home, switched on the machine and let my fingers fly. Within a few hours I had my first artificial neural network up and running and it worked great! Sure, it needed tweaking and the code was messy, but it worked and, what's more, I *knew* why it worked! I was a happy man that day I can tell you.

It's that "Ah Ha!" feeling I want to pass on to you in this book. Hopefully, you got a taste for it when we covered genetic algorithms, but if you think that felt good, just wait until neural networks click into place!

A Biological Neural Network— The Brain

As artificial neural networks attempt to mimic the way a biological brain works, it's appropriate that I spend a few paragraphs talking about the old gray matter in our skulls. You don't have to know this stuff, but I recommend reading it because it will probably aid your visualization of the mechanisms I will be describing when I start discussing artificial brains. And besides, it's interesting.

Your brain is not just one big lump of gray blancmange working as a single processing unit like the CPU in a computer. If you were given a cadaver, freshly preserved in formaldehyde, and with a bone saw, you carefully removed the top of its head, inside the skull you would see the familiar wrinkled mass of brain tissue. The outer layer of the brain—the bit that is all wrinkled like a walnut—is a sheet of tissue named the cortex. If you were to now dip your fingers inside the skull, carefully remove the brain and slice open the cortex with a surgeon's knife, you would see two layers: a gray layer and a white layer (hence the expression "gray matter"—it's actually pinkish without the formaldehyde). The gray layer is only a few millimeters thick and is tightly packed with billions of tiny cells called *neurons*. The white layer, which takes up most of the space in the cortex, consists of all the myriad connections between the neurons. The cortex is wrinkled up like a walnut in order to cram a large surface area into a small space. This enables the cortex to hold many more neurons than it could if it were smooth. The human brain contains about 100 billion of these tiny processing units; an ant's brain contains about 250,000.

Table 7.1 shows the neuron counts of some other common animals.

In the first nine months of a human's life, these cells are created at the astounding rate of 25,000 per minute. They're quite unlike any other cells in the body because each has a wire-like thread called an *axon*, sometimes extending many centimeters, which is used to transmit signals to other neurons. Each neuron consists of a star-shaped bulb, called the *soma*, that contains the nucleus of the cell, the axon, and a multitude of other smaller threads (called *dendrites*) branching in every direction. The axon forks into many smaller branches, which terminate in *synaptic terminals*. See Figure 7.1.

Table 7.1   Comparison of Neurons

Animal	Number of Neurons
Snail	10,000
Bee	100,000
Hummingbird	10x7
Mouse	10 x 8
Human	10 x 10
Elephant	10 x 11

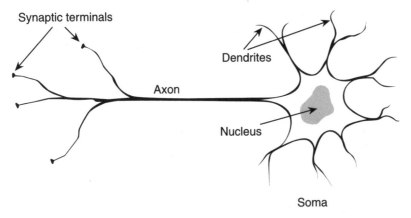

Synaptic terminals

Dendrites

Axon

Nucleus

Soma

Figure 7.1

The biological neuron.

Each neuron is connected via its dendrites to approximately 10,000 other neurons. That makes a possible 1,000,000,000,000,000 connections wired up inside your head—the equivalent of over 100 million modern telephone exchanges. It's no wonder we occasionally get headaches!

Interesting Fact

It has been estimated that if you were to stretch all the axons and dendrites from one human brain out in a straight line, they would reach from the earth to the moon, and then back again. If you did the same with all the axons and dendrites from all the humans on Earth, they would stretch to the nearest galaxy!

The neurons exchange signals using an electrochemical process. Incoming signals are received at the junctions where the synaptic terminals and the dendrites meet. These junctions are known as the synapses. How these signals move about the brain is a fairly complicated process but the important thing, as far as we're concerned, is that, just like a modern computer, which operates by manipulating a series of 1s and 0s, the brain's neurons either fire or they don't. The strength of the emitted signal does not vary—only the frequency. The neuron sums all the incoming signals from the synapses in some mysterious way, and if the total signal exceeds a threshold value, the neuron fires and an electrical signal is sent shooting down the axon. If the total is less than the threshold, the neuron doesn't fire. Well, that's a slight over-simplification, but the explanation will suffice for our purposes.

It's this massive amount of connectivity that gives the brain its incredible power. Although each neuron only operates at about 100Hz, because each one functions in parallel as an independent processing unit, the human brain has some remarkable properties:

It can learn without supervision. One of the incredible things about our brains is that they learn—and they can learn with no supervision. If a neuron is stimulated at high frequency for a long period of time, the strength of that connection is altered by some process that makes it much easier for that neuron to fire the next time it is stimulated. This mechanism was postulated 50 years ago by Donald Hebbs in his book *The Organization of Behavior*. He wrote:

> *"When an axon of cell A… excites cell B and repeatedly or persistently takes part in firing it, some growth process or metabolic change takes place in one or both cells so that A's efficiency as one of the cells firing B is increased."*

The opposite of this is if a neuron is left unstimulated for some time, the effectiveness of its connection slowly decays. This process is known as plasticity.

It is tolerant to damage. The brain can still perform complex tasks even when large portions of it are damaged. One famous experiment taught rats to navigate a maze. Scientists then consecutively removed larger and larger parts of their brains. They found the rats could still find their way around even when a huge portion of their brain was removed, proving among other things, that the knowledge stored in the brain is not localized. Other experiments have shown that if small lesions are made in the brain, neurons have the ability to regrow their connections.

It can process information extremely efficiently. Although the speed of the electrochemical signals between neurons is very slow compared with a digital CPU, the brain can simultaneously process massive amounts of data as neurons work in parallel. For example, the visual cortex processes images entering through our retina in about 100ms. Given the 100Hz operating frequency of your average neuron, that's only about ten time steps! This is an incredible feat considering the amount of data received through our eyes.

It can generalize. One of the things that brains are extremely good at (unlike digital computers) is recognizing patterns and generalizing based on the information it already knows. For example, we can read another person's handwriting even if we have never seen it before.

It is conscious. Consciousness is a widely and heatedly debated topic among neuro-scientists and AI researchers. Volumes have been written on the subject, yet there is no real consensus as to what consciousness actually *is*. We can't even agree on whether only humans are conscious or if we also consider our cousins in the animal kingdom to be conscious. Is an orangutan conscious? Is your cat conscious? What about the fish you ate for dinner last week?

So, an *artificial neural network* (ANN for short) attempts to mimic this amount of parallelism within the constraints of a modern digital computer, and in doing so, displays a number of similar properties to a biological brain. Let's take a look at how they tick.

The Digital Version

ANNs are built the same way as natural brains in that they use many little building blocks called *artificial neurons*. An artificial neuron is just like a simplified version of a real neuron, but simulated electronically. How many artificial neurons are used in an ANN can vary tremendously. Some neural nets use less than ten and some may require many thousands of neurons. It really depends on what they are going to be used for.

Interesting Fact

One man, a guy named Hugo de Garis, ran an extremely ambitious project to create and train a network of up to one billion neurons. The neurons were very cleverly created by using cellular automata in a machine custom built for the job: the CAM Brain Machine. (CAM is an acronym for Cellular Automata Machine.) He boasted that it would have the intelligence of a cat.

Unfortunately, the company employing him went bust before his dream was realized, although many neural network researchers feel he was reaching for the stars. He is now working in Utah as the head of the Utah Brain project. Time will tell if anything interesting becomes of his ideas.

I guess by now you're probably wondering what an artificial neuron looks like. Well, it doesn't really look like anything; it's just an abstraction, but check out Figure 7.2, it depicts one way of representing an artificial neuron.

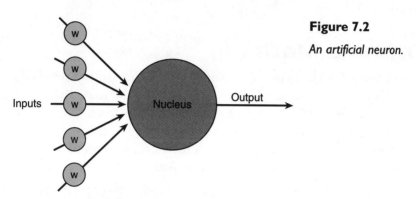

Figure 7.2

An artificial neuron.

The w's in the gray circles represent floating-point numbers called *weights*. Each input into the artificial neuron has a weight associated with it and it's these weights that determine the overall activity of the neural network. For the moment, imagine that all these weights are set to small random values—let's say between -1 and 1. Because a weight can be either positive or negative, it can exert an *excitory* influence over the input it's associated with, or it can exert an *inhibitory* influence. As the inputs enter the neuron, they are multiplied by their respective weights. A function in the nucleus—the *activation function*—then sums all these new, weight-adjusted input values to give the *activation value* (again a floating-point number, which can be negative or positive). If this activation value is above a certain threshold, let's use the number one as an example, the neuron outputs a signal and will output a one. If the activation is less than one, the artificial neuron outputs a zero. This is one of the simplest types of activation functions found in artificial neurons and it's called a *step function*. If you look at Figure 7.3, I'm sure you'll be able to guess why.

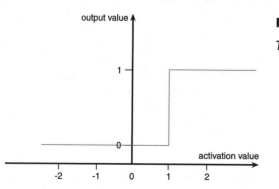

Figure 7.3

The step activation function.

Don't worry too much if none of this is making much sense to you at the moment. The trick is this: don't try to make sense of it, just go with the flow for awhile. Eventually, at some point during this chapter, it will start to click. For now, just relax and keep on reading.

Now for Some Math

I'm going to try to keep the mathematics down to an absolute minimum, but it's going to be useful if you learn some notation. I'll feed you the math little by little and introduce new concepts when you get to the relevant sections. This way, I hope your mind can absorb all the ideas a little more comfortably and you'll be able to see how we put the math to work at each stage in the development of a neural net. First, let's look at a way of expressing what I've told you so far.

An artificial neuron (I'll just refer to them as neurons from here on) can have any number of inputs numbered from one to n—where n is the total number of inputs. Each input can be expressed mathematically as:

$$x_1, x_2, x_3, x_4, x_5 \ldots, x_n$$

> **NOTE**
>
> The inputs into a neural network and the set of weights for each individual neuron can be thought of as n-dimensional vectors. You will often see them referred to in this way in the more technical literature.

The weights can be expressed similarly as:

$$w_1, w_2, w_3, w_4, w_5 \ldots, w_n$$

Remember, the activation is the sum of all the weights × inputs. This can now be written as:

$$a = w_1x_1 + w_2x_2 + w_3x_3 + w_4x_4 + w_5x_5 + \ldots + w_nx_n$$

This way of writing down summations can be simplified by using the Greek letter Σ, that I mentioned in Chapter 5, "Building a Better Genetic Algorithm."

$$a = \sum_{i=0}^{i=n} w_i x_i$$

Just to clarify, here's what it looks like in code. Assuming an array of inputs and weights are already initialized as x[n] and w[n], then:

```
double activation = 0;
for (int i=0; i<n; ++i)
{
```

```
    activation += x[i] * w[i];
}
```

Figure 7.4 represents the equations as a diagram. Remember, if the activation
exceeds the threshold, the neuron outputs a one; if the activation is below the
threshold, the neuron outputs a zero. This is equivalent to a biological neuron
firing or not firing. Imagine a neuron with five inputs, and all its weights initialized
to random values ($-1 < w < 1$). Table 7.2 shows how the activation is calculated.

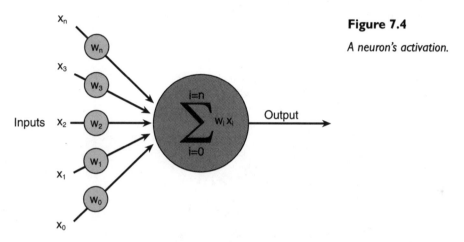

Figure 7.4

A neuron's activation.

If you assume the activation threshold is one, then this neuron would output a one
(because $1.1 > 1$).

Make sure you understand exactly how the activation function is calculated before
reading any further.

Table 7.2 Calculating the Activation of a Neuron

Input	Weight	Input × Weight	Running Total
1	0.5	0.5	0.5
0	-0.2	0	0.5
1	-0.3	-0.3	0.2
1	0.9	0.9	1.1
0	0.1	0	1.1

Okay, I Know *What* a Neuron Is, but What Do I *Do* with It?

Just as biological neurons in the brain connect to other neurons, these artificial neurons are connected together in some way to create the neural network. There are many, varied ways of connecting neurons but the easiest to understand and the most widely used is by connecting the neurons together in layers, as in Figure 7.5. This type of ANN is called a *feedforward network*. It gets its name from the way each layer of neurons feed their outputs into the next layer until an output is given.

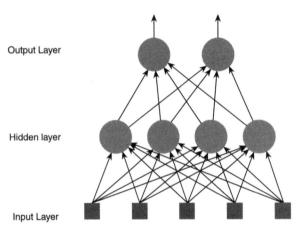

Output Layer

Hidden layer

Input Layer

Figure 7.5

A feedforward network.

As you can see, each input is sent to every neuron in the hidden layer, and then the output from each neuron in the hidden layer is connected to every neuron in the next layer. There can be any number of hidden layers within a feedforward network, but one is usually enough to cope with most of the problems you will tackle. In fact, some problems don't require any hidden units at all; you can simply connect the inputs straight into the output neurons. Also, the number of neurons I chose for Figure 7.5 was completely arbitrary. There can be any number of neurons in each layer; it all depends on the problem. Because the speed of the network decreases as more neurons are added, and because of other reasons I'll be explaining in Chapter 9, it's desirable to keep the network as small as possible.

I can imagine by now you may be feeling a little dazed by all this information. I reckon the best thing to do at this point is to give you a real world application of a neural network in the hopes of getting your own brain cells firing! Sound good? Okay, here goes...

You may have heard or read that neural networks are commonly used for pattern recognition. This is because they are great at mapping an input state (the pattern it's trying to recognize) to an output state (the pattern it's been trained to recognize). Here's how it's done. Let's take the example of character recognition. Imagine a panel made up of a grid of lights 8×8. Each light can be switched on or off, so the panel can be used to display numeric characters. The character "4" is shown in Figure 7.6.

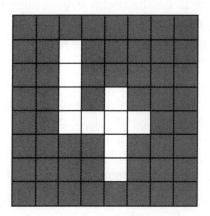

Figure 7.6

The character display grid.

To solve the problem, a neural net must be designed that will accept the state of the panel as an input, and then output either a one or a zero—a one to indicate that the ANN thinks the character "4" is being displayed, and zero if it thinks it is not being displayed. Therefore, the neural net will have 64 inputs (each one representing a particular cell in the panel) and a hidden layer consisting of a number of neurons (more on this later), all feeding their output into just one neuron in the output layer. I sure hope you can picture this in your head because the thought of drawing all those little circles and lines for you is not a happy one <smile>.

Once the neural network architecture has been created, it must be *trained* to recognize the character "4". One way of doing this is to initialize the neural net with random weights and then feed it a series of inputs that represent, in this example, the different panel configurations. For each configuration, we check to see what its output is and adjust the weights accordingly. If the input pattern we feed it is not a "4", then we know the neural network should output a zero. So for every non "4" character, the weights are adjusted slightly so the output tends toward zero. When it's presented with a pattern that represents the character "4", the weights are adjusted so the output tends toward the number one.

If you think about it, it would be easy to increase the number of outputs to ten. Then it would be possible to train the network to recognize all the digits 0 through 9. But why stop there? Let's increase the outputs further so the entire alphabet can be

recognized. This, in essence, is how handwriting recognition works. For each character, the network is trained to recognize many different versions of that letter. Eventually the network will not only be able to recognize the letters it has been trained with,
but it will also show the remarkable property of being able to *generalize*. That is to say,
if a letter is drawn slightly differently than the letters in the training set, the network
will still stand a pretty good chance of recognizing it. It's this ability to generalize that
has made the neural network an invaluable tool that can be applied to a myriad of
applications, from face recognition and medical diagnosis to horse racing prediction
and bot navigation in computer games (and in hardware robots).

This type of training is called *supervised learning* and the data the network is trained
with is called a *training set*. There are many different ways of adjusting the weights; the
most common for this type of problem is called *backpropagation*. I'll be talking about
backprop later in the book when I show you how you can train a neural network to
recognize mouse gestures. However, the rest of this chapter will be focused on a type
of training that requires little or no supervision at all: *unsupervised learning*.

So now that I've shown you some of the background theory, let's have some fun and
do something with it. Let me introduce you to the first code project.

The Smart Minesweeper Project

The first example I'm going to talk you through is how to use a neural network to
control the behavior of AI guided minesweepers. The minesweepers will live in a
very simple world. It will just be them and a random scattering of mines.

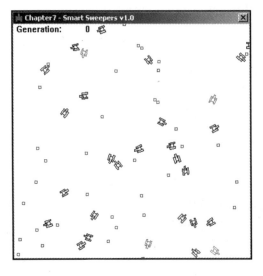

Figure 7.7

The demo program in action.

Although the figure is in black and white, the best performing minesweepers show up in red when you run the program. The mines, as you have probably guessed, are the little squares. The goal of the project is to create a neural network that will *evolve* to find the mines without any help from us at all. To do this, the weights of the networks will be encoded into genomes and a genetic algorithm will be used to evolve them. Cool, huh?

> **TIP**
>
> **Important:** If you have skipped pages to get here and you don't understand how to use genetic algorithms, please go back and read up on them before going any further!

First of all, let me explain the architecture of the ANN. We need to determine the number of inputs, the number of outputs, and the number of hidden units/layers.

Choosing the Outputs

So, how is the ANN going to control the movements of the minesweepers? Well, imagine that the minesweepers run on tracks just like a tank. See Figure 7.8.

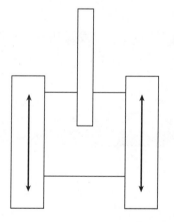

Figure 7.8

Controlling the minesweeper.

The rotation and velocity of the minesweepers are adjusted by altering the relative speeds of the tracks. Therefore, the neural network will require two outputs—one for the left track and one for the right.

Ah but... I hear a few of you mutter. *How can we control how fast the tracks move if the network can only output a one or a zero?* And you'd be right; the minesweepers wouldn't move at all realistically if the previously described step function determined the outputs. Fortunately, I have a trick up my sleeve. Instead of using a step threshold as the activation function, the minesweepers artificial neurons are going to use a function that provides a continuously graded output between zero and one. There are a few functions that do this, but the one we are going to use is called the *logistic sigmoid* function. Basically, what this function does is soften the output of each neuron into a curve symmetrical around 0.5, as shown in Figure 7.9.

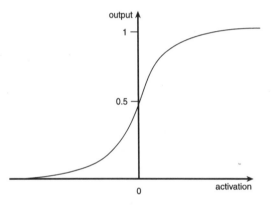

Figure 7.9

The sigmoid curve.

As the neuron's activation tends toward infinity and minus infinity, the sigmoid function tends toward one and zero. Negative activation values give results of less than 0.5; positive activation values give results greater than 0.5. Written down, the sigmoid function looks like this:

NOTE

The word *sigmoid* or *sigmoidal* is from the Greek word "sigma" and is just another way of saying something is S shaped.

$$\text{output} = \frac{1}{1 + e^{-a/p}}$$

Although this equation may look intimidating to some of you, it's really very simple. e is a mathematical constant that approximates to 2.7183, the a is the activation into the neuron, and p is a number that controls the shape of the curve. p is usually set to 1. Higher values of p give a flatter response curve; lower values produce a steeper curve. See Figure 7.10. Very low values produce a curve similar to a step function. p can be a useful value to play around with when you start tweaking your neural networks, but in this example we'll leave it set at 1.

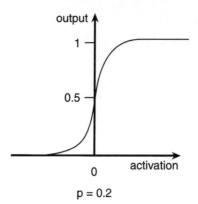
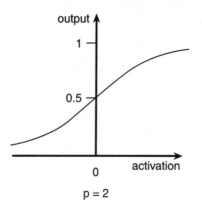

Figure 7.10

Different sigmoid response curves.

Choosing the Inputs

Okay, so the outputs are sorted—now for the inputs. To determine what inputs the network requires, we have to think like a minesweeper. What information does it need so it can figure out how to head for the mines? The first list of inputs you may think of could possibly be these:

- The minesweeper's position (x, y)
- The position of the closest mine (x, y)
- A vector representing the minesweeper's heading (x, y)

This makes a total of six inputs. But, using these inputs, the network has to work quite hard before it performs satisfactorily because it has to find a mathematical relationship between all six inputs. It's always a good exercise to try and figure out a way of using the least amount of inputs that still convey the information required for the network to solve the problem. The fewer inputs your networks use, the fewer neurons are required. Fewer neurons mean faster training and fewer calculations, which makes for a speedier network.

A little bit of extra thought can reduce the inputs to four, representing the two vectors shown in Figure 7.11.

It's a good idea to standardize all the inputs into a neural network. What I mean by this is not that all the inputs should be scaled to the interval 0 to 1, but that each input should carry the same amount of emphasis. Take the inputs we've discussed for the minesweeper, for example. The look-at vector is always a normalized vector of length 1. This means that its x and y components are always in the interval 0 to 1. The vector to the closest mine, however, has a much larger magnitude; one of the components may even be as large as the window width or height. If this data is input

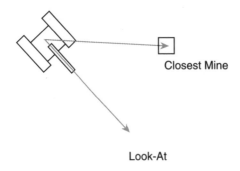

Figure 7.11

Choosing the inputs.

Closest Mine

Look-At

into the network in its raw state, the network would be much more sensitive to the higher valued inputs and give a poor performance. So, before the information is input into the neural network, the data is scaled/standardized so that the magnitudes are similar. In this particular example, the vector to the closest mine is normalized. This makes for much better performance.

> **TIP**
>
> Sometimes you will get the best performance from your neural networks if you rescale the input data so that it centers on zero. This little tip is always worth considering when designing your networks. I haven't done it this way for this minesweeper project because I wanted to use a more intuitive approach.

How Many Hidden Neurons?

Now that the number of input and output neurons has been decided, the next step is to determine the number of hidden layers and the number of neurons per hidden layer the network should have. There is no rule for doing this; it all comes down to developing a "feel" again. Some books and articles do give guidelines for determining the number of hidden neurons but the consensus among the experts in this field is that you should take any suggestions like this with a grain of salt. Basically, it comes down to trial and error. You will normally find that one hidden layer is plenty for most problems you encounter, so the skill is mostly about choosing the best number of neurons for that single layer. The fewer the better because, as I've already mentioned, fewer neurons make for a faster network. Normally I would do several runs using varied numbers of hidden neurons to determine the optimum amount. The neural net I've coded for this chapter's first code project uses ten hidden neurons (although this isn't the optimum <smile>). You should play around with this figure and also the number of hidden layers to see what effect they have on the minesweeper's evolution. Anyway, enough of the theory, let's take a look at some code. You can find all the source code I'll be describing in the next few pages in the Chapter7/Smart Sweepers v1.0 folder on the CD.

CNeuralNet.h

The CNeuralNet.h file contains definitions for an artificial neuron structure, a structure to define a layer of artificial neurons, and the neural network itself. First, let's take a peek at the artificial neuron structure.

SNeuron

This is a very simple structure. The artificial neuron just has to keep a record of how many inputs there are going into it and a std:vector of doubles representing the weights. Remember, there is a weight for every input into the neuron.

```
struct SNeuron
{
  //the number of inputs into the neuron
  int          m_NumInputs;

  //the weights for each input
```

```
vector<double>  m_vecWeight;

//ctor
SNeuron(int NumInputs);
};
```

This is what the constructor for the SNeuron struct looks like:

```
SNeuron::SNeuron(int NumInputs): m_NumInputs(NumInputs+1)
{
  //we need an additional weight for the bias hence the +1
  for (int i=0; i<NumInputs+1; ++i)
  {
    //set up the weights with an initial random value
    m_vecWeight.push_back(RandomClamped());
  }
}
```

As you can see, the constructor takes the number of inputs going into the neuron as an argument and creates a vector of random weights—one weight for each input. All the weights are clamped between -1 and 1.

What's that? I hear you say. *There's an extra weight there!* Well, I'm glad you spotted that because that extra weight is quite important. But to explain why it's there, I'm going to have to do some more math. Remember that the activation was the sum of all the inputs×weights and that the output of the neuron was dependent upon whether this activation exceeded a *threshold* value (t). This can be represented as the equation:

$$w_1x_1 + w_2x_2 + w_3x_3 + \ldots w_nx_n \geq t$$

where the above is the condition for outputting a one. Because all the weights for the network have to be evolved, it would be great if the threshold amount could be evolved too. To make this easy, you use a simple trick to get the threshold to appear as a weight. Subtract the t from either side of the equation:

$$w_1x_1 + w_2x_2 + w_3x_3 + \ldots w_nx_n - t \geq 0$$

Written another way, this equation can be made to look like this:

$$w_1x_1 + w_2x_2 + w_3x_3 + \ldots w_nx_n + (-1)t \geq 0$$

So I hope you can see how the threshold can now be thought of as a weight that is always multiplied by an input of -1. This is usually referred to as the *bias* and this is why each neuron is initialized with an additional weight. Now when you evolve the network, you don't have to worry about the threshold value because it is built in with the weights and will take care of itself. Good, eh? Just to make absolutely sure you know what our new artificial neuron looks like, have a look at Figure 7.12.

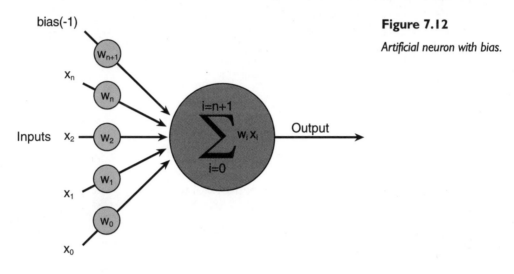

Figure 7.12

Artificial neuron with bias.

SNeuronLayer

The SNeuronLayer structure is very simple; it defines a layer of SNeurons as shown by the neurons enclosed by the dotted line in Figure 7.13.

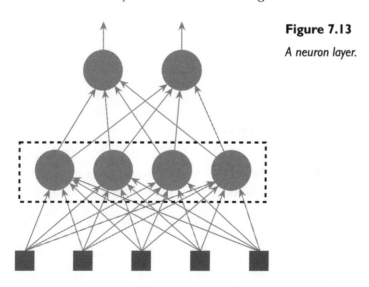

Figure 7.13

A neuron layer.

Here is the source for the definition, which shouldn't require any further explanation:

```
struct SNeuronLayer
{
  //the number of neurons in this layer
  int              m_NumNeurons;

  //the layer of neurons
  vector<SNeuron>  m_vecNeurons;

  SNeuronLayer(int NumNeurons, int NumInputsPerNeuron);
};
```

CNeuralNet

This is the class that creates the neural network object. Let me run you through the definition:

```
class CNeuralNet
{

private:

  int                m_NumInputs;

  int                m_NumOutputs;

  int                m_NumHiddenLayers;

  int                m_NeuronsPerHiddenLyr;

  //storage for each layer of neurons including the output layer
  vector<SNeuronLayer>  m_vecLayers;
```

All the private members should be self-explanatory. The class just needs to define the number of inputs, outputs, hidden layers, and neurons per hidden layer.

```
public:

  CNeuralNet();
```

The constructor initializes the private member variables from the ini file, then calls CreateNet to build the network.

```
//builds the network from SNeurons
void  CreateNet();
```

I'll show you this function's code in a moment.

```
//gets the weights for the NN
vector<double>  GetWeights()const;
```

Because the network weights will be evolved, a method needs to be created that will return all the weights present in the network as a vector of real numbers. These real numbers will be encoded into a genome for each neural network. I'll show you exactly how the weights are encoded when I start talking about the genetic algorithm used in this project.

```
//returns total number of weights in net
int             GetNumberOfWeights()const;

//replaces the weights with new ones
void               PutWeights(vector<double> &weights);
```

This does the opposite of GetWeights. When an epoch of the genetic algorithm has been run, the new generation of weights has to be inserted back into the neural networks. The PutWeight method does this for us.

```
//sigmoid response curve
inline double   Sigmoid(double activation, double response);
```

Given the sum of all the inputs × weights for a neuron, this method puts them through the sigmoid activation function.

```
//calculates the outputs from a set of inputs
vector<double>  Update(vector<double> &inputs);
```

I'll be commenting on the Update function in just a moment.

```
}; //end of class definition
```

CNeuralNet::CreateNet

I didn't comment on a couple of the CNeuralNet methods because I wanted to show you their code in entirety. The first of these is the CreateNet method. This builds the neural network from SNeurons gathered together in SNeuronLayers like this:

```cpp
void CNeuralNet::CreateNet()
{
  //create the layers of the network
  if (m_NumHiddenLayers > 0)
  {
    //create first hidden layer
    m_vecLayers.push_back(SNeuronLayer(m_NeuronsPerHiddenLyr, m_NumInputs));

    for (int i=0; i<m_NumHiddenLayers-1; ++i)
    {
      m_vecLayers.push_back(SNeuronLayer(m_NeuronsPerHiddenLyr,
                                        m_NeuronsPerHiddenLyr));
    }

    //create output layer
    m_vecLayers.push_back(SNeuronLayer(m_NumOutputs, m_NeuronsPerHiddenLyr));
  }

  else
  {
    //create output layer
    m_vecLayers.push_back(SNeuronLayer(m_NumOutputs, m_NumInputs));
  }
}
```

CNeuralNet::Update

The Update function is the main workhorse of the neural network. Here, the inputs into the network are passed in as an std::vector of doubles. The Update function then loops through each layer processing each neuron summing up the inputs×weights and calculating each neuron's activation by putting the total through the sigmoid function, as we have discussed in the last few pages. The Update function returns a std::vector of doubles that correspond to the outputs from the ANN.

Spend a couple of minutes or so acquainting yourself with the code for the Update function so you know exactly what's going on:

```cpp
vector<double> CNeuralNet::Update(vector<double> &inputs)
{
  //stores the resultant outputs from each layer
  vector<double> outputs;

  int cWeight = 0;

  //first check that we have the correct amount of inputs
  if (inputs.size() != m_NumInputs)
  {
    //just return an empty vector if incorrect.
    return outputs;
  }

  //For each layer...
  for (int i=0; i<m_NumHiddenLayers + 1; ++i)
  {

    if ( i > 0 )
    {
      inputs = outputs;
    }

    outputs.clear();

    cWeight = 0;

    //for each neuron sum the inputs * corresponding weights. Throw
    //the total at the sigmoid function to get the output.
    for (int j=0; j<m_vecLayers[i].m_NumNeurons; ++j)
    {
      double netinput = 0;

      int NumInputs = m_vecLayers[i].m_vecNeurons[j].m_NumInputs;

      //for each weight
      for (int k=0; k<NumInputs - 1; ++k)
```

```
    {
        //sum the weights x inputs
        netinput += m_vecLayers[i].m_vecNeurons[j].m_vecWeight[k] *
                    inputs[cWeight++];
    }

    //add in the bias
    netinput += m_vecLayers[i].m_vecNeurons[j].m_vecWeight[NumInputs-1] *
                CParams::dBias;
```

Don't forget that the last weight in each neuron's weight vector is the weight for the bias, which as we have already discussed, is always set to -1. I have included the bias in the ini file so you can play around with it to see what effect it has on the performance of the networks you create. Normally though, this value should never be altered.

```
    //we can store the outputs from each layer as we generate them.
    //The combined activation is first filtered through the sigmoid
    //function
    outputs.push_back(Sigmoid(netinput, CParams::dActivationResponse));

    cWeight = 0;
    }
  }

  return outputs;
}
```

Encoding the Networks

In the first few chapters, you've seen how to encode genetic algorithms in various ways. But I didn't show you a straightforward example of real number encoding because I knew I'd be showing you here. Encoding a neural network of the feedforward design I've been talking about is easy. The neural network is encoded by reading all the weights from left to right and from the first hidden layer upward and storing them in a vector. So if we had a network that looked like Figure 7.14, the encoded vector of weights would be:

0.3, -0.8, -0.2, 0.6, 0.1, -0.1, 0.4, 0.5

I did not include a bias in this network just to keep things simple. When doing this for real, though, you must always include a bias or you'll almost certainly not get the results you desire.

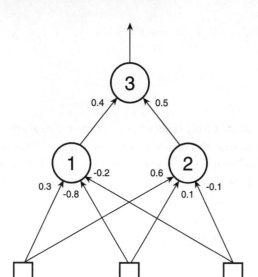

Figure 7.14

Encoding the weights.

Okay so far? Great, let's move on to the genetic algorithm used to manipulate the encoded genes...

The Genetic Algorithm

Now that all the weights are in a string just like a binary encoded genome, a genetic algorithm may be applied as discussed earlier in the book. The GA is run after the minesweepers have been allowed to trundle about for a user-defined amount of frames. (I like to call them ticks for some reason.) You can find the setting for this, iNumTicks, in the ini file.

Following is the code for the genome structure. You should find that it looks very familiar by now.

```
struct SGenome
{
  vector <double>  vecWeights;

  double           dFitness;

  SGenome():dFitness(0){}

  SGenome( vector <double> w, double f): vecWeights(w), dFitness(f){}

  //overload '<' used for sorting
```

```
    friend bool operator<(const SGenome& lhs, const SGenome& rhs)
    {
      return (lhs.dFitness < rhs.dFitness);
    }
};
```

As you can see, the SGenome structure is almost identical to every other genome structure shown in the book, except this time the chromosome is a std::vector of doubles. Therefore, the crossover and selection operators may be applied as normal. The mutation operator is slightly different in that the value of the weight is perturbed by a random number, which can be a maximum of dMaxPerturbation. dMaxPerturbation is declared in the ini file. The mutation rate is also set much higher for floating point genetic algorithms. For this project, it's set at 0.1.

Here's what the mutation function looks like from the minesweeper project's genetic algorithm class:

```
void CGenAlg::Mutate(vector<double> &chromo)
{
  //traverse the weight vector and mutate each weight dependent
  //on the mutation rate
  for (int i=0; i<chromo.size(); ++i)
  {
    //do we perturb this weight?
    if (RandFloat() < m_dMutationRate)
    {
      //add or subtract a small value to the weight
      chromo[i] += (RandomClamped() * CParams::dMaxPerturbation);
    }
  }
}
```

As in previous projects, I've kept the genetic algorithm for version 1.0 of the Smart Minesweepers project very simple so that there's lots of room for you to improve it with the techniques you've learned so far. As with most of the other projects, v1.0 just uses roulette wheel selection with elitism and single-point crossover.

NOTE

When the program is running, the weights may evolve to be any size; they are not constrained in any way.

The CMinesweeper Class

This is the class that defines a minesweeper. Just like the lunar lander class described in the last chapter, the minesweeper class keeps a record of the minesweeper's position, speed, and rotation. It also keeps track of the minesweeper's look-at vector; the components of which are used as two of the inputs into its neural net. This is a normalized vector calculated each frame from the minesweeper's rotation and indicates which way the minesweeper is pointing, as shown in Figure 7.11.

Here is the declaration of the CMinesweeper class:

```
class CMinesweeper
{
private:

  //the minesweeper's neural net
  CNeuralNet  m_ItsBrain;

  //its position in the world
  SVector2D   m_vPosition;

  //direction sweeper is facing
  SVector2D   m_vLookAt;

  //its rotation(surprise surprise)
  double      m_dRotation;

  double      m_dSpeed;

  //to store output from the ANN
  double      m_lTrack,
              m_rTrack;
```

m_lTrack and m_rTrack store the current frame's output from the network. These are the values that determine the minesweeper's velocity and rotation.

```
  //the sweeper's fitness score
  double      m_dFitness;
```

Every time the minesweeper finds a mine, its fitness score increases.

```
  //the scale of the sweeper when drawn
  double      m_dScale;

  //index position of closest mine
  int         m_iClosestMine;
```

The CController class has a member that is a std::vector of all the mines. m_iClosestMine is an index into that vector representing the closest mine to the minesweeper.

```
public:

  CMinesweeper();

  //updates the ANN with information from the sweepers environment
  bool        Update(vector<SVector2D> &mines);

  //used to transform the sweepers vertices prior to rendering
  void        WorldTransform(vector<SPoint> &sweeper);

  //returns a vector to the closest mine
  SVector2D   GetClosestMine(vector<SVector2D> &objects);

  //checks to see if the minesweeper has found a mine
  int         CheckForMine(vector<SVector2D> &mines, double size);


  void        Reset();


  //-----------------accessor functions
  SVector2D   Position()const{return m_vPosition;}
  void        IncrementFitness(double val){m_dFitness += val;}
  double      Fitness()const{return m_dFitness;}
  void        PutWeights(vector<double> &w){m_ItsBrain.PutWeights(w);}
  int         GetNumberOfWeights()const{return m_ItsBrain.GetNumberOfWeights();}
};
```

The CMinesweeper::Update Function

The only `CMinesweeper` class method I need to show you in more detail is the `Update` function. This function is called each frame and updates the neural network of the minesweeper, among other things. Let's take a look at the guts of this function:

```
bool CMinesweeper::Update(vector<SVector2D> &mines)
{
  //this will store all the inputs for the NN
  vector<double> inputs;

  //get vector to closest mine
  SVector2D vClosestMine = GetClosestMine(mines);

  //normalize it
  Vec2DNormalize(vClosestMine);
```

First of all, the function calculates a vector to the closest mine and then normalizes it. (Remember, when a vector is normalized its length becomes 1.) The minesweeper's look-at vector doesn't need to be normalized in this way because its length is always 1. Because both vectors have been effectively scaled to within the same limits, the inputs can be considered to be standardized, as I discussed earlier.

```
  //add in the vector to the closest mine
  inputs.push_back(vClosestMine.x);
  inputs.push_back(vClosestMine.y);

  //add in the sweeper's look at vector
  inputs.push_back(m_vLookAt.x);
  inputs.push_back(m_vLookAt.y);

  //update the brain and get the output from the network
  vector<double> output = m_ItsBrain.Update(inputs);
```

The look-at vector and the vector to the closest mine are then input into the neural network. The `CNeuralNet::Update` function updates the minesweeper's network with this information and returns a `std::vector` of doubles as the output.

```
  //make sure there were no errors in calculating the
  //output
  if (output.size() < CParams::iNumOutputs)
  {
```

```
    return false;
}

//assign the outputs to the sweepers left & right tracks
m_lTrack = output[0];
m_rTrack = output[1];
```

After checking to make sure there are no errors when updating the neural network, the program assigns the outputs to m_lTrack and m_rTrack. These values represent the forces being exerted on the left track and right track of the minesweeper.

```
//calculate steering forces
double RotForce = m_lTrack - m_rTrack;

//clamp rotation
Clamp(RotForce, -CParams::dMaxTurnRate, CParams::dMaxTurnRate);

m_dSpeed = (m_lTrack + m_rTrack);
```

The vehicle's rotational force is calculated by subtracting the force exerted by the right track from the force exerted by the left track. This is then clamped to make sure it doesn't exceed the maximum turn rate specified in the ini file. The vehicle's speed is simply the sum of the left track and right track. Now that we know the minesweeper's rotational force and speed, its position and rotation can be updated accordingly.

```
//update the minesweepers rotation
m_dRotation += RotForce;

//update Look At
m_vLookAt.x = -sin(m_dRotation);
m_vLookAt.y = cos(m_dRotation);

//update position
m_vPosition += (m_vLookAt * m_dSpeed);

//wrap around window limits
if (m_vPosition.x > CParams::WindowWidth) m_vPosition.x = 0;
if (m_vPosition.x < 0) m_vPosition.x = CParams::WindowWidth;
if (m_vPosition.y > CParams::WindowHeight) m_vPosition.y = 0;
if (m_vPosition.y < 0) m_vPosition.y = CParams::WindowHeight;
```

To keep things as simple as possible, I've made the window wrap around. This way the code doesn't have to do any collision response stuff. Although wrap-around space is a pretty weird concept for us humans, the minesweepers take to it like ducks to water.

```
    return true;
}
```

The CController Class

The CController class is the class that ties everything together. Figure 7.15 shows the relationship of the different classes to the controller class.

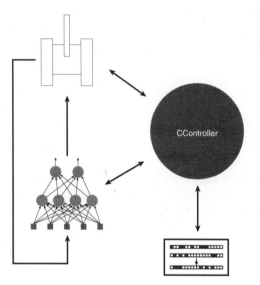

Figure 7.15

Program flow for the minesweeper project.

Here's the definition of the class:

```
class CController
{
private:

    //storage for the population of genomes
    vector<SGenome>        m_vecThePopulation;

    //and the minesweepers
```

```
vector<CMinesweeper> m_vecSweepers;

//and the mines
vector<SVector2D>    m_vecMines;

//pointer to the genetic algorithm object
CGenAlg*             m_pGA;

int                  m_NumSweepers;

int                  m_NumMines;

//total number of weights used in the neural net
int                  m_NumWeightsInNN;

//vertex buffer for the sweeper shape's vertices
vector<SPoint>       m_SweeperVB;

//vertex buffer for the mine shape's vertices
vector<SPoint>       m_MineVB;

//stores the average fitness per generation for use
//in graphing.
vector<double>       m_vecAvFitness;

//stores the best fitness per generation
vector<double>       m_vecBestFitness;

//pens we use for the stats
HPEN                 m_RedPen;
HPEN                 m_BluePen;
HPEN                 m_GreenPen;
HPEN                 m_OldPen;

//handle to the application window
HWND                 m_hwndMain;

//toggles the speed at which the simulation runs
```

```
        bool                    m_bFastRender;

        //cycles per generation
        int                 m_iTicks;

        //generation counter
        int                 m_iGenerations;

        //window dimensions
        int         cxClient, cyClient;

        //this function plots a graph of the average and best fitnesses
        //over the course of a run
        void    PlotStats(HDC surface);

public:

        CController(HWND hwndMain);

        ~CController();

        void    Render(HDC surface);

        void    WorldTransform(vector<SPoint> &VBuffer,
                            SVector2D     vPos);

        bool    Update();

        //accessor methods
        bool    FastRender(){return m_bFastRender;}
        void    FastRender(bool arg){m_bFastRender = arg;}
        void    FastRenderToggle(){m_bFastRender = !m_bFastRender;}
};
```

When an instance of the CController class is created, a lot of stuff happens:

- The CMinesweeper objects are created.
- The number of weights used in the neural networks is calculated and then this figure is used in the initialization of an instance of the genetic algorithm class.

- The random chromosomes (the weights) from the GA object are retrieved and inserted (by careful brain surgery) into the minesweeper's neural nets.
- The mines are created and scattered about in random locations.
- All the GDI pens are created for the render function.
- The vertex buffers for the minesweeper shape and mine shape are created.

Now that everything is initialized, the Update method can be called each frame to handle the evolution of the minesweepers.

The CController::Update Method

This method is called each frame. The first half of the function iterates through the minesweepers, calling their update functions and updating the minesweepers' fitness scores if a mine has been found. In addition, because m_vecThePopulation contains copies of all the genomes, the relevant fitness scores are adjusted here too. If the required number of frames has passed for the completion of a generation, the method runs an epoch of the genetic algorithm producing a new generation of weights. These weights are used to replace the old weights in the minesweeper's neural nets and each minesweeper's parameters are reset ready for a new generation.

```
bool CController::Update()
{
  //run the sweepers through CParams::iNumTicks amount of cycles. During
  //this loop each sweeper's NN is constantly updated with the appropriate
  //information from its surroundings. The output from the NN is obtained
  //and the sweeper is moved. If it encounters a mine its fitness is
  //updated appropriately as is the fitness of its corresponding genome.
  if (m_iTicks++ < CParams::iNumTicks)
  {
    for (int i=0; i<m_NumSweepers; ++i)
    {
      //update the NN and position
      if (!m_vecSweepers[i].Update(m_vecMines))
      {
        //error in processing the neural net, exit
        MessageBox(m_hwndMain, "Wrong amount of NN inputs!", "Error", MB_OK);

        return false;
```

```
      }

      //see if this minesweeper has found a mine
      int GrabHit = m_vecSweepers[i].CheckForMine(m_vecMines,
                                                  CParams::dMineScale);

      if (GrabHit >= 0)
      {
        //we have discovered a mine so increase fitness
        m_vecSweepers[i].IncrementFitness();

        //mine found so replace the mine with another at a random position
        m_vecMines[GrabHit] = SVector2D(RandFloat() * cxClient,
                                        RandFloat() * cyClient);
      }

      //update the genomes fitness score
      m_vecThePopulation[i].dFitness = m_vecSweepers[i].Fitness();
    }
  }
  //Another generation has been completed.
  //Time to run the GA and update the sweepers with their new NNs
  else
  {
    //update the stats to be used in our stat window
    m_vecAvFitness.push_back(m_pGA->AverageFitness());
    m_vecBestFitness.push_back(m_pGA->BestFitness());

    //increment the generation counter
    ++m_iGenerations;

    //reset cycles
    m_iTicks = 0;

    //run the GA to create a new population
    m_vecThePopulation = m_pGA->Epoch(m_vecThePopulation);

    //insert the new (hopefully)improved brains back into the sweepers
```

```
    //and reset their positions etc
    for (int i=0; i<m_NumSweepers; ++i)
    {
       m_vecSweepers[i].m_ItsBrain.PutWeights(m_vecThePopulation[i].vecWeights);

       m_vecSweepers[i].Reset();
    }
  }
  return true;
}
```

In summary, here's what the program is doing each epoch:

1. For each minesweeper and for iNumTicks iterations, call the Update function and increment the minesweeper's fitness score accordingly.

2. Retrieve the vector of weights for the minesweeper's ANN.

3. Use the genetic algorithm to evolve a new population of network weights.

4. Insert the new weights into the minesweeper's ANN.

5. Go to Step 1 until reasonable performance is achieved.

And finally, Table 7.3 lists the default parameter settings for the Smart Sweepers v1.0 program.

Running the Program

When you run the program, the "F" key toggles between a display showing the minesweepers learning how to find the mines and a stats display that shows a simple graph of the best and average fitness scores generated over the length of the run.

When the graph is displayed, the program runs in accelerated time.

A Couple of Performance Improvements

Although the minesweepers learn to find the mines quite well, there are a couple of things I'd like to show you which will improve their performance.

Improvement Number One

First, the single-point crossover operator leaves a lot to be desired. As it stands, this operator is cutting the genome anywhere along its length, and often the genome will be cut straight through the middle of the weights for a particular neuron.

Table 7.3 Default Project Settings for Smart Sweepers v1.0

Neural Network

Parameter	Setting
Number of inputs	4
Number of outputs	2
Number of hidden layers	1
Number of hidden neurons	10
Activation response	1

Genetic Algorithm

Parameter	Setting
Population size	30
Selection type	Roulette wheel
Crossover type	Single point
Crossover rate	0.7
Mutation rate	0.1
Elitism(on/off)	On
Number of elite(N/copies)	4/1

General

Parameter	Setting
Number of ticks/epoch	2000

To clarify, examine the weights in Figure 7.16. This is the simple network I showed you earlier to demonstrate the encoding.

Presently, the crossover operator could make a cut anywhere along the length of this vector, so there is a very high chance the split may be made in the middle of the weights for a neuron—say between the weights 0.6 and -0.1 of neuron two. This may

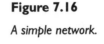

Figure 7.16

A simple network.

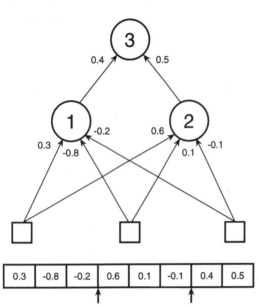

0.3	-0.8	-0.2	0.6	0.1	-0.1	0.4	0.5

not be favorable because, if you think of the neurons as individual units, then any improvement gained so far may be disturbed. In effect, the crossover operator could be acting very much like a disruptive mutation operator.

To combat this, I've created another type of crossover operator that only cuts at the boundaries of neurons. (In the example given in Figure 7.16, these would be at gene positions 3, 6, and 8 shown by the little arrows.) To implement this, I've added another method to the CNeuralNet class: CalculateSplitPoints. This function creates a vector of all the network weight boundaries and it looks like this:

```
vector<int> CNeuralNet::CalculateSplitPoints() const
{
  vector<int> SplitPoints;

  int WeightCounter = 0;

  //for each layer
  for (int i=0; i<m_NumHiddenLayers + 1; ++i)
  {
    //for each neuron
    for (int j=0; j<m_vecLayers[i].m_NumNeurons; ++j)
    {
```

```
    //for each weight
    for (int k=0; k<m_vecLayers[i].m_vecNeurons[j].m_NumInputs; ++k)
    {
      ++WeightCounter;
    }

    SplitPoints.push_back(WeightCounter - 1);
    }
  }

  return SplitPoints;
}
```

The constructor of the CController class calls this method when it's creating the minesweepers and passes the vector of split points to the genetic algorithm class. They are stored in a std::vector named m_vecSplitPoints. The genetic algorithm then uses these split points to implement a two-point crossover operator as follows:

```
void CGenAlg::CrossoverAtSplits(const vector<double> &mum,
                                const vector<double> &dad,
                                vector<double>       &baby1,
                                vector<double>       &baby2)
{
  //just return parents as offspring dependent on the rate
  //or if parents are the same
  if ( (RandFloat() > m_dCrossoverRate) || (mum == dad))
  {
    baby1 = mum;
    baby2 = dad;

    return;
  }

  //determine two crossover points
  int Index1 = RandInt(0, m_vecSplitPoints.size()-2);
  int Index2 = RandInt(Index1, m_vecSplitPoints.size()-1);

  int cp1 = m_vecSplitPoints[Index1];
  int cp2 = m_vecSplitPoints[Index2];

  //create the offspring
```

```
    for (int i=0; i<mum.size(); ++i)
    {
      if ( (i<cp1) || (i>=cp2) )
      {
        //keep the same genes if outside of crossover points
        baby1.push_back(mum[i]);
        baby2.push_back(dad[i]);
      }

      else
      {
        //switch over the belly block
        baby1.push_back(dad[i]);
        baby2.push_back(mum[i]);
      }
    }

  return;
}
```

In my experience, I have found that treating the neurons as individual units when implementing crossover gives better results than splitting the genomes at random points along the length of the chromosome.

Improvement Number Two

The other performance improvement I want to discuss with you is another way of looking at those network inputs. The example you've already seen uses four inputs into the network: a look-at vector and a vector to the closest mine. There is, however, a way of getting those inputs down to just one.

If you think about it, the minesweepers only need to know one piece of information to locate the mines and that is an angle that indicates how much to the left or right the mine is (congratulations, by the way, if you'd already thought about this). Because we have already calculated a look-at vector and the vector to the closest mine, calculating the angle (θ) between them is trivial—it's just the dot product of those vectors, as I discussed in Chapter 6, "Moon Landings Made Easy." See Figure 7.17.

Unfortunately, the dot product only gives the magnitude of the angle; it doesn't indicate on which side of the minesweeper the angle lays. Therefore, I've written

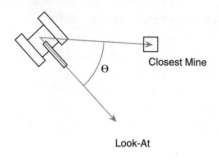

Figure 7.17

Calculating the angle to the closest mine.

Closest Mine

θ

Look-At

another vector function that returns the sign of one vector relative to another. The function prototype looks like this:

```
inline int Vec2DSign(SVector2D &v1, SVector2D &v2);
```

You can find the source in the SVector2D.h file if you are interested in the mechanics. But, basically, if v2 is clockwise of v1, the function returns 1. If it's anticlockwise, the function returns -1. Combining the dot product and Vec2DSign enable the inputs to be distilled to their essence, and the network can now accept just one input. Here's what the relevant section of the new CMinesweeper::Update function looks like:

```
//get vector to closest mine
SVector2D vClosestMine = GetClosestMine(mines);

//normalize it
Vec2DNormalize(vClosestMine);

//calculate dot product of the look at vector and Closest mine
//vector. This will give us the angle we need to turn to face
//the closest mine
double dot = Vec2DDot(m_vLookAt, vClosestMine);

//calculate sign
int sign   = Vec2DSign(m_vLookAt, vClosestMine);

inputs.push_back(dot*sign);
```

You can see how much these two changes speed up the evolution by running the executable in the Chapter7/Smart Sweepers v1.1 folder.

An important thing to note is that the network takes longer to evolve with four inputs because it has to find out more relationships between the input data and how it should behave. In effect, it is actually *learning* how to do the dot product and sign calculation. So, when designing your own networks, you have to carefully balance pre-calculating a lot of the input data (which may be heavy on the CPU but leads to faster evolution times) and letting the network figure out the complex relationships between the input data (which usually takes longer to evolve but can often be much less CPU intensive).

Last Words

I hope you enjoyed your first foray into the wonderful world of neural networks. I bet you're amazed at how simple they can be to use, eh? I know I was.

In the next few chapters, I'll be expanding on your knowledge, showing you new training approaches and even ways of evolving the structure of a neural net. First though, it would be a good idea for you to fool around with the suggestions at the end of this chapter.

Stuff to Try

1. In v1.0, instead of using the look-at vector as an input, just use the rotation value, thereby reducing the number of inputs by one. How does this affect the evolution? Why do you think that is?

2. Try using six inputs describing the raw x/y coordinates of the minesweepers and the closest mine, and the minesweepers heading vector. Does the network still evolve to find a solution?

3. Change the activation response. Try low values, around 0.1 – 0.3, which will produce an activation function that acts very much like a step function. Then try higher values, which will give a more flattened response curve. How does this affect the evolution?

4. Instead of evolving behavior to pick up the mines, change the fitness function so the minesweepers avoid the mines.

5. Make sure you fool around with different settings and operators for the genetic algorithm!

6. Now add another object type—say people. Given this new environment, evolve vehicles that will avoid the people and yet still pick up the mines. (This is not as easy as you might think!)

CHAPTER 8

GIVING YOUR BOT SENSES

BLIND MAN: I am healed! The Master has healed me!

BRIAN: I didn't touch him!

BLIND MAN: I was blind but now I can see. Arghhhhh! [Thud]

—Monty Python's Life of Brian

By now you should be feeling fairly comfortable with how a neural network operates. If not, it's probably a good idea to go back, read the last chapter again, and then try your hand at some of the exercises.

In this chapter, I'll be spending some time discussing how neural networks can be applied to a couple of common game AI problems: obstacle avoidance and environment exploration. As a base, I'll be using the same code as the previous chapter but this time I've created a simple game world that has a number of obstacles scattered about for the minesweepers to negotiate. The obstacles are stored in a vertex buffer and rendered just like any other game object. Figure 8.1 shows the minesweepers' new world.

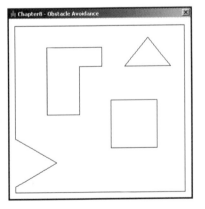

Figure 8.1

A brave new world.

The goal of this chapter is to show you how to create bots that are able to avoid all the obstacles and navigate their way around the game world. I'll start with how to avoid bumping into things.

Obstacle Avoidance

Obstacle avoidance is a very common task in game AI. It's the ability of a game agent to perceive its environment and to navigate without bumping into the objects in the game world. There are only a few games out there that do not require this ability to some degree.

To perform successful obstacle avoidance, the agent must be able to:

- observe its environment
- take action to avoid potential collisions

Let's first look at how a game agent may be given the sense of vision.

Sensing the Environment

So far the minesweepers have had very limited senses. In Chapter 7, "Neural Networks in Plain English," they were blind to all but the closest mine. To enable them to perceive obstacles, we are going to have to give them a way of "seeing" the world around them. The way I've chosen to do this is by giving each minesweeper a number of sensors. The sensors are line segments that radiate outward from the minesweepers' bodies. See Figure 8.2.

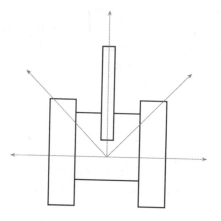

Figure 8.2

A minesweeper gets sensors.

The number of segments and their length can be adjusted, but the default is for five sensors that radiate outward for 25 pixels. Each frame, a function is called which tests for an intersection between each sensor and the line segments that make up the obstacles in the game world. Every minesweeper has a buffer, m_vecdSensors, which is a std::vector of distances to any obstacle it may encounter. The distances are measured between zero and one. The closer the object is to the minesweeper, the closer to zero the reading returned by the sensor will be. Figure 8.3 shows some approximate readings a sensor may return.

Figure 8.3

Typical sensor readings.

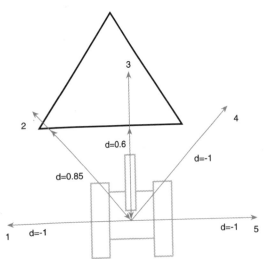

As you can see, the sensor returns -1 if no obstacle line segments are encountered. To indicate whether the minesweeper has actually collided with an object (as opposed to just detecting it), a test is made to see if the reading returned by each sensor is below a certain value defined in CParams.h as dCollisionDist. This value is calculated from the scale of the minesweeper and the length of the sensor segments. It is a fairly crude way of detecting for collisions, but it's quick (all the calculations having already been completed) and it suffices for the purposes of this demonstration. Let's take a look at the code that does all the testing:

```
void CMinesweeper::TestSensors(vector<SPoint> &objects)
{
```

The function is passed a vector of SPoints that describe all the obstacles/objects the minesweeper is allowed to perceive. These are defined at the beginning of CController.cpp.

```
    m_bCollided = false;
```

This is the flag that lets the minesweeper know if it collided or not.

```
    //first we transform the sensors into world coordinates
    m_tranSensors = m_Sensors;
    WorldTransform(m_tranSensors, 1);
```

The line segments that describe the sensor segments are created in the method CMinesweeper::CreateSensors and stored in the vertex buffer m_Sensors. Therefore, just like any other game object, each frame these sensors need to be transformed into world coordinates before they are tested against the segments that make up the obstacles. The transformed vertices are stored in m_transSensors.

```
//flush the sensors
m_vecdSensors.clear();

//now to check each sensor against the objects in the world
for (int sr=0; sr<m_tranSensors.size(); ++sr)
{
  bool bHit = false;
```

This flag is set if a sensor intersects with an obstacle.

```
  double dist = 0;

  for (int seg=0; seg<objects.size(); seg+=2)
  {
    if (LineIntersection2D(SPoint(m_vPosition.x, m_vPosition.y),
                           m_tranSensors[sr],
                           objects[seg],
                           objects[seg+1],
                           dist))
    {
      bHit = true;

      break;
    }
  }
```

This part of the code iterates through each sensor segment and calls the function LineIntersection2D to perform an intersection test. You can find the code for this function in the collision.h and collision.cpp files. (If you are interested in the finer workings of this function, see the comp.graphics.algorithms FAQ in the FAQs folder on the CD.) If an intersection is detected, the loop exits to avoid any further unnecessary calculations.

```
  if (bHit)
  {
```

```
       m_vecdSensors.push_back(dist);

       //implement very simple collision detection
       if (dist < CParams::dCollisionDist)
       {
         m_bCollided = true;
       }
     }
```

If a sensor/obstacle intersection has been detected, the collision test is undertaken as described earlier, and m_bCollided is set accordingly.

```
     else
     {
       m_vecdSensors.push_back(-1);
     }
   }//next sensor
}
```

This function is called at the beginning of CMinesweeper::Update. The sensor readings are then used as inputs into the sweepers' neural nets.

The Fitness Function

This time the fitness function has to reflect how often the minesweepers collide with an obstacle. The better the fitness score, the better the minesweeper is at avoiding obstacles. One way of doing it is to penalize a sweeper every time a collision is detected. This works fine but results in negative fitness scores. You can work with negative fitness scores just the same as you can with positive ones, but from experience I've learned that it's easy for hard-to-spot bugs to creep into your code when working with negative scores. Therefore, if I can find a way I'll use a fitness function that always produces positive scores.

With this in mind, the first fitness function you may think of is to simply reward the minesweeper for every frame that passes without a collision. Something like:

```
if (!Collided)
{
  Fitness += 1;
}
```

Look reasonable? What type of behavior do you think this type of fitness function will produce? Give it a few moments of thought and then take a look at the SmartSweepers v2.0 code on the CD.

If you predicted the behavior you've just observed, well done. If not, don't worry. A lot of people don't realize the best way for the minesweepers to maximize their fitness is to just spin around in circles. What an easy life!

A way to prevent the minesweepers from spinning madly around has to be found. We have to tame those suckers. Fortunately, this is pretty easy to do. All that's needed is to give a minesweeper a reward for every frame where its rotation is less than a certain value. Like this:

```
if (fabs(Rotation) < RotationTolerance)
{
    Fitness += 1;
}
```

If you now run the executable for SmartSweepers v2.1, you'll see how this has produced much more reasonable behavior. At last, the minesweepers are starting to bend to our will!

Because I wanted to display the fitness score onscreen, I've broken it down into two bonuses: m_dSpinBonus and m_dCollisionBonus. These are added together at the end of every epoch to calculate the final fitness scores. When you run the program, you'll see the scores allocated to these two bonuses at the top of the screen. Figure 8.4 shows a screenshot of the minesweepers in action.

Because this method of scoring typically generates fitness scores that are close together over the population distribution, I've used tournament selection as the selection method for the genetic algorithm. If a fitness proportionate selection technique is used, then the fitness scores would almost certainly have to be preprocessed in some way to give good results.

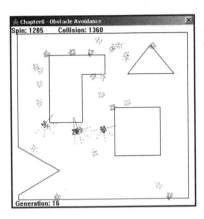

Figure 8.4

The minesweepers learning to avoid obstacles.

As you will discover, learning to avoid obstacles is a fairly easy task for a neural network to learn. In this example, the best minesweepers max out their fitness score within a handful of generations.

Here are the default settings used for this project:

As you'll have noticed by now, although the minesweepers learn to avoid obstacles, they don't really do very much and usually end up either following the edge of one of the obstacles or bouncing from one obstacle to the other. After all, they don't have any incentive to do anything else. A more useful behavior would be if the minesweepers could learn to *explore* their environment in addition to learning how to avoid the objects in the environment. To do that, we have to give them a *memory*.

Giving Your Bots a Memory

A memory can be created using a simple data structure to represent the environment. In this example, the environment is broken down into a number of equally sized cells that are then stored in a 2D `std::vector`, as shown in Figure 8.5.

This can now be used as a type of memory map to store relevant information. In this example, the number of ticks a minesweeper has spent frequenting a cell is recorded. In this way, the minesweeper can index into a cell and know whether it has been there before. To explore the environment, the minesweepers must evolve neural networks that favor unvisited cells.

Table 8.1   Default Project Settings for Smart Sweepers v2.1

Neural Network

Parameter	Setting
Number of inputs	5
Number of outputs	2
Number of hidden layers	1
Number of hidden neurons	6
Activation response	1

Genetic Algorithm

Parameter	Setting
Population size	40
Selection type	Tournament
Num tourney competitors	5
Crossover type	Two point
Crossover rate	0.7
Mutation rate	0.1
Elitism (on/off)	On
Number of elite (N/copies)	4/1

General

Parameter	Setting
Number of sensors	5
Sensor range	25
Number of ticks/epoch	2000

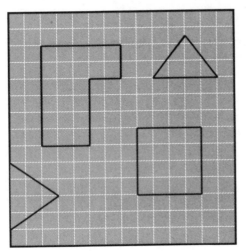

Figure 8.5

Memory cells.

The memory map is implemented in the class called `CMapper`. Here is the definition:

```
class CMapper
{
private:

  //the 2d vector of memory cells
  vector<vector<SCell> > m_2DvecCells;
```

The `SCell` structure is simply a structure that holds a `RECT` describing the coordinates of the cell, and an integer, `iTicksSpentHere`, that keeps track of how much time has been spent there. The `SCell` struct also has methods to increment and to clear `iTicksSpentHere`.

```
  int     m_NumCellsX;
  int     m_NumCellsY;
  int     m_iTotalCells;

  //the dimensions of each cell
  double  m_dCellSize;

public:

  CMapper():m_NumCellsX(0),
            m_NumCellsY(0),
```

```
            m_iTotalCells(0)
{}


//this must be called after an instance of this class has been
//created. This sets up all the cell coordinates.
void     Init(int MaxRangeX, int MaxRangeY);


//this method is called each frame and updates the time spent
//at the cell at this position
void     Update(double xPos, double yPos);


//returns how many ticks have been spent at this cell position
int      TicksLingered(double xPos, double yPos) const;


//returns the total number of cells visited
int      NumCellsVisited()const;


//returns if the cell at the given position has been visited or
//not
bool     BeenVisited(double xPos, double yPos) const;


//This method renders any visited cells in shades of red. The
//darker the red, the more time has been spent at that cell
void     Render(HDC surface);


void     Reset();


int      NumCells(){return m_iTotalCells;}
};
```

Now that the minesweepers have a memory, they need a way of using it to remember where they've been. This is simple to implement because the endpoints of the sensors have already been calculated in the last version. The ends of these sensors may be used to "feel" around inside the memory map and sample the information found there—similar to the way an insect uses its antennae. See Figure 8.6.

The readings from these feelers are stored in a std::vector called m_vecFeelers and then input into the neural network along with the range readings from the original

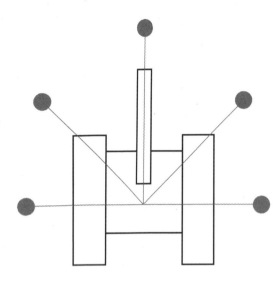

Figure 8.6

The minesweeper grows antennae.

sensors. The code to do this can be found in the `CMinesweeper::TestSensors` method. Here's what the additional lines of code look like:

```
//check how many times the minesweeper has visited the cell
//at the current position
int HowOften = m_MemoryMap.TicksLingered(m_tranSensors[sr].x,
                                         m_tranSensors[sr].y);

if (HowOften == 0)
{
  m_vecFeelers.push_back(-1);

  continue;
}

if (HowOften < 10)
{
  m_vecFeelers.push_back(0);

  continue;
}

if (HowOften < 20)
{
```

```
    m_vecFeelers.push_back(0.2);

    continue;
}

if (HowOften < 30)
{
    m_vecFeelers.push_back(0.4);

    continue;
}

if (HowOften < 50)
{
    m_vecFeelers.push_back(0.6);

    continue;
}

if (HowOften < 80)
{
    m_vecFeelers.push_back(0.8);

    continue;
}

m_vecFeelers.push_back(1);
```

Because it's preferable to standardize the inputs into the network, any values added to m_vecFeelers are scaled to $-1 < n < 1$. If the minesweeper has never visited a cell before, the feeler reading for that cell will return a value of -1. If the cell has been visited, the feeler returns a scaled value between 0 and 1. The more time spent in the cell, the higher the value will be.

You may wonder why it's important to have this sliding scale. After all, the feeler could simply return -1 for an unvisited cell or 1 for a visited cell. The reason can best be explained with the use of a couple of diagrams. Let's assume the latter case is true and that the feelers only give readings of -1 or 1. Now take a look at Figure 8.7.

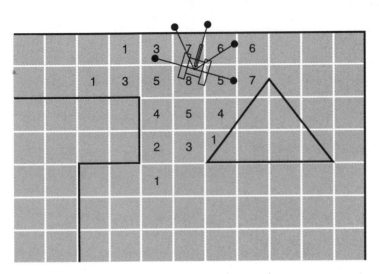

Figure 8.7

Uh Oh!

The numbers show how much time has been spent by the minesweeper in each cell. The unnumbered cells represent unvisited cells. The figure shows a very common scenario for a minesweeper. Now because the feeler will only read 1 for each visited cell, the poor old minesweeper is going to get hopelessly stuck here because it hasn't a clue how to find its way out. Wherever its feelers feel, they are always going to return the same value.

However, when a sliding scale is used for the feeler readings, you can see how the neural network has the potential to learn how to direct the minesweeper toward less frequented cells and find a way out. See Figure 8.8.

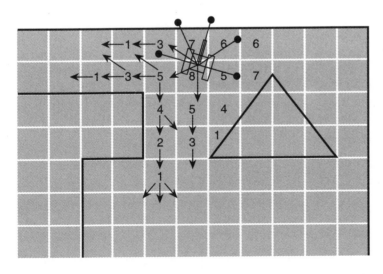

Figure 8.8

Feeling the way to freedom.

I've also included one other input into the neural network and that's the member variable m_bCollided. This is explicitly telling the minesweeper whether it is presently in collision with an obstacle, and helps the performance somewhat. (When you play around with the code, remove this input and note how the network takes longer to evolve.)

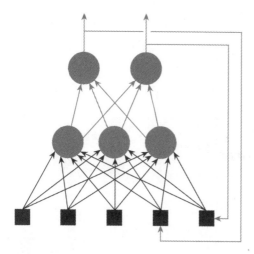

Figure 8.9

A recurrent network.

TIP

Some tasks may benefit from a small amount of very short-term memory. This can be achieved simply and quickly by feeding back the neural network's output. For example, with the minesweepers, you would create a network with an additional two inputs, and then use the previous generation's outputs (m_lTrack and m_rTrack) as the additional two inputs. This type of network, one that feeds back to itself in someway, is called a *recurrent* network. See Figure 8.9.

This idea can be extended to feedback any number of the previous generation's outputs, although, this will slow down the processing of the network a great deal and is best avoided. In a game, you want your networks to be as speedy as possible. (Somehow, I think you already knew that!)

The Fitness Function

A fitness function could be used that combines the fitness function from version 2.1 along with another score for the number of memory cells visited. However, quicker results can be achieved if *only* the number of cells visited is considered. To visit as many cells as possible, the minesweepers will automatically learn how to avoid obstacles and spinning because doing either of these two activities will only slow them down and produce lower scores! Smart, huh?

Now's a good time to run the executable from version 2.2 and see what happens. By the time the genetic algorithm has performed 100-150 epochs, the minesweepers will be zipping along very nicely.

Table 8.2 shows the default settings I've used for this project.

Table 8.2   Default Project Settings for Smart Sweepers v2.2

Neural Network

Parameter	Setting
Number of inputs	11
Number of outputs	2
Number of hidden layers	1
Number of hidden neurons	10
Activation response	1

Genetic Algorithm

Parameter	Setting
Population size	50
Selection type	Tournament
Num tourney competitors	5
Crossover type	Two point
Crossover rate	0.7
Mutation rate	0.1
Elitism (on/off)	On
Number of elite (N/copies)	4/1

General

Parameter	Setting
Number of sensors	5
Sensor range	25
Number of ticks/epoch	2500

Summary

By now I hope the neurons inside your own head are firing away like a 4th of July fireworks display. If I've done my job correctly, you should be having difficulty sleeping at night because of all the groovy ideas flying around your skull. And the more you get comfortable with the technology, the more areas you'll see where it may be appropriate to apply what you've learned. It needn't be a big thing, like using one enormously complicated network to control every aspect of a FPS bot— that's being a little optimistic (although someone has already tried it). You can use them for just handling specific parts of a game agent's AI.

Neural networks, in my opinion, are better used in a modular way. For example, you could train up separate networks for particular sorts of behavior, such as pursuit, flee, explore, and gather, and then use another neural network as a sort of state machine to choose which of the behaviors is relevant at any given time. Or even use a simple finite state machine to choose which network is appropriate.

One excellent use would be to use a neural net to calculate the bot aiming for a *Quake*-type first-person shooter game. If you've played the bots currently available, you'll almost certainly have come to the conclusion that the aiming AI leaves a lot to be desired. When the bots are played at the better skill levels, 30% of the shots they pull off are ridiculously unlikely—they are just *too* accurate. It's like going up against Clint Eastwood in *A Fistful of Dollars*! But you could easily design a network with inputs like visibility (bright/foggy/dark), amount of target visible, distance to target and the currently selected weapon, and an output that determines a radius of distance from the center of the target. This network could then be trained to give much more realistic aiming behavior.

Or how about using a neural network to control the computer-controlled cars in a racing game? In fact, this has already been done. The cars in *Colin McRae Rally 2.0* are driven by neural networks that have been trained to follow racing lines.

Some of the ideas I've mentioned would be very difficult to implement using a genetic algorithm to evolve the network weights. Sometimes a *supervised* training method is the best approach to a problem, and that's what I'm going to be talking about in the next chapter.

Stuff to Try

1. Incorporate some of the project settings into the genomes so they can be evolved by the genetic algorithm. For example, you could evolve the number of sensors and their lengths.

2. Add some items for the minesweepers to find.

3. Evolve minesweepers that avoid other minesweepers.

4. Create a neural network to pilot the lunar lander from Chapter 6.

5. Evolve neural networks that play the light cycle game from *Tron*. This is not as easy as it first appears. In fact, you are almost certainly doomed to failure, but trust me, you may fail the task, but the lesson will be valuable. Can you work out where the difficulty may lie with this problem before you begin?

6. Try adding visualizations to the programs so you can watch the neural networks and weights in real time.

CHAPTER 9

A SUPERVISED TRAINING APPROACH

There are 10 kinds of people in this world…

Those who understand binary and those who do not.

In this chapter, I'm going to show you a completely different way of training a neural network. Up to now, you've been using an *unsupervised* training technique. The alternative is to train your networks using a *supervised* technique. A supervised training approach can be used when you already have examples of data you can train the network with. I mentioned this in Chapter 7, "Neural Networks in Plain English," when I described how a network may be trained to recognize characters. It works like this: An input pattern is presented to the network and the output examined and compared to the target output. If the output differs from the target output, then all the weights are altered slightly so the next time the same pattern is presented, the output will be a little closer to the expected outcome. This is repeated many times with each pattern the network is required to learn until it performs correctly.

To show you how the weights are adjusted, I'm going to resort to using a simple mathematical function: the XOR function. But don't worry, after you've learned the principle behind the learning mechanism, I'll show you how to apply it to something much more exciting.

The XOR Function

For those of you unfamiliar with Boolean logic, the XOR (exclusive OR) function is best described with a table:

The XOR function has played a significant role in the history of neural networks. Marvin Minsky demonstrated in 1969 that a network consisting of just an input layer and an output layer could never solve this simple problem. This is because the XOR function is one of a large set of functions that are *linearly inseparable*. A function that is linearly inseparable is one, which when plotted on a 2D graph, cannot be separated with a straight line. Figure 9.1 shows graphs for the XOR function and the AND function. The AND function only outputs a 1 if both inputs are 1 and, as you can see, is a good example of a function that is linearly separable.

Table 9.1   The XOR Problem

A	B	A XOR B
1	1	0
0	0	0
1	0	1
0	1	1

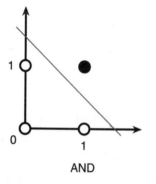

AND

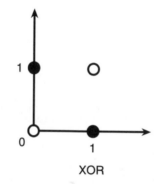

XOR

Figure 9.1

The XOR and AND function. The gray line shows the linear separability of the AND function.

Interesting Fact

Boolean algebra was invented by George Boole in the mid-nineteenth century. He was working with numbers that satisfy the equation $x^2 = x$ when he came up with his particular brand of logic. The only numbers that satisfy that equation are 1 and 0, or on and off, the two states of a modern digital computer. This is why you come across Boolean operators so often in conjunction with computers.

Although people were aware that adding layers between the input and output layers could, in theory, solve problems of this type, no one knew how a multilayer network like this could be trained. At this point, connectionism went out of fashion and the study of neural networks went into decline. Then in the mid seventies, a man named Werbos figured out a learning method for multilayer networks called the *backpropagation* learning method. Incredibly, this went more or less unnoticed until the early eighties when there was a great resurgence of interest in the field, and once again neural networks were the "in thing" to study among computer scientists.

How Does Backpropagation Work?

Backpropagation, or backprop for short, works like this: First create a network with one or more hidden layers and randomize all the weights—say to values between -1 and 1. Then present a pattern to the network and note its output. The difference between this value and the target output value is called the *error value*. This error value is then used to determine how the weights from the layer below the output layer are adjusted so if the same input pattern is presented again, the output will be a little closer to the correct answer. Once the weights for the current layer have been adjusted, the same thing is repeated for the previous layer and so on until the first hidden layer is reached and all the weights for every layer have been adjusted slightly. If done correctly, the next time the input pattern is presented, the output will be a little bit closer to the target output. This whole process is then repeated with all the different input patterns many times until the error value is within acceptable limits for the problem at hand. The network is then said to be *trained*.

To clarify, the training set required for an ANN to learn the XOR function would be a series of vectors like this:

This set of matched input/output patterns is used to train the network as follows:

1. Initialize weights to small random values.
2. For each pattern, repeat Steps a to e.
   a. Present to the network and evaluate the output, o.
   b. Calculate the error between o and the target output value (t).
   c. Adjust the weights in the output layer.
      For each hidden layer repeat d and e.

Table 9.2   The XOR Training Set

Input data	Output data (target)
(1, 1)	(0)
(1, 0)	(1)
(0, 1)	(1)
(0, 0)	(0)

    d. Calculate the error in the hidden layer.

    e. Adjust the weights in the hidden layer.

3. Repeat Step 2 until the sum of all the errors in Step b is within an acceptable limit.

This is how this learning method got its name; the error is propagated backward through the network. See Figure 9.2.

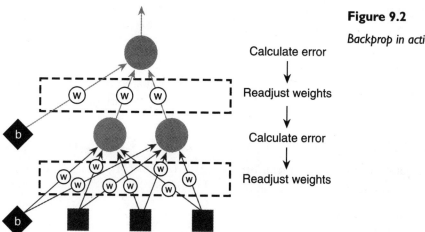

Figure 9.2

Backprop in action.

Calculate error

↓

Readjust weights

↓

Calculate error

↓

Readjust weights

The derivation of the equations for the backprop learning algorithm is difficult to understand without some knowledge of calculus, and it's not my intention to go into that aspect here. I'm just going to show you what the equations are and how to use them. If you find that you become interested in the more theoretical side of this algorithm, then you'll find plenty of references to good reading material in the bibliography.

First I'll show you the equations, then I'll run through the XOR problem putting in actual figures, and you'll get to see backprop in action.

There are basically two sets of equations: one to calculate the error and weight adjustment for the output layer and the other to calculate the error and weight adjustments for the hidden layers. To make things less complicated, from now on I'll be discussing the case of a network with only one hidden layer. You'll almost certainly find that one hidden layer is adequate for most of the problems you'll encounter, but if two or more layers are ever required then it's not too difficult to alter the code to accommodate this.

Adjusting the Weights for the Output Layer

First, let's look at the equation to adjust the weights leading into the output layer. The output from a neuron, k, will be given as o_k and target output from a neuron will be given as t_k. To begin with, the error value, E_k, for each neuron is calculated.

$$E_k = (t_k - o_k) \times o_k (1 - o_k)$$

To change the weight between a unit j in the hidden layer and an output unit k, use the following formula:

$$W_{jk} + = L \times E_k \times o_j$$

in which L is a small positive value known as the *learning rate*. The bigger the learning rate, the more the weight is adjusted. This figure has to be adjusted by hand to give the best performance. I'll talk to you more about the learning rate in a moment.

Adjusting the Weights for the Hidden Layer/s

The equations for calculating the weight adjustments for a neuron, j, in a hidden layer go like this. As before, the error value is calculated first.

$$E_j = o_k (1 - o_k) \times \sum_{k=1}^{k=n} E_k w_{jk}$$

in which n is the number of units in the output layer.

Knowing the error value, the weight adjustment from the hidden unit j, to the input units i, can be made:

$$w_{ij} + = L \times E_j \times o_i$$

This entire process is repeated until the error value over all the training patterns has been reduced to an acceptable level.

An Example

Now that you know what the equations are, let's quickly run through an example for a network created to solve the XOR problem. The smallest network you can build that has the capability of solving this problem is shown in Figure 9.3. This network is a little unusual in that it is *fully connected*—the inputs are connected directly to the output as well as to the hidden neuron. Although this is not the type of network you will be building very often, I'm using it here because its size enables me to concisely show you the calculations required for backprop.

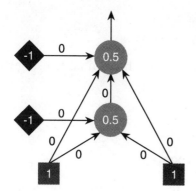

Figure 9.3

Training an XOR network.

Assume the network has been initialized with all the weights set to zero (normally, they would be set to small random values). For the sake of this demonstration, I'll just be running through the calculations using one pattern from the training set, (1, 1), so the expected target output is therefore a 0. The numbers in the neurons show the activation from that neuron. Don't forget, the sigmoid activation function gives a result of 0.5 for a zero input.

As we have discussed, the training will follow these steps:

1. Calculate the error values at the output neurons.
2. Adjust the weights using the result from Step 1 and the learning rate L.
3. Calculate the error values at the hidden neurons.
4. Adjust the weights using the result from Step 3 and the learning rate L.
5. Repeat until the error value is within acceptable limits.

Now to plug in some numbers.

Step one. 0 is the target output t_k and 0.5 is the network output o_k, so using the equation:

$$E_k = (t_k - o_k) \times o_k (1 - o_k)$$

$$\text{error} = (0 - 0.5) \times 0.5 \times (1 - 0.5) = -0.125$$

Step two. Adjust the weights going into the output layer using the equation:

$$W_{jk} + = L \times E_k \times o_j$$

Calculating the new weights into the output layer going from left to right and using a learning rate of 0.1.

$$\text{New weight(bias)} = 0 + 0.1 \times -0.125 \times -1 = 0.0125$$
$$\text{New weight1} = 0 + 0.1 \times -0.125 \times 1 = -0.0125$$

New weight2 = 0 + 0.1 × -0.125 × 0.5 = -0.00625

New weight3 = 0 + 0.1 × -0.125 × 1 = -0.0125

Step three. Calculate the error value for the neuron in the hidden layer using the equation:

$$E_j = O_k(1 - O_k) \times \sum_{k=1}^{k=n} E_k W_{jk}$$

error = 0.5 × (1 − 0.5) × -0.125 × 0.00625 = -0.000195

Notice how I've used the *updated* weight computed in Step two for w to calculate the error. This is not essential. It's perfectly reasonable to step through the network calculating all the errors first and then adjust the weights. Either way works. I do it this way because it feels more intuitive when I write the code.

Step four. Adjust the weights going into the hidden layer. Again, going from left to right and using the equation:

$$w_{ij} += L \times E_j \times O_i$$

New weight(bias) = 0 + 0.1 × 0.000195 × -1 = 0.0000195

New weight1 = 0 + 0.1 × -0.000195 × 1 = -0.0000195

New weight2 = 0 + 0.1 × -0.000195 × 1 = -0.0000195

After this single iteration of the learning method, the network looks like Figure 9.4.

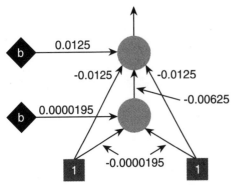

Figure 9.4

The XOR network after one iteration of backprop.

The output this updated network gives is 0.496094. Just a little bit closer to the target output of 0 than the original output of 0.5.

Step five. Go to step one.

The idea is to keep iterating through the learning process until the error value drops below an acceptable value. The number of iterations can be very large and is proportional to the size of the learning rate: the smaller the learning rate, the more iterations backprop requires. However, when increasing the learning rate, you run the risk of the algorithm falling into a local minima.

The example shown only ran one input pattern (1,1) through the algorithm. In practice, each pattern would be run through the algorithm every iteration. The entire process goes like this:

1. Create the network.
2. Initialize the weights to small random values with a mean of 0.
3. For each training pattern:

> calculate the error value for the neurons in the output layer
>
> adjust the weights of the output layer
>
> calculate the error value for neurons in the hidden layer
>
> adjust the weights of the hidden layer

4. Repeat Step 3 until the error is below an acceptable value.

Changes to the CNeuralNet Code

To implement backpropagation, the CNeuralNet class and related structures have to be altered slightly to accommodate the new training method. The first change is to the SNeuron structure so that a record of each neuron's error value and activation can be made. These values are accessed frequently by the algorithm.

```
struct SNeuron
{
  //the number of inputs into the neuron
  int             m_iNumInputs;

  //the weights for each input
  vector<double>  m_vecWeight;

  //the activation of this neuron
  double          m_dActivation;

  //the error value
```

```
    double          m_dError;

    //ctor
    SNeuron(int NumInputs);
};
```

The `CNeuralNet` class has also changed to accommodate the new learning algorithm. Here is the header for the new version with comments against the changes. I've removed any extraneous methods (used in the last two chapters) for clarity.

```
//define a type for an input or output vector (used in
//the training method)
typedef vector<double> iovector;
```

A training set consists of a series of `std::vectors` of doubles. This `typedef` just helps to make the code more readable.

```
class CNeuralNet
{

private:

    int         m_iNumInputs;

    int         m_iNumOutputs;

    int         m_iNumHiddenLayers;

    int         m_iNeuronsPerHiddenLyr;

    //we must specify a learning rate for backprop
    double      m_dLearningRate;

    //cumulative error for the network (sum (outputs - expected))
    double      m_dErrorSum;

    //true if the network has been trained
    bool        m_bTrained;

    //epoch counter
```

```cpp
int         m_iNumEpochs;

//storage for each layer of neurons including the output layer
vector<SNeuronLayer>  m_vecLayers;

//given a training set this method performs one iteration of the
//backpropagation algorithm. The training sets comprise of series
//of vector inputs and a series of expected vector outputs. Returns
//false if there is a problem.
bool          NetworkTrainingEpoch(vector<iovector> &SetIn,
                                    vector<iovector> &SetOut);


void          CreateNet();

//sets all the weights to small random values
void          InitializeNetwork();

//sigmoid response curve
inline double   Sigmoid(double activation, double response);


public:


CNeuralNet::CNeuralNet(int    NumInputs,
                       int    NumOutputs,
                       int    HiddenNeurons,
                       double LearningRate);


//calculates the outputs from a set of inputs
vector<double>  Update(vector<double> inputs);

//trains the network given a training set. Returns false if
//there is an error with the data sets
bool          Train(CData* data, HWND hwnd);

//accessor methods
bool          Trained()const{return m_bTrained;}
```

```
double          Error()const  {return m_dErrorSum;}
int             Epoch()const  {return m_iNumEpochs;}
};
```

Before we move on to the first code project, let me list the actual code implementation of the backprop algorithm. This method takes a training set (which is a series of std::vectors of doubles representing each input vector and its matching output vector) and runs the set through one iteration of the backprop algorithm. A record of the cumulative error for the training set is kept in m_dErrorSum. This error is calculated as the sum of the squares of each output minus its target output. In the literature, this method of calculating the error is usually abbreviated to SSE (Sum of the Squared Errors).

The CNeuralNet::Train method calls NetworkTrainingEpoch repeatedly until the SSE is below a predefined limit. At this point, the network is considered to be trained.

```
bool CNeuralNet::NetworkTrainingEpoch(vector<iovector> &SetIn,
                                      vector<iovector> &SetOut)
{
  //create some iterators
  vector<double>::iterator  curWeight;
  vector<SNeuron>::iterator curNrnOut, curNrnHid;

  //this will hold the cumulative error value for the training set
  m_dErrorSum = 0;

  //run each input pattern through the network, calculate the errors and update
  //the weights accordingly
  for (int vec=0; vec<SetIn.size(); ++vec)
  {
    //first run this input vector through the network and retrieve the outputs
    vector<double> outputs = Update(SetIn[vec]);

    //return if error has occurred
    if (outputs.size() == 0)
    {
      return false;
    }

    //for each output neuron calculate the error and adjust weights
    //accordingly
```

```cpp
  for (int op=0; op<m_iNumOutputs; ++op)
  {
    //first calculate the error value
    double err = (SetOut[vec][op] - outputs[op]) * outputs[op]
                 * (1 - outputs[op]);

    //update the error total. (when this value becomes lower than a
    //preset threshold we know the training is successful)
    m_dErrorSum += (SetOut[vec][op] - outputs[op]) *
                   (SetOut[vec][op] - outputs[op]);

    //keep a record of the error value
    m_vecLayers[1].m_vecNeurons[op].m_dError = err;

    curWeight = m_vecLayers[1].m_vecNeurons[op].m_vecWeight.begin();
    curNrnHid = m_vecLayers[0].m_vecNeurons.begin();

    //for each weight up to but not including the bias
    while(curWeight != m_vecLayers[1].m_vecNeurons[op].m_vecWeight.end()-1)
    {
      //calculate the new weight based on the backprop rules
      *curWeight += err * m_dLearningRate * curNrnHid->m_dActivation;

      ++curWeight; ++curNrnHid;
    }

    //and the bias for this neuron
    *curWeight += err * m_dLearningRate * BIAS;
  }

//**moving backwards to the hidden layer**
  curNrnHid = m_vecLayers[0].m_vecNeurons.begin();

  int n = 0;

  //for each neuron in the hidden layer calculate the error signal
  //and then adjust the weights accordingly
  while(curNrnHid != m_vecLayers[0].m_vecNeurons.end())
  {
```

```
        double err = 0;

        curNrnOut = m_vecLayers[1].m_vecNeurons.begin();

        //to calculate the error for this neuron we need to iterate through
        //all the neurons in the output layer it is connected to and sum
        //the error * weights
        while(curNrnOut != m_vecLayers[1].m_vecNeurons.end())
        {
          err += curNrnOut->m_dError * curNrnOut->m_vecWeight[n];

          ++curNrnOut;
        }

        //now we can calculate the error
        err *= curNrnHid->m_dActivation * (1 - curNrnHid->m_dActivation);

        //for each weight in this neuron calculate the new weight based
        //on the error signal and the learning rate
        for (int w=0; w<m_iNumInputs; ++w)
        {
          //calculate the new weight based on the backprop rules
          curNrnHid->m_vecWeight[w] += err * m_dLearningRate * SetIn[vec][w];
        }

        //and the bias
        curNrnHid->m_vecWeight[m_iNumInputs] += err * m_dLearningRate * BIAS;

        ++curNrnHid;
        ++n;
      }

  }//next input vector
  return true;
}
```

Well, now that you've seen the theory, let's start another fun project to illustrate
how to implement it.

RecognizeIt—Mouse Gesture Recognition

Imagine you're playing a real-time strategy game and instead of having to memorize a zillion shortcut keys for troop attack and defense patterns, all you have to do is make a gesture with your mouse and your soldiers comply by rearranging themselves into the appropriate formation. Make a "V" gesture and your soldiers obediently shuffle into a "V" formation. A few minutes later they become threatened so you make a box-like gesture and they shuffle together with their shields and pikes facing outward. One more sweep of your hand and they divide into two groups. This can be achieved by training a neural network to recognize any gestures the user makes with the mouse, thereby eliminating the usual "click fest" that these sort of games usually require to get anything done. Also, the user need not be tied down to using just the built-in gestures; it's pretty easy to let the users define their own custom gestures too. Cool, huh? Let me tell you how it's done…

> **NOTE**
>
> If you are impatient and want to try the demo program before you read any further, you can find an executable in the Chapter9/Executables/ RecognizeIt V1.0 folder on the CD.
>
> First, you must wait until the network is trained. Then, to make a gesture, press the right mouse button and while it is still depressed make the gesture. Then release the mouse button.
>
> All the pre-defined gestures are shown in Figure 9.7. If the network recognizes your gesture, the name of the gesture will appear in blue in the upper left-hand corner. If the network is unsure, it will have a guess.
>
> The other versions of the RecognizeIt program you can see on the CD utilize improvements and/or alternative methods described later in this chapter.

To solve this problem, we have to:

1. Find a way of representing gestures in such a way that they may be input into a neural network.
2. Train the neural network with some predefined gestures using the method of representation from 1.
3. Figure out a way of knowing when the user is making a gesture and how to record it.
4. Figure out a way of converting the raw recorded mouse data into a format the neural network can recognize.
5. Enable the user to add his own gestures.

Representing a Gesture with Vectors

The first task is to work out how the mouse gesture data can be presented to the ANN. There are a few ways you can do this, but the method I've chosen is to represent the mouse path as a series of 12 vectors. Figure 9.5 shows how the mouse gesture for **Right Arrow** can be represented as a series of vectors.

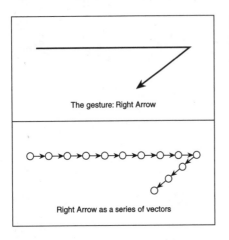

Figure 9.5

Gestures as vectors.

The gesture: Right Arrow

Right Arrow as a series of vectors

To aid training, these vectors are then normalized before becoming part of the training set. Therefore, all the inputs into the network have, as in previous examples, been standardized. This also gives the added advantage, when we come to process the gestures made by the user, of evenly distributing the vectors through the gesture pattern, which will aid the ANN in the recognition process.

The neural network will have the same number of outputs as there are patterns to recognize. If, for example, there are only four predefined gestures the network is required to learn: **Right, Left, Down,** and **Up** as shown in Figure 9.6, the network would have 24 inputs (to represent the 12 vectors) and four outputs.

The training set for these patterns is shown in Table 9.3.

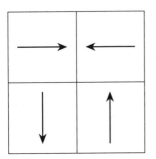

Figure 9.6

*The gestures **Right, Left, Down,** and **Up**.*

Table 9.3   Training Set to Learn the Gestures: Right, Left, Down, and Up

Gesture	Input data	Output data
Right	(1,0, 1,0, 1,0, 1,0, 1,0, 1,0, 1,0, 1,0, 1,0, 1,0, 1,0, 1,0)	(1,0,0,0)
Left	(-1,0, -1,0, -1,0, -1,0, -1,0, -1,0, -1,0, -1,0, -1,0, -1,0, -1,0, -1,0)	(0,1,0,0)
Down	(0,1, 0,1, 0,1, 0,1, 0,1, 0,1, 0,1, 0,1, 0,1, 0,1, 0,1, 0,1)	(0,0,1,0)
Up	(0,-1, 0,-1, 0,-1, 0,-1, 0,-1, 0,-1, 0,-1, 0,-1, 0,-1, 0,-1, 0,-1)	(0,0,0,1)

As you can see, if the user makes the gesture for **Right,** the neural net should output a 1 from the first output neuron and zero from the others. If the gesture is **Down,** the network should output a 1 from the third output neuron and zero from the others. In practice though, these types of "clean" outputs are rarely achieved because the data from the user will be slightly different every time. Even when repeatedly making a simple gesture like the gesture for **Right,** it's almost impossible for a human to draw a perfect straight line every time! Therefore, to determine what pattern the network *thinks* is being presented to it, all the outputs are scanned and the one with the highest output is the most likely candidate. If that neuron is the highest, but only outputting a figure like 0.8, then most likely the gesture is not one that the network recognizes. If the output is above 0.96 (this is the default #defined in the code project as MATCH_TOLERANCE), there is a very good chance that the network recognizes the gesture.

All the training data for the program is encapsulated in a class called CData. This class creates a training set from the predefined patterns (defined as constants at the beginning of CData.cpp) and also handles any alterations to the training set when, for example, a user defined gesture is added. I'm not going to list the source for CData here but please take a look at the source on the CD if you require further clarification of how this class creates a training set. You can find all the source code for this first attempt at gesture recognition in the Chapter9/RecognizeIt v1.0 folder.

Training the Network

Now that you know how to represent a gesture as a series of vectors and have created a training set, it's a piece of cake to train the network. The training set is passed to the CNeuralNet::Train method, which calls the backprop algorithm repeatedly with the training data until the SSE (Sum of the Squared Errors) is below the value #defined as ERROR_THRESHOLD (default is 0.003). Here's what the code looks like:

```cpp
bool CNeuralNet::Train(CData* data, HWND hwnd)
{
  vector<vector<double> > SetIn  = data->GetInputSet();
  vector<vector<double> > SetOut = data->GetOutputSet();

  //first make sure the training set is valid
  if ((SetIn.size()      != SetOut.size())   ||
      (SetIn[0].size()   != m_iNumInputs)    ||
      (SetOut[0].size() != m_iNumOutputs))
  {
    MessageBox(NULL, "Inputs != Outputs", "Error", NULL);

    return false;
  }

  //initialize all the weights to small random values
  InitializeNetwork();

  //train using backprop until the SSE is below the user defined
  //threshold
  while( m_dErrorSum > ERROR_THRESHOLD )
  {
    //return false if there are any problems
    if (!NetworkTrainingEpoch(SetIn, SetOut))
    {
      return false;
    }

    //call the render routine to display the error sum
    InvalidateRect(hwnd, NULL, TRUE);
    UpdateWindow(hwnd);
  }

  m_bTrained = true;

  return true;
}
```

When you load up the source into your own compiler, you should play with the settings for the learning rate. The default value is 0.5. As you'll discover, lower values slow the learning process but are almost always guaranteed to converge. Larger values speed up the process but may get the network trapped in a local minimum. Or, even worse, the network may not converge at all. So, like a lot of the other parameters you've encountered so far in this book, it's worth spending the time tweaking this value to get the right balance.

Figure 9.7 shows all the predefined gestures the network learns when you run the program.

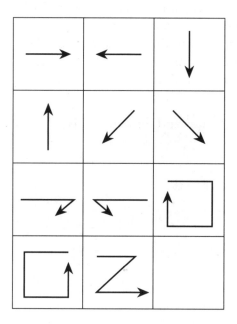

Figure 9.7

Predefined gestures.

Recording and Transforming the Mouse Data

To make a gesture, the user depresses the right mouse button and draws a pattern. The gesture is finished when the user releases the right mouse button. The gesture is simply recorded as a series of POINTS in a std::vector. The POINTS structure is defined in windef.h as:

```
typedef struct tagPOINTS {
    SHORT x;
    SHORT y;
} POINTS;
```

Unfortunately, this vector can be any size at all, depending entirely on how long the user keeps the mouse button depressed. This is a problem because the number of inputs into a neural network is fixed. We, therefore, need to find a way of reducing the number of points in the path to a fixed predetermined size. While we are at it, it would also be useful to "smooth" the mouse path data somewhat to take out any small kinks the user may have made in making the gesture. This will help the user to make more consistent gestures.

As discussed earlier, the example program uses an ANN with 24 inputs representing 12 vectors. To make 12 vectors, you need 13 points (see Figure 9.5), so the raw mouse data has to be transformed in some way to reduce it to those 13 points. The method I've coded does this by iterating through all the points, finding the smallest span between the points and then inserting a new point in the middle of this shortest span. The two end points of the span are then deleted. This procedure reduces the number of points by one. The process is repeated until only the required number of points remains.

The code to do this can be found in the CController class and looks like this:

```
bool CController::Smooth()
{
  //make sure it contains enough points for us to work with
  if (m_vecPath.size() < m_iNumSmoothPoints)
  {
    //return
    return false;
  }

  //copy the raw mouse data
  m_vecSmoothPath = m_vecPath;

  //while there are excess points iterate through the points
  //finding the shortest spans, creating a new point in its place
  //and deleting the adjacent points.
  while (m_vecSmoothPath.size() > m_iNumSmoothPoints)
  {
    double ShortestSoFar = 99999999;

    int PointMarker = 0;

    //calculate the shortest span
```

```
for (int SpanFront=2; SpanFront<m_vecSmoothPath.size()-1; ++SpanFront)
{
  //calculate the distance between these points
  double length =
  sqrt( (m_vecSmoothPath[SpanFront-1].x - m_vecSmoothPath[SpanFront].x) *
        (m_vecSmoothPath[SpanFront-1].x - m_vecSmoothPath[SpanFront].x) +

        (m_vecSmoothPath[SpanFront-1].y - m_vecSmoothPath[SpanFront].y)*
        (m_vecSmoothPath[SpanFront-1].y - m_vecSmoothPath[SpanFront].y));

  if (length < ShortestSoFar)
  {
    ShortestSoFar = length;

    PointMarker = SpanFront;
  }
}


//now the shortest span has been found calculate a new point in the
//middle of the span and delete the two end points of the span
POINTS newPoint;

newPoint.x = (m_vecSmoothPath[PointMarker-1].x +
              m_vecSmoothPath[PointMarker].x)/2;

newPoint.y = (m_vecSmoothPath[PointMarker-1].y +
              m_vecSmoothPath[PointMarker].y)/2;

m_vecSmoothPath[PointMarker-1] = newPoint;

m_vecSmoothPath.erase(m_vecSmoothPath.begin() + PointMarker);
}

return true;
}
```

This method of reducing the number of points is not perfect because it doesn't account for features in a shape, such as corners. Therefore, you'll notice that when you draw a gesture like **Clockwise Square,** the smoothed mouse path will tend to have rounded corners. However, this algorithm is fast, and because the ANN is trained using smoothed data, enough information is retained for the neural network to recognize the patterns successfully.

Adding New Gestures

The program also lets the user define his own gestures. This is simple to do provided the gestures are all sufficiently unique, but I wanted to write a paragraph or two about it because it addresses an important point about adding data to a training set. If you have a trained neural network and you need to add an additional pattern for that network to learn, it's usually a bad idea to try and run the backprop algorithm again for just that additional pattern. When you need to add data, first add it to the existing training set and start afresh. Wipe any existing network you have and completely retrain it with the new training set.

A user may add a new gesture by pressing the L key and then making a gesture as normal. The program will then ask the user if he or she is happy with the entered gesture. If the user is satisfied, the program smoothes the gesture data, adds it to the current training set, and retrains the network from scratch.

The CController Class

Before I move on to some of the improvements you can make to the program, let me show you the header file for the CController class. As usual, the CController class is the class that ties all the other classes together. All the methods for handling, transforming, and testing the mouse data can be found here.

```
class CController
{

private:

  //the neural network
  CNeuralNet*     m_pNet;

  //this class holds all the training data
  CData*          m_pData;

  //the user mouse gesture paths - raw and smoothed
  vector<POINTS> m_vecPath;
```

```
vector<POINTS> m_vecSmoothPath;

//the smoothed path transformed into vectors
vector<double> m_vecVectors;

//true if user is gesturing
bool    m_bDrawing;

//the highest output the net produces. This is the most
//likely candidate for a matched gesture.
double  m_dHighestOutput;

//the best match for a gesture based on m_dHighestOutput
int     m_iBestMatch;

//if the network has found a pattern this is the match
int     m_iMatch;

//the raw mouse data is smoothed to this number of points
int     m_iNumSmoothPoints;

//the number of patterns in the database;
int     m_iNumValidPatterns;

//the current state of the program
mode    m_Mode;
```

The program can be in one of four states: TRAINING when a training epoch is
underway, ACTIVE when the network is trained and the program is ready to recognize gestures, UNREADY when the network is untrained, and finally LEARNING
when the user is entering a custom-defined gesture.

```
//local copy of the application handle
HWND    m_hwnd;

//clears the mouse data vectors
void    Clear();

//given a series of points this method creates a path of
```

```
//normalized vectors
void    CreateVectors();

//preprocesses the mouse data into a fixed number of points
bool    Smooth();

//tests for a match with a pre-learnt gesture by querying the
//neural network
bool    TestForMatch();

//dialog box procedure. A dialog box is spawned when the user
//enters a new gesture.
static BOOL CALLBACK DialogProc(HWND    hwnd,
                                UINT    msg,
                                WPARAM  wParam,
                                LPARAM  lParam);

//this temporarily holds any newly created pattern names
static string m_sPatternName;


public:

  CController(HWND hwnd);

  ~CController();

  //call this to train the network using backprop with the current data
  //set
  bool TrainNetwork();

  //renders the mouse gestures and relevant data such as the number
  //of training epochs and training error
  void Render(HDC &surface, int cxClient, int cyClient);

  //returns whether or not the mouse is currently drawing
  bool Drawing()const{return m_bDrawing;}

  //this is called whenever the user depresses or releases the right
```

```
//mouse button.
//If val is true then the right mouse button has been depressed so all
//mouse data is cleared ready for the next gesture. If val is false a
//gesture has just been completed. The gesture is then either added to
//the current data set or it is tested to see if it matches an existing
//pattern.
//The hInstance is required so a dialog box can be created as a child
//window of the main app instance. The dialog box is used to grab the
//name of any user defined gesture
bool Drawing(bool val, HINSTANCE hInstance);

//clears the screen and puts the app into learning mode, ready to accept
//a user defined gesture
void LearningMode();

//call this to add a point to the mouse path
void AddPoint(POINTS p)
{
  m_vecPath.push_back(p);
}
};
```

Some Useful Tips and Techniques

There are many tips and tricks that enable your network to learn quicker or to help it generalize better, and I'm going to spend the next few pages covering some of the more popular ones.

Adding Momentum

As you've seen, the backprop algorithm attempts to reduce the error of the neural network a little each epoch. You can imagine the network having an error land-scape, similar to the fitness landscapes of genetic algorithms. Each iteration, backprop determines the gradient of the error at the current point in the landscape and attempts to move the error value toward a global minimum. See Figure 9.8.

Unfortunately, most error landscapes are not nearly so smooth and are more likely to represent the curve shown in Figure 9.9. Therefore, if you are not careful, your algorithm can easily get stuck in a local minima.

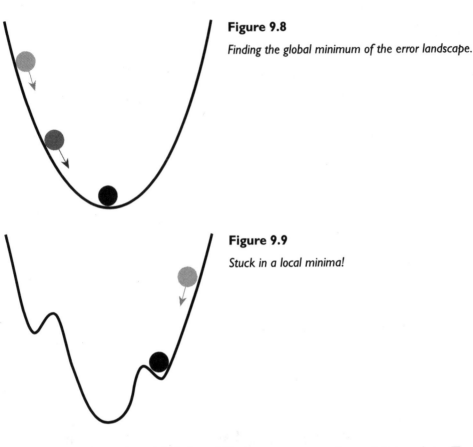

Figure 9.8

Finding the global minimum of the error landscape.

Figure 9.9

Stuck in a local minima!

One way of preventing this is by adding *momentum* to the weight update. To do this, you simply add a fraction of the previous time-step's weight update to the current weight update. This will help the algorithm zip past any small fluctuations in the error landscape, thereby giving a much better chance of finding the global minimum. Using momentum also has the added bonus of reducing the number of epochs it takes to train a network. In this example, momentum reduces the number of epochs from around 24,000 to around 15,000.

The equation shown earlier for the weight update:

$$w_{ij} \mathrel{+}= L \times E_j \times o_i$$

with momentum added becomes:

$$w_{ij} \mathrel{+}= L \times E_j \times o_i + m \times \Delta w_{ij}$$

in which the [CapDelta]w_{ij} is the previous time-step's weight update, and *m* represents the fraction to be added. *m* is typically set to 0.9.

Momentum is pretty easy to implement. The SNeuron structure has to be changed to accommodate another std::vector of doubles, in which the previous time-step's weight updates are stored. Then additional code is required for the backprop training itself. You can find the source code in the folder Chapter9/RecognizeIt v2.0 (with momentum) on the CD.

Overfitting

As you may have realized by now, a neural network is basically a function approximator. Given a training set, the ANN attempts to find the function that will fit the input data to the output data. One of the problems with neural networks is that they can learn to do this too well and lose the ability to generalize. To show you what I mean, imagine a network that is learning to approximate the function that fits the data shown in graph A in Figure 9.10.

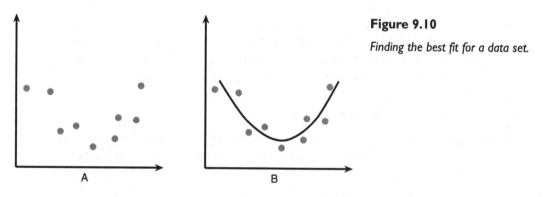

Figure 9.10

Finding the best fit for a data set.

The simplest curve that fits the data is shown in graph B, and this is the curve you ideally want the network to learn. However, if the network is designed incorrectly, you may end up with it *overfitting* the data set. If this is the case, you may end up with it learning a function that describes the curve shown in Figure 9.11.

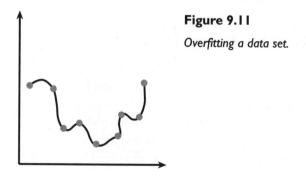

Figure 9.11

Overfitting a data set.

With a network like this, although it's done a great job of fitting the data it has been trained with, it will have great difficulty predicting exactly where any new data presented to it may fit. So what can you do to prevent overfitting? Here are a few techniques you can try:

Minimizing the number of neurons. The first thing you should do is reduce the number of hidden neurons in your network to a minimum. As previously mentioned, there is no rule of thumb for judging the amount; as usual, you'll need to determine it by good old trial and error. I've been using just six hidden units for the RecognizeIt app and I got there by starting off with 12 and reducing the number until the performance started to degrade.

Adding jitter. In this context, *jitter* is not some long-forgotten dance from the '50s, but a way of helping the network to generalize by adding noise (random fluctuations around a mean of zero) to the training data. This prevents the network from fitting any specific data point too closely and therefore, in some situations can help prevent overfitting. The example found in Chapter 9/RecognizeIt v3.0 (with jitter) has a few additional lines of code in the `CNeuralNet::Update` method that adds noise to the input data. The maximum amount of noise that can be added is #defined as `MAX_NOISE_TO_ADD`. However, adding jitter to the mouse gesture application only makes a very small amount of difference. You will find you will get better results with jitter when using large training sets.

Early stopping. Early stopping is another simple technique and is a great one to use when you have a large amount of training data. You split the training data into two sets: a training set and a *validation* set. Then, using a small learning rate and a network with plenty of hidden neurons—there's no need to worry about having too many in this case—train the network using the training set, but this time make periodic tests against the validation set. The idea is to stop the training when the *error from testing against the validation set* begins to increase as opposed to reducing the SSE below a predefined value. This method works well when you have a large enough data set to enable splitting and can be very fast.

The Softmax Activation Function

Some problems, like the mouse gesture application, are *classification* problems. That is to say, given some data, the network's job is to place it into one of several categories. In the example of the RecognizeIt program, the neural network has to decide which category of pattern the user's mouse gestures fall into. So far we've just been choosing the output with the highest value as the one representing the best match. This is fine, but sometimes it's more convenient if the outputs represent a *probability* of the data falling into the corresponding category. To represent a probability, all the outputs must add up to one. To achieve this, a completely different activation function must be used for the output neurons: the *softmax* activation function. It works like this:

For a network with n output units, the activation of output neuron o_i is given by

$$\text{output} = \frac{\exp(w_i x_j)}{\sum_0^n \exp(w_n x_n)}$$

in which $w_i x_i$ is the sum of all the inputs $\times$ weights going into that neuron.

This can be a fairly confusing equation, so let me run through it again to make sure you understand what's going on. To get the output from any particular output neuron, you must first sum all the weights $\times$ inputs for every output neuron in the neural network. Let's call that total A. Once you've done that, to calculate the output, you iterate through each output neuron in turn and divide the exponential of that neuron's A with the sum of the exponentials of all the output neurons' As. And just to make doubly sure, here's what it looks like in code:

```
double expTot = 0;

//first calculate the exp for the sum of the outputs
for (int o=0; o<outputs.size(); ++o)
{
    expTot += exp(outputs[o]);
}

//now adjust each output accordingly
for (o=0; o<outputs.size(); ++o)
{
    outputs[o] = exp(outputs[o])/expTot;
}
```

Got it? Great. If you check the CNeuralNet::Update method in version 4.0 of the RecognizeIt source found in the Chapter9/RecognizeIt v4.0 (softmax) folder on the CD, you'll see how I've altered it to accommodate the softmax activation function.

Although you can use the sum squared error function (SSE), as used previously, a better error function to use when utilizing softmax is the *cross-entropy* error function. You don't have to worry where this equation comes from, just be assured that this is the better error function to apply when your network is designed to produce probabilities. It looks like this:

$$E = \sum_{j=0}^{n} t_j \log y_j$$

Where n is the number of output neurons, t is the target value, and y is the actual output.

Applications of Supervised Learning

As you have learned, supervised techniques are useful whenever you have a series of input patterns that need to be mapped to matching output patterns. Therefore, you can use this technique for anything from Pong to beat'emups and racing games.

As an example, let's say you are working on a racing game and you want your neural network to drive the cars as well as that spotty-chinned games tester your company employs who does nothing but race your cars and discuss Star Trek all day long. You get the guy to drive the car, and this time while he's zipping full blast around the course, you create a training set by recording any relevant data. Each frame (or every N frames), for the input training set, you would record information like:

- Distance to left curb
- Distance to right curb
- Current speed
- Curvature of current track segment
- Curvature of next track segment
- Vector to best driving line

And for the output training set, you would record the driver's responses:

- Amount of steering left or right
- Amount of throttle
- Amount of brake
- Gear change

After a few laps and over a few different courses, you will have amassed enough data to train a neural network to behave in a similar fashion. Given enough data and the correct training, the neural network should be able to generalize what it has learned and handle tracks it has never seen before. Cool, huh?

A Modern Fable

Before I finish this chapter, I'd like to leave you with a little story. Apparently, the story is a true one but I haven't been able to get that confirmed. However, please keep the story in mind when you are training your own neural networks because I'm sure you wouldn't want to make the same mistake as the military <smile>.

Once upon a time, a few Wise Men thought it would be a terrific idea to mount a camera on the side of a tank and continually scan the environment for possible threats, like... well, another bigger tank hiding behind a tree. They thought this would be a great idea because they knew computers were exceptional at doing repetitive tasks. Computers never grow tired or complacent. They never grow bored and they never need a break. Unfortunately, computers are terrible at recognizing things. The Wise Men knew this also, but they also knew about neural networks. They'd heard good things about this newfangled technology and were prepared to spend some serious money on it. And they made it so.

The following day, the Wise Men decreed that two sets of images be made. One set of images were of tanks partially hidden among trees and the other set were of trees alone, standing tall and proud. The Wise Men examined the images and saw that they were good. Half of the images from each set were put away for safe keeping in a darkened room with the door firmly locked and the windows barred—for the Wise Men were big on security.

On the third day, a state-of-the-art mainframe computer was purchased and its towering bulk was lowered by crane into a specially constructed room. One of the Wise Men's underlings flicked a switch and the gigantic machine whirred into life, along with five tons of air conditioning equipment and a state-of-the-art shiny steel coffee machine. A team of incredibly intelligent programmers were hired at great cost and flown in from all the corners of the world. The programmers observed the machine with its many flickering lights, whirring magnetic tapes, and glowing terminals, and saw that it was good.

On the fourth day, the programmers brought forth an artificial neural network according to their kind. After many hours of testing to make sure it was working properly and without bugs, they started to feed the network the images of the tanks and the trees. Each time an image was shown to the network, the machine had to guess if there was a tank among the trees or not. At first, the machine did poorly but the clever programmers punished the machine for its mistakes, and in no time at all it was improving in leaps and bounds. By the end of the fourth day, the network was getting every single answer correct. Life was good.

Although, the coffee, by now had grown thick and rank.

On the morning of the fifth day, the clever programmers double-checked the results and called the Wise Men forth. The Wise Men watched the machine accurately recognizing the tanks and saw that it was good. Then they commanded that the doors of the darkened room be flung open and the remaining images be brought forth. The clever programmers were apprehensive because although they had known this moment would come, they did not know what to expect. Would the neural network perform well or not? It was impossible to say because although they had designed the network, they didn't really have a clue what was happening inside. And so, with trembling hands, the clever programmers fed the machine the new images one by one.

Verily, they were all much relieved and happy to see that every answer was good and much joy was felt in their hearts.

The sixth day dawned and the Wise Men were concerned, for they knew that things never go this well in the world of mortals. And so they decreed that a new set of images be taken and be brought forth with all speed. The new images were presented to the machine, but to their horror the answers were completely random. *"Oh no!"* cried the clever programmers. *"Verily we hath truly made a mighty screw up!"*

One Wise Man pointed his bony index finger at the all-of-a-sudden-not-so-clever-programmers, who promptly vanished in a puff of smoke.

On the seventh and eighth day, and for many more days thereafter, the Wise Men and a newly hired team of clever programmers wondered how it had all gone so wrong. No one could guess until one day an observant programmer noticed that the images with tanks in the initial set of photos were all taken on a cloudy day, whilst the images without the tanks were all taken on a sunny day. The machine had simply learned to distinguish between a sunny day and an overcast one!

Stuff to Try

1. Try adjusting the learning rate and other parameters to see what effect they have on the network training. While you are doing this, make sure you try altering the activation response of the sigmoid function to see how changing the response curve affects the learning.

2. Train a neural network to play Pong. First, figure out a way of training it using a supervised approach. Once you've cracked that, write some code to evolve networks to play Pong as per the last couple of chapters.

3. Train a network to play tic-tac-toe as above.

CHAPTER 10

REAL-TIME EVOLUTION

As soon as we started programming, we found to our surprise that it wasn't as easy to get programs right as we had thought. Debugging had to be discovered. I can remember the exact instant when I realized that a large part of my life from then on was going to be spent in finding mistakes in my own programs.

—*Maurice Wilkes discovers debugging, 1949*

So far, you've learned how to evolve behavior that progresses through a series of epochs. This is fine if it's acceptable to develop the behavior of your game agents offline or via epochs that are undertaken during natural breaks in a game (such as between levels), but now I'm going to show you a simple technique that you can use to evolve genomes *while* the game is being played. This can be used wherever you have a large number of game agents constantly getting destroyed and created. The advantage of this type of evolution is that it can adapt to accommodate varying game dynamics, such as different human players or changes to the game environment it may not have encountered offline. For example, the tank units in your favorite real-time strategy game could learn to adapt their behavior according to the playing style of their opponents.

The technique I'm going to describe is a breeze to implement. In short, to evolve a population online, all you have to do is keep a pool of genomes (the population) stored in a container that is always kept sorted. Individuals used in the game are spawned from this pool. Immediately after an individual is killed off in the game, it's replaced by mutating one of the better performers in the population (chosen from amongst the top 20%, say). In this way, the population doesn't evolve in waves as each epoch is processed, but rather, continuously, in a constant cycle of birth and death. For this reason, this technique requires a fast turnaround of game agents in order to work properly. If your game agents die off at too slow a rate, then it's unlikely they will evolve at a satisfactory pace. If, however, your game agents get killed off swiftly, like in a shoot-em-up or some types of units in real-time strategy games, this method of evolution may be used to good effect.

Brainy Aliens

To illustrate the principle, I'm going to show you how this technique can be used to evolve the motion of the aliens in a Space Invaders-type arcade game.

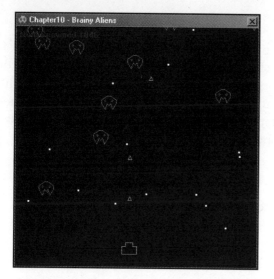

Figure 10.1

Brainy Aliens in action.

I've kept the example simple. There's only a bunch of aliens flying around the screen and their enemy—you. The aliens must learn to stay alive as long as possible. They die if they get shot or if they fly off the top or bottom of the screen. The longer they live, the higher their fitness score.

The program uses two containers of aliens. The first container, a std::multiset, contains a sorted pool of aliens, and the second, a std::vector, contains the invaders that are currently active within the game. See Figure 10.2.

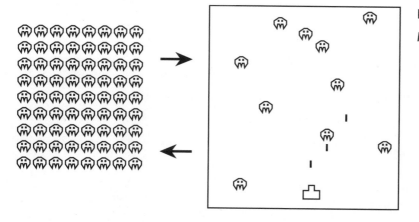

Figure 10.2

Real-time evolution.

When an alien dies, it is removed from the game and, if its fitness score is better than the worst performer in the population, its genomes are added to the pool. Its place in the game is then taken by mutating one of the better performers to date.

Implementation

You can find the source code to this project in the 'Chapter10/Brainy Aliens'
folder. There are three game object classes: CGun, CBullet, and CAlien, as well as the
usual CNeuralNet and CController classes. The CGun and CBullet classes are straightforward, and the comments within the code should be sufficient to understand them,
but I'll describe CAlien and CController in more detail so you understand exactly
how everything works. First, let me show you how the aliens are controlled.

Roswell Revisited: An Alien Brain Autopsy

Before I describe the inner workings of an alien mind, take a quick look at the
definition for the CAlien class.

```
class CAlien
{

private:

  CNeuralNet      m_ItsBrain;

  //its position in the world
  SVector2D       m_vPos;

  SVector2D       m_vVelocity;

  //its scale
  double          m_dScale;

  //its mass
  double          m_dMass;

  //its age (= its fitness)
  int             m_iAge;

  //its bounding box(for collision detection)
  RECT            m_AlienBBox;

  //vertex buffer for the alien's local coordinates
```

```cpp
    vector<SPoint>  m_vecAlienVB;

    //vertex buffer to hold the alien's transformed vertices
    vector<SPoint>  m_vecAlienVBTrans;

    //when set to true a warning is displayed informing of
    //an input size mismatch to the neural net.
    bool            m_bWarning;

    void            WorldTransform();

    //checks for collision with any active bullets. Returns true if
    //a collision is detected
    bool            CheckForCollision(vector<CBullet> &bullets)const;

    //updates the alien's neural network and returns its next action
    action_type  GetActionFromNetwork(const vector<CBullet> &bullets,
                                       const SVector2D       &GunPos);

    //overload '<' used for sorting
    friend bool operator<(const CAlien& lhs, const CAlien& rhs)
    {
        return (lhs.m_iAge > rhs.m_iAge);
    }


public:

    CAlien();

    void Render(HDC &surface, HPEN &GreenPen, HPEN &RedPen);

    //queries the alien's brain and updates it position accordingly
    bool Update(vector<CBullet> &bullets, const SVector2D &GunPos);

    //resets any relevant member variables ready for a new run
    void Reset();

    //this mutates the connection weights in the alien's neural net
```

```
void Mutate();

//-------------------------------------accessor methods
SVector2D    Pos()const{return m_vPos;}
double       Fitness()const{return m_iAge;}
};
```

The architecture of each alien brain is shown in Figure 10.3. By default, there can only be three bullets on the screen at any one time. To detect where these are, an alien's neural network has three pairs of inputs, each representing a vector to a bullet. In addition, each neural network has two inputs representing the vector to the gun turret. If a bullet is inactive (not on the screen), the matching inputs of the neural network also receive a vector to the gun turret.

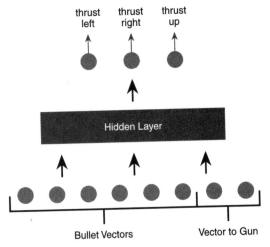

Figure 10.3

Inside an alien brain.

The aliens have mass and are affected by gravity. To move, they can fire thrusters, which blast them up, left, and right. There are four actions an alien can chose from each frame. These are

- Thrust up
- Thrust left
- Thrust right
- Drift

An alien's neural network has three outputs, each one acting like a switch for one of the first three actions shown in the list. To be considered switched on, an output must have an activation greater than 0.9. If more than one output is above 0.9, the highest valued is chosen. If all the switches are off, the alien just drifts with gravity.

The actions are enumerated as the type, `action_type`.

```
enum action_type{thrust_left,
                 thrust_right,
                 thrust_up,
                 drift};
```

For example, the action for the network with the outputs shown on the left in Figure 10.4 would be `thrust_right`, and the action for the network on the right would be `drift`.

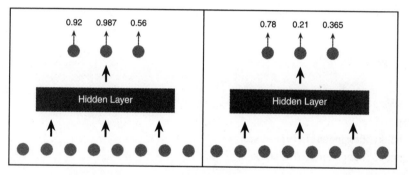

Figure 10.4

Example actions.

Here's what the method to update and receive instructions from the alien brain looks like.

```
action_type CAlien::GetActionFromNetwork(const vector<CBullet> &bullets,
                                         const SVector2D        &GunPos)
{
  //the inputs into the net
  vector<double> NetInputs;

  //This will hold the outputs from the neural net
  static vector<double> outputs(0,3);

  //add in the vector to the gun turret
  int XComponentToTurret = GunPos.x - m_vPos.x;
  int YComponentToTurret = GunPos.y - m_vPos.y;

  NetInputs.push_back(XComponentToTurret);
```

```
NetInputs.push_back(YComponentToTurret);

//now any bullets
for (int blt=0; blt<bullets.size(); ++blt)
{
  if (bullets[blt].Active())
  {

    double xComponent = bullets[blt].Pos().x - m_vPos.x;
    double yComponent = bullets[blt].Pos().y - m_vPos.y;

    NetInputs.push_back(xComponent);
    NetInputs.push_back(yComponent);
  }

  else
  {
    //if a bullet is innactive just input a vector pointing to
    //the gun turret
    NetInputs.push_back(XComponentToTurret);
    NetInputs.push_back(YComponentToTurret);
  }
}

//feed the inputs into the net and get the outputs
outputs = m_ItsBrain.Update(NetInputs);

//this is set if there is a problem with the update
if (outputs.size() == 0)
{
   m_bWarning = true;
}

//determine which action is valid this frame. The highest valued
//output over 0.9. If none are over 0.9 then just drift with
//gravity
```

```
    double BiggestSoFar = 0;

  action_type action = drift;

  for (int i=0; i<outputs.size(); ++i)
  {
    if( (outputs[i] > BiggestSoFar) && (outputs[i] > 0.9))
    {
      action = (action_type)i;

      BiggestSoFar = outputs[i];
    }
  }


  return action;
}
```

Because the program is only responsive at the edges of the sigmoid function's slope, the activation response for the sigmoid function is set lower in params.ini than usual, at 0.2. This makes the response curve much steeper and has the effect of making the networks much more sensitive to a change in the connection weights, which aids speedy evolution.

Now that you know how the neural networks are set up, let me show you how the evolutionary mechanism works.

Alien Evolution

As usual, CController is the class that ties everything together, but this time there is no familiar epoch function. All the spawning and mutation is now handled by the Update method. Before I show you that though, let me talk you through the definition of the CController class.

```
class CController
{
private:

  //the player's gun
  CGun*            m_pGunTurret;
```

The player can move the gun left and right using the cursor keys. To fire bullets, the player uses the space bar. If you examine the CGun class, you will also find a method called AutoGun. This moves the gun erratically left and right and fires at random. Because at the commencement of a run the aliens tend to be pretty stupid, AutoGun is used in conjunction with accelerated time to rapidly spawn aliens until the population reaches the required size (default 200).

```
//the pool of aliens
multiset<CAlien> m_setAliens;
```

This is the pool of genomes from which all the aliens are spawned. A multiset is a STL container that keeps all its elements ordered. See the following sidebar for further details about how multisets are used.

```
//the currently active aliens
vector<CAlien>    m_vecActiveAliens;
```

These are the aliens that are active in the game. When one dies, it is replaced by mutating one of the fitter members of m_setAliens.

```
int               m_iAliensCreatedSoFar;
```

This variable keeps track of all the newly created aliens at the start of a run. Each new alien is first tested for fitness in the game environment and then added to the multiset. When this figure has reached the required population size, aliens can be spawned from the multiset.

```
int               m_iNumSpawnedFromTheMultiset;

//vertex buffer for the stars
vector<SPoint>    m_vecStarVB;

//keeps track of the window size
int               m_cxClient,
                  m_cyClient;

//lets the program run as fast as possible
bool              m_bFastRender;

//custom pens used for drawing the game objects
HPEN              m_GreenPen;
HPEN              m_RedPen;
HPEN              m_GunPen;
```

```
  HPEN           m_BarPen;


  void    WorldTransform(vector<SPoint> &pad);

  CAlien  TournamentSelection();


public:

  CController(int cxClient, int cyClient);

  ~CController();

  //The workhorse of the program. Updates all the game objects and
  //spawns new aliens into the population.
  bool  Update();

  void  Render(HDC &surface);

  //resets all the controller variables and creates a new starting
  //population of aliens, ready for another run
  void  Reset();

  //-----------------------accessor functions
  bool FastRender(){return m_bFastRender;}
};
```

Because sets and multisets are implemented as binary trees, they do not allow direct element access because that could foul up the order of the tree. Instead, you may only access elements using iterators.

Here's an example that inserts ten random integers into a multiset and then outputs the elements to the screen in order.

```cpp
#include <iostream>
#include <set>

using namespace std;

int main()
{
   const int SomeNumbers[10] = {12, 3, 56, 10, 3, 34, 8, 234, 1, 17};

   multiset<int> MySet;

   //first, add the numbers
   for (int i= 0; i<10; ++i)
   {
     MySet.insert(SomeNumbers[i]);
   }

   //create an iterator
   multiset<int>::iterator CurrentElement = MySet.begin();

   //and use it to access the elements
   while (CurrentElement != MySet.end())
   {
     cout  << *CurrentElement << ", ";

     ++CurrentElement;
   }

   return 1;
}
```

When run, the output of this program is

```
1, 3, 3, 8, 10, 12, 17, 34, 56, 234
```

The CController::Update Method

This is the workhorse of the program. After updating the gun turret and the stars, this method iterates through all the aliens kept in m_vecActiveAliens and calls their update function. The CAlien::Update function queries each alien's brain to see what action should be undertaken this time-step and then updates the alien's position accordingly. If the alien has been shot or if it has moved beyond the window boundaries, it's removed from the game and added to the population pool (its fitness is equal to the amount of time it remained alive, measured in ticks). Because a std::multiset is used as the container for the pool, any newly added aliens are automatically inserted into their correctly sorted position (by fitness). If the required population size has been met, the code then deletes the last member—the weakest alien—of the multiset to keep the size of the pool constant.

Now the code must replace the dead alien with a new one. To do this, it uses tournament selection to choose an alien from the best 20% (default value) of the population pool. It then mutates this individual's weights depending on the mutation rate and adds it to m_vecActiveAliens. The size of m_vecActiveAliens is, therefore, always kept constant. The default number of aliens shown on screen at any one time can be set using the parameter CParams::iNumOnScreen.

Take a look at the following code listing which will help clarify your understanding of this process.

> **NOTE**
>
> I have omitted the crossover operator in this program because I wanted to demonstrate that successful evolution still occurs without it and when using this technique, you want your spawning code to run as fast as possible.
>
> In the next chapter, I'll be explaining another reason why omitting the crossover operator may be a good idea when evolving neural nets.

```cpp
bool CController::Update()
{
  //switch the autogun off if enough offspring have been
  //spawned
  if (m_iNumSpawnedFromTheMultiset > CParams::iPreSpawns)
  {
    m_pGunTurret->AutoGunOff();

    m_bFastRender = false;
```

```cpp
  }

  //get update from player for the turret movement
  //and update any bullets that may have been fired
  m_pGunTurret->Update();

  //move the stars
  for (int str=0; str<m_vecStarVB.size(); ++str)
  {
    m_vecStarVB[str].y -= 0.2;

    if (m_vecStarVB[str].y < 0)
    {
      //create a new star
      m_vecStarVB[str].x = RandInt(0, CParams::WindowWidth);
      m_vecStarVB[str].y = CParams::WindowHeight;
    }
  }

  //update the aliens
  for (int i=0; i<m_vecActiveAliens.size(); ++i)
  {

    //if alien has 'died' replace with a new one
    if (!m_vecActiveAliens[i].Update(m_pGunTurret->m_vecBullets,
                            m_pGunTurret->m_vPos))
    {

      //first we need to re-insert into the breeding population so
      //that its fitness score and genes are recorded.
      m_setAliens.insert(m_vecActiveAliens[i]);

      //if the required population size has been reached, delete the
      //worst performer from the multiset
      if (m_setAliens.size() >= CParams::iPopSize)
      {
        m_setAliens.erase(--m_setAliens.end());
      }
```

```
    ++m_iNumSpawnedFromTheMultiset;

    //if early in the run then we are still trying out new aliens
    if (m_iAliensCreatedSoFar <= CParams::iPopSize)
    {
      m_vecActiveAliens[i] = CAlien();

      ++m_iAliensCreatedSoFar;
    }

    //otherwise select from the multiset and apply mutation
    else
    {
      m_vecActiveAliens[i] = TournamentSelection();

      m_vecActiveAliens[i].Reset();

      if (RandFloat() < 0.8)
      {
        m_vecActiveAliens[i].Mutate();
      }
    }
  }
}//next alien

  return true;
}
```

And that's all there is to it! As you will find when you play around with the program, the aliens evolve all sorts of ways of staying alive as long as possible and learn to adapt to your attempts at killing them.

Running the Program

When you run the Brainy Aliens program, it will initially boot up in accelerated time mode. This allows the population of aliens to evolve a little before you get a go at killing them. The default number of pre-spawns is 200 and a blue bar at the bottom of the display indicates the program's progress. At this point, although you can't see it, the autogun is operating, blasting mindlessly away at random. When the blue bar reaches the right hand side of the screen, the program will hand over the control of the gun to you and you'll be able to shoot away to your hearts content.

Table 10.1 shows the default project settings.

Table 10.1   Default Project Settings for Brainy Aliens

Parameters for the Neural Networks

Parameter	Setting
Num hidden layers	1
Num neurons per hidden layer	15
Activation response	0.2

Parameters Affecting Evolution

Parameter	Setting
Mutation rate	0.2
Max mutation perturbation	1
Alien pool size	200
Percent considered fit to spawn	20%
Number of tournament competitors	10
Number of pre-spawns	200

Other Parameters

Parameter	Setting
Bullet speed	4
Max number of displayed aliens	10
Max available bullets	3

Stuff to Try

1. As usual, make sure you experiment with varying amounts of hidden units and layers to observe what effect they have on the performance of the aliens.

2. Evolve separate neuro controllers for each alien for dropping bombs on the gun turret.

3. Experiment with different types of fitness functions.

4. Create a game that has "waves" of aliens. This way you can combine normal GA techniques to breed the population between waves, and you get the best of both worlds!

CHAPTER 11

Evolving Neural Network Topology

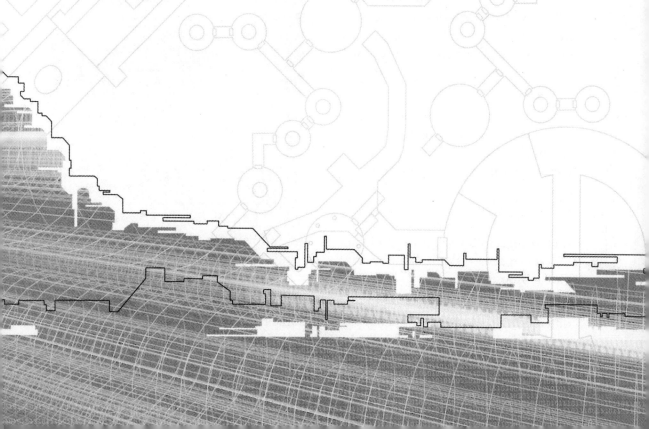

It would appear that we have reached the limits of what it is possible to achieve with computer technology, although one should be careful with such statements, as they tend to sound pretty silly in 5 years time.

—*John Von Neumann 1949*

As you have learned, the architecture—or topology—of a neural network plays an important role in how effective it is. You've also learned that choosing the parameters for that architecture is more of an art than a science and usually involves an awful lot of hands-on tweaking. Although you can develop a "feel" for this, wouldn't it be great if your networks *evolved* to find the best topology along with the network weights? A network that is simple enough to learn whatever it is you want it to learn, yet not so simple that it loses its ability to generalize?

When using an evolutionary algorithm to evolve neural network topology, we can imagine an undulating fitness landscape where each point in search space represents a certain type of architecture. The goal of an EANN (Evolutionary Artificial Neural Network), therefore, is to traverse that landscape as best it can before alighting upon the global optima.

NOTE

This problem has been tackled in a few *non*-evolutionary ways. Researchers have attempted to create networks either *constructively* or *destructively*. A destructive algorithm commences with an oversized ANN with many neurons, layers, and links and attempts to reduce its size by systematically pruning the network during the training process. A constructive process is one that approaches the problem from the opposite end, by starting with a minimal network and adding neurons and links during training. However, these methods have been found to be prone to converging upon local optima and, what's more, they are still usually fairly restrictive in terms of network architecture. That is to say, only a fraction of the full spectrum of possible topologies is usually available for these techniques to explore.

A fair amount of time and thought has been put into this problem by a number of different researchers, and I'm going to spend the first part of this chapter describing some of the many techniques available. The second part of the chapter will be spent describing a simple implementation of what I consider to be one of the better methods.

As with every other problem tackled with evolutionary algorithms, any potential solution has to figure out a way of encoding the networks, a way of assigning fitness scores, and valid operators for performing genome mutation and/or crossover. I say *or* crossover because a few methods dispose with this potentially troublesome operator altogether, preferring to rely entirely on mutation operators to navigate the search space. So before I describe some of the popular EANNs, let me show you why this operator can be so problematic.

The Competing Conventions Problem

One of the main difficulties with encoding candidate networks is called the *competing conventions* problem—sometimes referred to as the structural-functional mapping problem. Simply put, this is where a system of encoding may provide several different ways of encoding networks that exhibit identical functionality. For example, imagine a simple encoding scheme where a network is encoded as the order in which the hidden neurons appear in a layer. Figure 11.1 shows a couple of examples of simple networks.

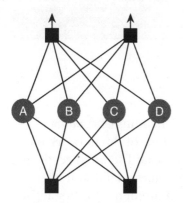

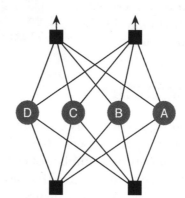

Figure 11.1

A simple encoding scheme.

Network 1   Network 2

Using the simple scheme I've just proposed, Network 1 may be encoded as:

A B C D

and Network 2 as:

D C B A

If you look carefully, you'll notice that, although the order of the neurons is different—and therefore the genomes are different—both networks are essentially identical. They will both exhibit exactly the same behavior. And this is where the problem lies, because if you now attempt to apply a crossover operator to these two networks, lets say at the midpoint of the genome, the resultant offspring will be:

A B B A or **D C C D**

This is an undesirable result because not only have both offspring inherited duplicated neurons, they have also lost 50% of the functionality of their parents and are unlikely to show a performance improvement. (Even if one of them did go on to produce such '70s classics as *Super Trooper* and *Dancing Queen*. <smile>).

Obviously, the larger the networks are, the more frequently this problem is encountered. And this results in a more negative effect on the population of genomes. Consequently, it is a problem researchers do their best to avoid when designing an encoding scheme.

> **NOTE**
>
> There is an alternative camp of opinion to the competing convention problem. Some researchers believe that any steps taken to avoid this problem may actually create more problems. They feel it's preferable to simply ignore the problem and allow the evolutionary process to handle the disposal of the "handicapped" networks, or to ditch the crossover operator altogether and rely entirely on mutation to traverse the search space.

Direct Encoding

There are two methodologies of EANN encoding: *direct* encoding and *indirect* encoding. The former attempts to specify the exact structure of the network by encoding the number of neurons, number of connections, and so on, directly into the genome. The latter makes use of growth rules, which may even define the network structure recursively. I'll be discussing those in a moment, but first let's take a look at some examples of direct encoding.

GENITOR

GENITOR is one of the simplest techniques to be found and is also one of the earliest. A typical version of this algorithm encodes the genome as a bit string. Each gene is encoded with nine bits. The first bit indicates whether there is a connection between neurons and the rest represent the weight (-127 to 127). Given the network shown in Figure 11.2, the genome is encoded as:

110010000   **0**00000010   **1**01000011   **0**00000101   **1**10000011

Where the bit in bold is the connectivity bit.

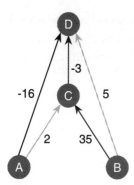

Figure 11.2

GENITOR encoding. The light gray connectivity lines indicate disabled connections.

The disadvantage of this technique, as with many of the encoding techniques developed to date, is that a maximal network topology must be designed for each problem addressed in order for all the potential connectivity to be represented within the genome. Additionally, this type of encoding will suffer from the competing conventions problem.

Binary Matrix Encoding

One popular method of direct encoding is to use a *binary adjacency matrix*. As an example, take a look at the network shown in Figure 11.3.

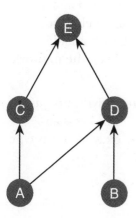

	A	B	C	D	E
A	0	0	1	1	0
B	0	0	0	1	0
C	0	0	0	0	1
D	0	0	0	0	1
E	0	0	0	0	0

Figure 11.3

Binary matrix representation for a simple 5-node network

As you can see, the connectivity for this network can be represented as a matrix of binary digits, where a 1 represents a connection between neurons and a 0 signifies no connection. The chromosome can then be encoded by just assigning each row (or column) of the matrix to a gene. Like so:

00110 00010 00001 00001 00000

However, because the network shown is entirely feedforward, this encoding is wasteful because half the matrix will always contain zeros. Realizing this, we can dispose of one-half of the matrix, as shown in Figure 11.4, and encode the chromosome as:

0110 010 01 1

which, I'm sure you will agree, is much more efficient!

	A	B	C	D	E
A	0	0	1	1	0
B	0	0	0	1	0
C	0	0	0	0	1
D	0	0	0	0	1
E	0	0	0	0	0

Figure 11.4

The adjusted matrix.

Once encoded, the bit strings may be run through a genetic algorithm to evolve the topologies. Each generation, the chromosomes are decoded and the resultant networks initialized with random weights. The networks are then trained and a fitness is assigned. If, for example, backprop is used as the training mechanism, the fitness function could be proportional to the error generated, with an additional penalty as the number of connections increases in order to keep the network size at a minimum.

Obviously, if your training approach can handle any form of connectivity, not just feedforward, then the entire matrix may be represented. Figure 11.5 shows an example of this. A genetic algorithm training approach would be okay with this type of network, but standard backpropagation would not.

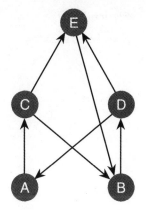

	A	B	C	D	E
A	0	0	1	0	0
B	0	0	0	1	0
C	0	1	0	0	1
D	1	0	0	0	1
E	0	1	0	0	0

Figure 11.5

Network with recurrent connectivity.

Some Related Problems

It has been demonstrated that when using matrix encoding (and some other forms of direct encoding), performance deteriorates as the size of the chromosome increases. Because the size increases in proportion to the square of the number of neurons, performance deteriorates pretty quickly. This is known as the *scalability* problem. Also, the user still has to decide how many neurons will make up the maximal architecture before the matrix can be created. In addition, this type of representation does not address the competing conventions problem discussed earlier. It's very likely, when using this encoding, that two or more chromosomes may display the same functionality. If these chromosomes are then mated, the resultant offspring has little chance of being fitter than either parent. For this reason, it's quite common for the crossover operator to be dismissed altogether with this technique.

Node-Based Encoding

Node-based encoding tackles the problem by encoding all the required information about each neuron in a single gene. For each neuron (or node), its gene will contain information about the other neurons it is connected to and/or the weights associated with those connections. Some node-based encoding schemes even go so far as to specify an associated activation function and learning rate. (A learning rate, don't forget, is used when the network is trained using a gradient descent method like backpropagation.)

Because the code project for this chapter uses node-based encoding, I'll be discussing this technique in a lot more detail later on, but for now, just so you get the idea, let's look at a simple example that encodes just the connectivity of a network.

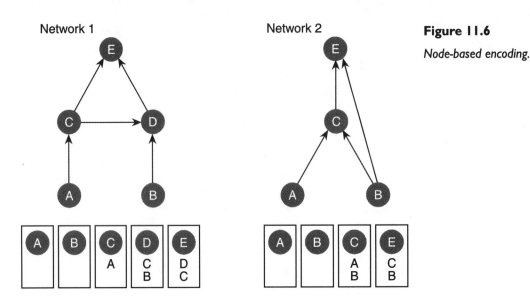

Figure 11.6
Node-based encoding.

Figure 11.6 shows two simple networks and their chromosomes. Each gene contains a node identifier and a list of incoming connections. In code, a simplified gene and genome structure would look something like this:

```
struct SGene
{
  int           NodeID;

  vector<Node*> vecpNodes;
}

struct SGenome
{
  vector<SGene> chromosome;

  double        fitness;
};
```

Mutation operators using this sort of encoding can be varied and are simple to implement. They include such mutations as adding a link, removing a link, adding a node, or removing a node. The crossover operator, however, is a different beast altogether. Care must be taken to ensure valid offspring are produced and that neurons are not left stranded without any incoming and outgoing connections. Figure 11.7 shows the resultant offspring if the two chromosomes from Figure 11.6 are mated after the third gene (the "C" gene).

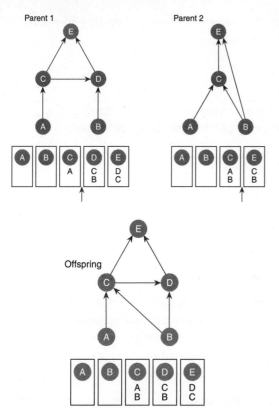

Figure 11.7

Crossover in action.

Once valid genetic algorithm operators have been defined, the neural networks encoded using the described scheme may be evolved as follows (assuming they are trained using a training set in conjunction with a gradient descent algorithm like backpropagation):

1. Create an initial random population of chromosomes.
2. Train the networks and assign a fitness score based on the overall error value of each network (target output – best trained output). It is also feasible to penalize the score as the networks grow in size. This will favor populations with fewer neurons and links.
3. Choose two parents using your favorite selection technique (fitness proportionate, tournament, and so on).
4. Use the crossover operator where appropriate.
5. Use the mutation operator/s where appropriate.
6. Repeat Steps 3,4, and 5 until a new population is created.
7. Go to Step 2 and keep repeating until a satisfactory network is evolved.

Later in the chapter, I'll be showing you how to use node-based encoding to evolve the topology *and* the connection weights at the same time.

Path-Based Encoding

Path-based encoding defines the structure of a neural network by encoding the routes from each input neuron to each output neuron. For example, given the network described by Figure 11.8, the paths are:

$$1 \rightarrow A \rightarrow C \rightarrow 3$$

$$1 \rightarrow D \rightarrow B \rightarrow 4$$

$$1 \rightarrow D \rightarrow C \rightarrow 3$$

$$2 \rightarrow D \rightarrow C \rightarrow 3$$

$$2 \rightarrow D \rightarrow B \rightarrow 4$$

Because each path always begins with an input neuron and always ends with an output neuron, this type of encoding guarantees there are no useless neurons referred to in the chromosome. The operator used for recombination is two-point crossover. (This ensures the chromosomes are always bound with an input and output neuron). Several mutation operators are typically used:

- Create a new path and insert into the chromosome.
- Choose a section of path and delete.
- Select a path segment and insert a neuron.
- Select a path segment and remove a neuron.

Because the networks defined by this type of encoding are not restricted to feedforward networks (links can be recurrent), a training approach such as genetic algorithms must be used to determine the ideal connection weights.

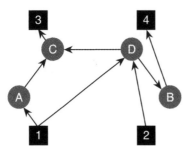

Figure 11.8

Path-based encoding.

Indirect Encoding

Indirect encoding methods more closely mimic the way genotypes are mapped to phenotypes in biological systems and typically result in more compact genomes. Each gene in a biological organism does not give rise to a single physical feature; rather, the interactions between different permutations of genes are expressed. Indirect encoding techniques try to emulate this mechanism by applying a series of *growth rules* to a chromosome. These rules often specify many connections simultaneously and may even be applied recursively. Let's take a look at a couple of these techniques, so you get a feel for how they can work.

Grammar-Based Encoding

This type of encoding uses a series of developmental rules that can be expressed as a type of grammar. The grammar consists of a series of left-hand side symbols (LHS) and right-hand side symbols (RHS). Whenever a LHS symbol is seen by the development process, it's replaced by a number of RHS symbols. The development process starts off with a *start symbol* (a LHS symbol) and uses one of the production rules to create a new set of symbols. Production rules are then applied to these symbols until a set of *terminal symbols* has been reached. At this point, the development process stops and the terminal symbols are expressed as a phenotype.

If you're anything like me, that last paragraph probably sounded like gobbledygook! This is a difficult idea to understand at first, and it's best illustrated with diagrams. Take a look at Figure 11.9, which shows an example of a set of production rules.

$$S \rightarrow \begin{matrix} A & B \\ C & D \end{matrix}$$

Figure 11.9

Example production rules for grammar-based encoding.

$$A \rightarrow \begin{matrix} c & p \\ a & c \end{matrix} \quad B \rightarrow \begin{matrix} a & a \\ a & e \end{matrix} \quad C \rightarrow \begin{matrix} a & a \\ a & a \end{matrix} \quad D \rightarrow \begin{matrix} a & a \\ a & b \end{matrix}$$

$$a \rightarrow \begin{matrix} 0 & 0 \\ 0 & 0 \end{matrix} \quad b \rightarrow \begin{matrix} 0 & 0 \\ 0 & 1 \end{matrix} \quad c \rightarrow \begin{matrix} 1 & 0 \\ 0 & 1 \end{matrix} \quad e \rightarrow \begin{matrix} 0 & 1 \\ 0 & 1 \end{matrix} \quad p \rightarrow \begin{matrix} 1 & 1 \\ 1 & 1 \end{matrix}$$

The **S** is the start symbol and the **1**s and **0**s are terminal symbols. Now examine Figure 11.10 to see how these rules are used to replace the start symbol **S** with more symbols in the grammar, and then how these symbols in turn are replaced by more symbols until the terminal symbols have been reached. As you can clearly see, what we have ended up with is a binary matrix from which a phenotype can be constructed. Cool, huh?

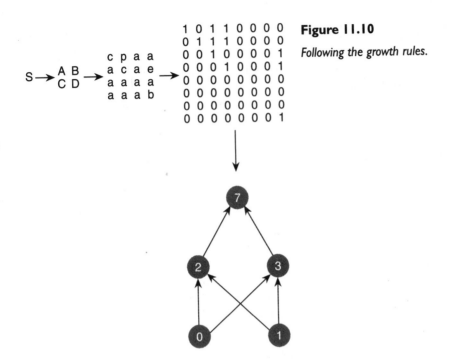

Figure 11.10

Following the growth rules.

A genetic algorithm is used to evolve the growth rules. Each rule can be expressed in the chromosome by four positions corresponding to the four symbols in the RHS of the rule. The actual position (its loci) of the rule along the length of the chromosome determines its LHS. The number of non-terminal symbols can be in any range. The inventors of this technique used the symbols **A** through **Z** and **a** through **p.** The rules that had terminal symbols as their RHS were predefined, so the chromosome only had to encode the rules consisting of non-terminal symbols. Therefore, the chromosome for the example shown in Figure 11.10 would be:

ABCD cpac aaae aaaa aaab

where the first four positions correspond to the start symbol **S**, the second four to the LHS symbol **A,** and so on.

Bi-Dimensional Growth Encoding

This is a rather unusual type of encoding. The neurons are represented by having a fixed position in two-dimensional space, and the algorithm uses rules to actually *grow* axons, like tendrils reaching through the space. A connection is made when an axon touches another neuron. This is definitely a method best illustrated with a diagram, so take a look at Figure 11.11 to see what's going on.

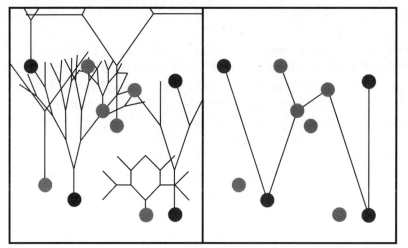

Figure 11.11

Axons growing outward from neurons located in 2D space.

The left-hand side of Figure 11.11 shows the neurons with all their axons growing outward, and the right-hand side shows where connections have been established.

The designers of this technique use a genome encoding which consists of 40 blocks, each representing a neuron. There are five blocks at the beginning of the genome to represent input neurons, five at the end to represent output neurons, and the remaining thirty are used as hidden neurons.

Each block has eight genes.

- Gene1 determines if the neuron is present or not.
- Gene2 is the X position of the neuron in 2D space.
- Gene3 is the Y position.
- Gene4 is the branching angle of the axon growth rule. Each time the axon divides, it divides using this angle.
- Gene5 is the segment length of each axon.
- Gene6 is the connection weight.
- Gene7 is the bias.
- Gene8 is a neuron type gene. This gene in the original experiment was used to determine which input the input neuron represented.

As you can imagine, this technique is tricky to implement and also pretty slow to evolve. So, although it's interesting, it's not really of much practical use.

And that ends your whistle-stop tour of encoding techniques. Next, I'll show you a fantastic way of using node-based encoding to grow your networks from scratch.

NEAT

NEAT is short for *Neuro Evolution of Augmenting Topologies* and has been developed by Kenneth Stanley Owen and Risto Miikkulainen at the University of Texas. It uses node-based encoding to describe the network structure and connection weights, and has a nifty way of avoiding the competing convention problem by utilizing the historical data generated when new nodes and links are created. NEAT also attempts to keep the size of the networks it produces to a minimum by starting the evolution using a population of networks of minimal topology and adding neurons and connections throughout the run. Because nature works in this way—by increasing the complexity of organisms over time—this is an attractive solution and is partly the reason I've chosen to highlight this technique in this chapter.

There's quite a bit of source code required to implement this concept, so the related code is listed as I describe each part of the NEAT paradigm. This way (if I do it in the proper order <smile>), the source will help to reinforce the textual explanations and help you to grasp the concepts quickly. You can find all the source code for this chapter in the Chapter11/NEAT Sweepers folder on the CD.

First, let me describe how the networks are encoded.

The NEAT Genome

The NEAT genome structure contains a list of *neuron genes* and a list of *link genes*. A link gene, as you may have guessed, contains information about the two neurons it is connected to, the weight attached to that connection, a flag to indicate whether the link is enabled, a flag to indicate if the link is recurrent, and an *innovation* number (more on this in a moment). A neuron gene describes that neuron's function within the network—whether it be an input neuron, an output neuron, a hidden neuron, or a bias neuron. Each neuron gene also possesses a unique identification number.

Figure 11.12 shows the gene lists for a genome describing a simple network.

SLinkGene

The link gene structure is called SLinkGene and can be found in genes.h. Its definition is listed here:

```
struct SLinkGene
{
   //the IDs of the two neurons this link connects
```

Weight:	1.2	Weight:	-3	Weight:	0.7	Weight:	-2.1	Weight:	1.1	Weight:	0.8	Weight:	-1
From:	1	From:	1	From:	2	From:	3	From:	3	From:	4	From:	5
To:	3	To:	4	To:	4	To:	4	To:	5	To:	5	To:	3
Enabled:	Y	Enabled:	Y	Enabled:	Y	Enabled:	Y	Enabled:	N	Enabled:	Y	Enabled:	Y
Recurrent:	N	Recurrent:	N	Recurrent:	N	Recurrent:	N	Recurrent:	N	Recurrent:	N	Recurrent:	Y
Innovation:	1	Innovation:	6	Innovation:	2	Innovation:	8	Innovation:	3	Innovation:	4	Innovation:	7

Link Genes

Figure 11.12

Encoding a network the NEAT way.

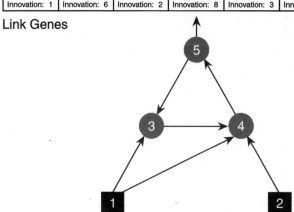

ID: 1	ID: 2	ID: 3	ID: 4	ID: 5
Type: input	Type: input	Type: hidden	Type: hidden	Type: output

Neuron Genes

```
int      FromNeuron,
         ToNeuron;

double  dWeight;

//flag to indicate if this link is currently enabled or not
bool    bEnabled;

//flag to indicate if this link is recurrent or not
bool     bRecurrent;

//I'll be telling you all about this value shortly
int      InnovationID;

SLinkGene(){}

SLinkGene(int    in,
          int    out,
```

```
                   bool    enable,
                   int     tag,
                   double w,
                   bool    rec = false):bEnabled(enable),
                                        InnovationID(tag),
                                        FromNeuron(in),
                                        ToNeuron(out),
                                        dWeight(w),
                                        bRecurrent(rec)
  {}


  //overload '<' used for sorting(we use the innovation ID as the criteria)
  friend bool operator<(const SLinkGene& lhs, const SLinkGene& rhs)
  {
    return (lhs.InnovationID < rhs.InnovationID);
  }
};
```

SNeuronGene

The neuron gene structure is called SNeuronGene and is found in genes.h. Here is its definition:

```
struct SNeuronGene
{
  //its identification number
  int        iID;

  //its type
  neuron_type NeuronType;
```

This is an enumerated type. The values are input, hidden, bias, output, and none. You will see how the none type is used when I discuss innovations in the next section.

```
  //is it recurrent?
  bool       bRecurrent;
```

A *recurrent neuron* is defined in NEAT as a neuron with a connection that loops back on itself. See Figure 11.13

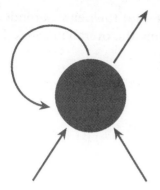

Figure 11.13

A neuron with two incoming links: an outgoing link and a looped recurrent link.

```
//sets the curvature of the sigmoid function
double    dActivationResponse;
```

In this implementation, the sigmoid function's activation response is also evolved separately for each neuron.

```
//position in network grid
double    dSplitY, dSplitX;
```

If you imagine a neural network laid out on a 2D grid, it's useful to know the coordinates of each neuron on that grid. Among other things, this information can be used to render the network to the display as a visual aid for the user.

When a genome is first constructed, all the neurons are assigned a SplitX and a SplitY value. I'll just stick to discussing the SplitY value for now, but the SplitX value is calculated in a similar way. Each input neuron is assigned a SplitY value of 0 and each output neuron a value of 1. When a neuron is added, it effectively splits a link, and so the new neuron is assigned a SplitY value halfway between its two neighbors. Figure 11.14 should help clarify this.

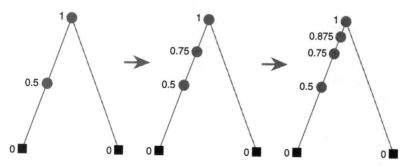

Figure 11.14

Some example SplitY *depths.*

As well as being used to calculate the display coordinates for the network render routine, this information is also invaluable for calculating the overall network depth and for determining if a newly created link is recurrent.

```
SNeuronGene(neuron_type type,
            int        id,
            double     y,
            double     x,
            bool       r = false):iID(id),
                                  NeuronType(type),
                                  bRecurrent(r),
                                  pNeuronMarker(NULL),
                                  dSplitY(y),
                                  dSplitX(x)
    {}
};
```

CGenome

Here's the definition of the genome class. There will be some methods and members you will not understand the purpose of just yet, but just take a quick glance at the class for now and move onto the next section.

(Please note, I have omitted the accessor methods for the sake of brevity).

```
class CGenome
{

private:

  //its identification number
  int                 m_GenomeID;

  //all the neurons which make up this genome
  vector<SNeuronGene>  m_vecNeurons;

  //and all the links
  vector<SLinkGene>    m_vecLinks;

  //pointer to its phenotype
```

```
CNeuralNet*              m_pPhenotype;


  //its raw fitness score
  double                 m_dFitness;


  //its fitness score after it has been placed into a
  //species and adjusted accordingly
  double                 m_dAdjustedFitness;


  //the number of offspring this individual is required to spawn
  //for the next generation
  double                 m_dAmountToSpawn;


  //keep a record of the number of inputs and outputs
  int                    m_iNumInputs,
                         m_iNumOutPuts;


  //keeps a track of which species this genome is in (only used
  //for display purposes)
  int                    m_iSpecies;


  //returns true if the specified link is already part of the genome
  bool    DuplicateLink(int NeuronIn, int NeuronOut);


  //given a neuron id this function just finds its position in
  //m_vecNeurons
  int     GetElementPos(int neuron_id);


  //tests if the passed ID is the same as any existing neuron IDs. Used
  //in AddNeuron
  bool    AlreadyHaveThisNeuronID(const int ID);



public:


  CGenome();


  //this constructor creates a minimal genome where there are output &
  //input neurons and every input neuron is connected to each output neuron
```

```
CGenome(int id, int inputs, int outputs);

//this constructor creates a genome from a vector of SLinkGenes
//a vector of SNeuronGenes and an ID number
CGenome(int                    id,
        vector<SNeuronGene>    neurons,
        vector<SLinkGene>      genes,
        int                    inputs,
        int                    outputs);


~CGenome();

//copy constructor
CGenome(const CGenome& g);

//assignment operator
CGenome& operator =(const CGenome& g);

//create a neural network from the genome
CNeuralNet*      CreatePhenotype(int depth);

//delete the neural network
void             DeletePhenotype();

//add a link to the genome dependent upon the mutation rate
void             AddLink(double      MutationRate,
                         double      ChanceOfRecurrent,
                         CInnovation &innovation,
                         int         NumTrysToFindLoop,
                         int         NumTrysToAddLink);

//and a neuron
void             AddNeuron(double      MutationRate,
                           CInnovation &innovation,
                           int         NumTrysToFindOldLink);

//this function mutates the connection weights
void             MutateWeights(double  mut_rate,
```

```
                        double   prob_new_mut,
                        double   dMaxPertubation);

  //perturbs the activation responses of the neurons
  void                MutateActivationResponse(double mut_rate,
                                              double MaxPertubation);

  //calculates the compatibility score between this genome and
  //another genome
  double              GetCompatibilityScore(const CGenome &genome);

  void                SortGenes();

  //overload '<' used for sorting. From fittest to poorest.
  friend bool operator<(const CGenome& lhs, const CGenome& rhs)
  {
    return (lhs.m_dFitness > rhs.m_dFitness);
  }
};
```

Operators and Innovations

Now that you've seen how a network structure is encoded, let's have a look at the ways a genome may be mutated. There are four mutation operators in use in this implementation of NEAT: a mutation to add a link gene to the genome, a mutation to add a neuron gene, a mutation for perturbing the connection weights, and a mutation that can alter the response curve of the activation function for each neuron. The connection weight mutation works very similarly to the mutation operators you've seen in the rest of the book, so I'll not show you the code. It simply steps through the connection weights and perturbs each one within predefined limits based on a mutation rate. There is one difference however, this time there is a probability the weight is *replaced with a completely new weight*. The chance of this occurring is set by the parameter dProbabilityWeightReplaced.

An *innovation* occurs whenever new structure is added to a genome, either by adding a link gene or by adding a neuron gene, and is simply a record of that change. A global database of all the innovations is maintained—each innovation having its own unique identification number. Each time a link or neuron addition occurs, the database is referenced to see if that innovation has been previously created. If it has, then the new gene is assigned the existing innovation ID number. If not, a new innovation is created, added to the database, and the gene is tagged with the newly created innovation ID.

As an example, imagine you are evolving a network that has two inputs and one output. The network on the left of Figure 11.15 describes the basic structure each member of the population possesses at the commencement of the run. The network on the right shows the result of a mutation that adds a neuron to the network. When neuron 4 is added, three innovations are created: an innovation for the neuron, and innovations for each of the new connections between neurons 1-4 and 4-3. (The old link gene between neurons 1 and 3 still exists in the genome, but it is disabled).

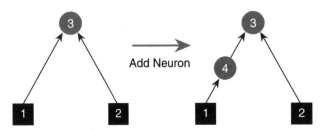

Figure 11.15

Mutation to add a neuron.

Each innovation is recorded in a SInnovation structure. The definition of this structure looks like this:

```
struct SInnovation
{
    //new neuron or new link?
    innov_type   InnovationType;

    int          InnovationID;

    int          NeuronIn;
    int          NeuronOut;

    int          NeuronID;

    neuron_type NeuronType;

    /*constructors and extraneous members omitted*/
};
```

The innovation type can be either new_neuron or new_link. You can find the definitions for SInnovation and the class CInnovation, which keeps track of all the innovations, in the file CInnovation.h.

Because NEAT grows structure by adding neurons and links, all the genomes in the initial population start off representing identical minimal topologies (but with different connection weights). When the genomes are created, the program automatically defines innovations for all the starting neurons and connections. As a result, the innovation database prior to the mutation shown in Figure11.15 will look a little like Table 11.1.

Input and output neurons are assigned a value of -1 for the in and out values to avoid confusion. Similarly, new links are assigned a neuron ID of -1 (because they're not neurons! <smile>).

After the addition of neuron 4, shown in Figure 11.15, the innovation database will have grown to include the new innovations shown in Table 11.2.

If at any time in the future a different genome stumbles across this identical mutation (adding neuron number 4), the innovation database is referenced and the correct innovation ID is assigned to the newly created gene. In this way, the genes contain a historical record of any structural changes. This information is invaluable for designing a valid crossover operator, as you shall see shortly.

Let me take you through the code for the AddLink and AddNeuron mutation operators.

Table 11.1 Innovations Before the Neuron Addition

Innovation ID	Type	In	Out	Neuron ID	Neuron Type
1	new_neuron	-1	-1	1	input
2	new_neuron	-1	-1	2	input
3	new_neuron	-1	-1	3	output
4	new_link	1	3	-1	none
5	new_link	2	3	-1	none

Table 11.2 Innovations After the Neuron Addition

Innovation ID	Type	In	Out	Neuron ID	Neuron Type
1	new_neuron	-1	-1	1	input
2	new_neuron	-1	-1	2	input
3	new_neuron	-1	-1	3	output
4	new_link	1	3	-1	none
5	new_link	2	3	-1	none
6	new_neuron	1	3	4	hidden
7	new_link	1	4	-1	none
8	new_link	4	3	-1	none

CGenome::AddLink

This operator adds one of three different kinds of links:

- A forward link
- A recurrent link
- A looped recurrent link

Figure 11.16 shows an example of each type of link.

Here's the code for adding links to genomes. I've added additional comments where necessary.

```
void CGenome::AddLink(double      MutationRate,
                      double      ChanceOfLooped,
                      CInnovation &innovation, //the database of innovations
                      int         NumTrysToFindLoop,
                      int         NumTrysToAddLink)
{
  //just return dependent on the mutation rate
  if (RandFloat() > MutationRate) return;

  //define holders for the two neurons to be linked. If we find two
  //valid neurons to link these values will become >= 0.
```

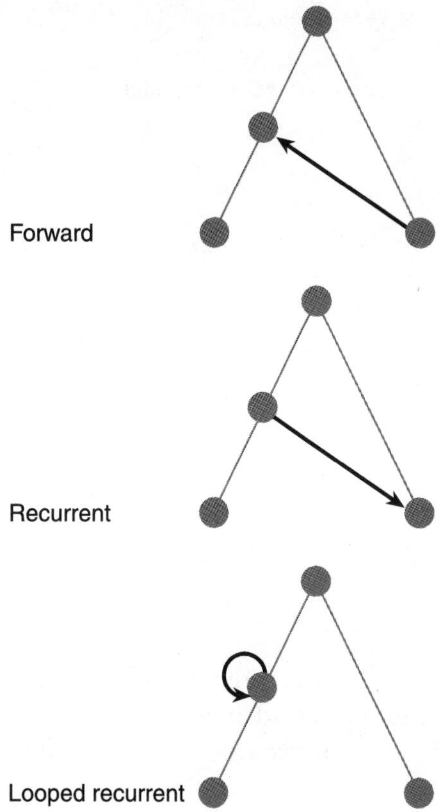

Figure 11.16

Different types of links.

Forward

Recurrent

Looped recurrent

```
int ID_neuron1 = -1;
int ID_neuron2 = -1;

//flag set if a recurrent link is selected to be added
bool bRecurrent = false;

//first test to see if an attempt should be made to create a
//link that loops back into the same neuron
if (RandFloat() < ChanceOfLooped)
{
  //YES: try NumTrysToFindLoop times to find a neuron that is not an
  //input or bias neuron and does not already have a loopback
  //connection
  while(NumTrysToFindLoop--)
  {
    //grab a random neuron
```

```
            int NeuronPos = RandInt(m_iNumInputs+1, m_vecNeurons.size()-1);

            //check to make sure the neuron does not already have a loopback
            //link and that it is not an input or bias neuron
            if (!m_vecNeurons[NeuronPos].bRecurrent &&
               (m_vecNeurons[NeuronPos].NeuronType != bias) &&
               (m_vecNeurons[NeuronPos].NeuronType != input))
            {
              ID_neuron1 = ID_neuron2 = m_vecNeurons[NeuronPos].iID;

              m_vecNeurons[NeuronPos].bRecurrent = true;

              bRecurrent = true;

              NumTrysToFindLoop = 0;
            }
          }
        }
```

First, the code checks to see if there is a chance of a looped recurrent link being added. If so, then it attempts NumTrysToFindLoop times to find an appropriate neuron. If no neuron is found, the program continues to look for two unconnected neurons.

```
      else
      {
        //No: try to find two unlinked neurons. Make NumTrysToAddLink
        //attempts
        while(NumTrysToAddLink--)
        {
```

Because some networks will already have existing connections between all its available neurons, the code has to make sure it doesn't enter an infinite loop when it tries to find two unconnected neurons. To prevent this from happening, the program only tries NumTrysToAddLink times to find two unlinked neurons. This value is set in CParams.cpp.

```
          //choose two neurons, the second must not be an input or a bias
          ID_neuron1 = m_vecNeurons[RandInt(0, m_vecNeurons.size()-1)].iID;

          ID_neuron2 =
```

```
          m_vecNeurons[RandInt(m_iNumInputs+1, m_vecNeurons.size()-1)].iID;

       if (ID_neuron2 == 2)
       {
          continue;
       }

       //make sure these two are not already linked and that they are
       //not the same neuron
       if ( !( DuplicateLink(ID_neuron1, ID_neuron2) ||
               (ID_neuron1 == ID_neuron2)))
       {
          NumTrysToAddLink = 0;
       }

       else
       {
          ID_neuron1 = -1;
          ID_neuron2 = -1;
       }
     }
   }

 //return if unsuccessful in finding a link
 if ( (ID_neuron1 < 0) || (ID_neuron2 < 0) )
 {
    return;
 }

 //check to see if we have already created this innovation
 int id = innovation.CheckInnovation(ID_neuron1, ID_neuron2, new_link);
```

Here, the code examines the innovation database to see if this link has already been discovered by another genome. CheckInnovation returns either the ID number of the innovation or, if the link is a new innovation, a negative value.

```
 //is this link recurrent?
 if (m_vecNeurons[GetElementPos(ID_neuron1)].dSplitY >
     m_vecNeurons[GetElementPos(ID_neuron2)].dSplitY)
```

```
{
    bRecurrent = true;
}
```

Here, the split values for the two neurons are compared to see if the link feeds forward or backward.

```
if ( id < 0)
{
    //we need to create a new innovation
    innovation.CreateNewInnovation(ID_neuron1, ID_neuron2, new_link);

    //now create the new gene
    int id = innovation.NextNumber() - 1;
```

If the program enters this section of code, then the innovation is a new one. Before the new gene is created, the innovation is added to the database and an identification number is retrieved. The new gene will be tagged with this identification number.

```
    SLinkGene NewGene(ID_neuron1,
                      ID_neuron2,
                      true,
                      id,
                      RandomClamped(),
                      bRecurrent);

    m_vecLinks.push_back(NewGene);
}

else
{
    //the innovation has already been created so all we need to
    //do is create the new gene using the existing innovation ID
    SLinkGene NewGene(ID_neuron1,
                      ID_neuron2,
                      true,
                      id,
                      RandomClamped(),
                      bRecurrent);

    m_vecLinks.push_back(NewGene);
```

```
    }

    return;
}
```

CGenome::AddNeuron

To add a neuron to a network, first a link must be chosen and then disabled. Two new links are then created to join the new neuron to its neighbors. See Figure 11.17.

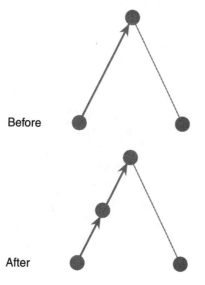

Figure 11.17

Adding a neuron to a network.

Before

After

This means that every time a neuron is added, *three* innovations are created (or repeated if they have already been discovered): one for the neuron gene and two for the connection genes.

```
void CGenome::AddNeuron(double      MutationRate,
                        CInnovation &innovations, //the innovation database
                        int         NumTrysToFindOldLink)
{
  //just return dependent on mutation rate
  if (RandFloat() > MutationRate) return;

  //if a valid link is found into which to insert the new neuron
  //this value is set to true.
```

```cpp
  bool bDone = false;

  //this will hold the index into m_vecLinks of the chosen link gene
  int   ChosenLink = 0;

  //first a link is chosen to split. If the genome is small the code makes
  //sure one of the older links is split to ensure a chaining effect does
  //not occur. Here, if the genome contains less than 5 hidden neurons it
  //is considered to be too small to select a link at random.
  const int SizeThreshold = m_iNumInputs + m_iNumOutPuts + 5;

  if (m_vecLinks.size() < SizeThreshold)
  {
    while(NumTrysToFindOldLink--)
    {
      //choose a link with a bias towards the older links in the genome
      ChosenLink = RandInt(0, NumGenes()-1-(int)sqrt(NumGenes()));

      //make sure the link is enabled and that it is not a recurrent link
      //or has a bias input
      int FromNeuron = m_vecLinks[ChosenLink].FromNeuron;

      if ( (m_vecLinks[ChosenLink].bEnabled)    &&
           (!m_vecLinks[ChosenLink].bRecurrent) &&
           (m_vecNeurons[GetElementPos(FromNeuron)].NeuronType != bias))
      {
        bDone = true;

        NumTrysToFindOldLink = 0;
      }
    }

    if (!bDone)
    {
      //failed to find a decent link
      return;
    }
  }
```

Early on in the development of the networks, a problem can occur where the same link is split repeatedly creating a chaining effect, as shown in Figure 11.18.

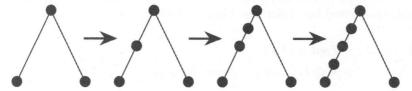

Figure 11.18

The chaining effect.

Obviously, this is undesirable, so the following code checks the number of neurons in the genome to see if the structure is below a certain size threshold. If it is, measures are taken to ensure that older links are selected in preference to newer ones.

```
else
{
  //the genome is of sufficient size for any link to be acceptable
  while (!bDone)
  {
    ChosenLink = RandInt(0, NumGenes()-1);

    //make sure the link is enabled and that it is not a recurrent link
    //or has a BIAS input
    int FromNeuron = m_vecLinks[ChosenLink].FromNeuron;

    if ( (m_vecLinks[ChosenLink].bEnabled) &&
         (!m_vecLinks[ChosenLink].bRecurrent) &&
         (m_vecNeurons[GetElementPos(FromNeuron)].NeuronType != bias))
    {
      bDone = true;
    }
  }
}

//disable this gene
m_vecLinks[ChosenLink].bEnabled = false;

//grab the weight from the gene (we want to use this for the weight of
//one of the new links so the split does not disturb anything the
//NN may have already learned
double OriginalWeight = m_vecLinks[ChosenLink].dWeight;
```

When a link is disabled and two new links are created, the old weight from the disabled link is used as the weight for one of the new links, and the weight for the other link is set to 1. In this way, the addition of a neuron creates as little disruption as possible to any existing learned behavior. See Figure 11.19.

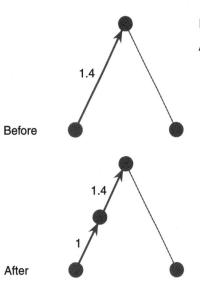

Figure 11.19

Assigning weights to the new link genes.

1.4

Before

1.4

1

After

```
//identify the neurons this link connects
int from =  m_vecLinks[ChosenLink].FromNeuron;
int to    = m_vecLinks[ChosenLink].ToNeuron;

//calculate the depth and width of the new neuron. We can use the depth
//to see if the link feeds backwards or forwards
double NewDepth = (m_vecNeurons[GetElementPos(from)].dSplitY +
                  m_vecNeurons[GetElementPos(to)].dSplitY) /2;

double NewWidth = (m_vecNeurons[GetElementPos(from)].dSplitX +
                  m_vecNeurons[GetElementPos(to)].dSplitX) /2;

//Now to see if this innovation has been created previously by
//another member of the population
int id = innovations.CheckInnovation(from,
                          to,
```

```
                              new_neuron);
```

```
/*it is possible for NEAT to repeatedly do the following:

    1. Find a link. Lets say we choose link 1 to 5
    2. Disable the link,
    3. Add a new neuron and two new links
    4. The link disabled in Step 2 may be re-enabled when this genome
       is recombined with a genome that has that link enabled.
    5  etc etc


Therefore, the following checks to see if a neuron ID is already being used.
If it is, the function creates a new innovation for the neuron. */
if (id >= 0)
{
  int NeuronID = innovations.GetNeuronID(id);

  if (AlreadyHaveThisNeuronID(NeuronID))
  {
    id = -1;
  }
}
```

AlreadyHaveThisNeuronID returns true if (you guessed it) the genome already has a
neuron with an identical ID. If this is the case, then a new innovation needs to be
created, so id is reset to -1.

```
if (id < 0)  //this is a new innovation
{
  //add the innovation for the new neuron
  int NewNeuronID = innovations.CreateNewInnovation(from,
                                                    to,
                                                    new_neuron,
                                                    hidden,
                                                    NewWidth,
                                                    NewDepth);

  //Create the new neuron gene and add it.
  m_vecNeurons.push_back(SNeuronGene(hidden,
```

```
                                    NewNeuronID,
                                    NewDepth,
                                    NewWidth));

//Two new link innovations are required, one for each of the
//new links created when this gene is split.

//---------------------------------first link

//get the next innovation ID
int idLink1 = innovations.NextNumber();

//create the new innovation
innovations.CreateNewInnovation(from,
                                NewNeuronID,
                                new_link);

//create the new gene
SLinkGene link1(from,
               NewNeuronID,
               true,
               idLink1,
               1.0);

m_vecLinks.push_back(link1);

//---------------------------------second link

//get the next innovation ID
int idLink2 = innovations.NextNumber();

//create the new innovation
innovations.CreateNewInnovation(NewNeuronID,
                                to,
                                new_link);

//create the new gene
SLinkGene link2(NewNeuronID,
```

```
                    to,
                    true,
                    idLink2,
                    OriginalWeight);


  m_vecLinks.push_back(link2);
}


else      //existing innovation
{
  //this innovation has already been created so grab the relevant neuron
  //and link info from the innovation database
  int NewNeuronID = innovations.GetNeuronID(id);

  //get the innovation IDs for the two new link genes
  int idLink1 = innovations.CheckInnovation(from, NewNeuronID, new_link);
  int idLink2 = innovations.CheckInnovation(NewNeuronID, to, new_link);

  //this should never happen because the innovations *should* have already
  //occurred
  if ( (idLink1 < 0) || (idLink2 < 0) )
  {
    MessageBox(NULL, "Error in CGenome::AddNode", "Problem!", MB_OK);

    return;
  }

  //now we need to create 2 new genes to represent the new links
  SLinkGene link1(from, NewNeuronID, true, idLink1, 1.0);
  SLinkGene link2(NewNeuronID, to, true, idLink2, OriginalWeight);

  m_vecLinks.push_back(link1);
  m_vecLinks.push_back(link2);

  //create the new neuron
  SNeuronGene NewNeuron(hidden, NewNeuronID, NewDepth, NewWidth);

  //and add it
```

```
    m_vecNeurons.push_back(NewNeuron);
  }

  return;
}
```

How Innovations Help in the Design of a Valid Crossover Operator

As I discussed at the beginning of this chapter, the crossover operator for EANNs can often be more trouble than it's worth. In addition to ensuring that crossover does not produce invalid networks, care must also be taken to avoid the competing conventions problem. The designers of NEAT have managed to steer clear of both these evils by using the innovation IDs as historical gene markers. Because each innovation has a unique ID, the genes can be tracked chronologically, which means similar genes in different genomes can be aligned prior to crossover. To see this clearly, take a look at Figure 11.20.

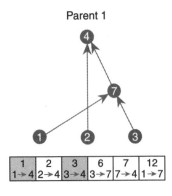

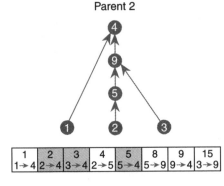

Figure 11.20

Two phenotypes with different innovations. The gray genes are disabled. The number at the top of each gene is that gene's innovation number.

The genes shown are the link genes for each phenotype. As you can see, the phenotypes have very different topologies, yet we can easily create an offspring from them by matching up the innovation numbers of the genomes before swapping over the appropriate genes, as shown in Figure 11.21.

Those genes that do not match in the middle of the genomes are called *disjoint* genes, whereas those that do not match at the end are called *excess* genes. Crossover proceeds a little like multi-point crossover, discussed earlier in the book. As the operator iterates down the length of each genome, the offspring inherits matching genes randomly. Disjoint and excess genes are only inherited from the fittest parent.

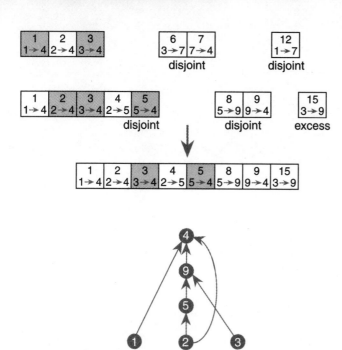

Figure 11.21

The crossover operator in action.

This way, NEAT ensures only valid offspring are created and that the competing convention problem is avoided. Neat, huh? (sorry, couldn't resist! <smile>)

Let me show you the code for the crossover operator, so you can check out the complete process.

```
CGenome Cga::Crossover(CGenome& mum, CGenome& dad)
{
  //first, calculate the genome we will using the disjoint/excess
  //genes from. This is the fittest genome. If they are of equal
  //fitness use the shorter (because we want to keep the networks
  //as small as possible)
  parent_type best;

  if (mum.Fitness() == dad.Fitness())
  {
    //if they are of equal fitness and length just choose one at
    //random
    if (mum.NumGenes() == dad.NumGenes())
    {
      best = (parent_type)RandInt(0, 1);
```

```cpp
      }

      else
      {
        if (mum.NumGenes() < dad.NumGenes())
        {
          best = MUM;
        }

        else
        {
          best = DAD;
        }
      }
    }

    else
    {
      if (mum.Fitness() > dad.Fitness())
      {
        best = MUM;
      }

      else
      {
        best = DAD;
      }
    }

    //these vectors will hold the offspring's neurons and genes
    vector<SNeuronGene>  BabyNeurons;
    vector<SLinkGene>    BabyGenes;

    //temporary vector to store all added neuron IDs
    vector<int> vecNeurons;

    //create iterators so we can step through each parents genes and set
    //them to the first gene of each parent
    vector<SLinkGene>::iterator curMum = mum.StartOfGenes();
```

```cpp
vector<SLinkGene>::iterator curDad = dad.StartOfGenes();

//this will hold a copy of the gene we wish to add at each step
SLinkGene SelectedGene;

//step through each parents genes until we reach the end of both
while (!((curMum == mum.EndOfGenes()) && (curDad == dad.EndOfGenes())))
{

  //the end of mum's genes have been reached
  if ((curMum == mum.EndOfGenes())&&(curDad != dad.EndOfGenes()))
  {
    //if dad is fittest
    if (best == DAD)
    {
      //add dads genes
      SelectedGene = *curDad;
    }

    //move onto dad's next gene
    ++curDad;
  }

  //the end of dad's genes have been reached
  else if ( (curDad == dad.EndOfGenes()) && (curMum != mum.EndOfGenes()))
  {
    //if mum is fittest
    if (best == MUM)
    {
      //add mums genes
      SelectedGene = *curMum;
    }

    //move onto mum's next gene
    ++curMum;
  }

  //if mums innovation number is less than dads
  else if (curMum->InnovationID < curDad->InnovationID)
```

```cpp
  {
    //if mum is fittest add gene
    if (best == MUM)
    {
      SelectedGene = *curMum;
    }

    //move onto mum's next gene
    ++curMum;
  }

  //if dad's innovation number is less than mum's
  else if (curDad->InnovationID < curMum->InnovationID)
  {
    //if dad is fittest add gene
    if (best = DAD)
    {
      SelectedGene = *curDad;
    }

    //move onto dad's next gene
    ++curDad;
  }

  //if innovation numbers are the same
  else if (curDad->InnovationID == curMum->InnovationID)
  {
    //grab a gene from either parent
    if (RandFloat() < 0.5f)
    {
      SelectedGene = *curMum;
    }

    else
    {
      SelectedGene = *curDad;
    }

    //move onto next gene of each parent
```

```cpp
    ++curMum;
    ++curDad;
  }


  //add the selected gene if not already added
  if (BabyGenes.size() == 0)
  {
    BabyGenes.push_back(SelectedGene);
  }

  else
  {
    if (BabyGenes[BabyGenes.size()-1].InnovationID !=
        SelectedGene.InnovationID)
    {
      BabyGenes.push_back(SelectedGene);
    }
  }


  //Check if we already have the neurons referred to in SelectedGene.
  //If not, they need to be added.
  AddNeuronID(SelectedGene.FromNeuron, vecNeurons);
  AddNeuronID(SelectedGene.ToNeuron, vecNeurons);

}//end while

//now create the required neurons. First sort them into order
sort(vecNeurons.begin(), vecNeurons.end());

for (int i=0; i<vecNeurons.size(); i++)
{
  BabyNeurons.push_back(m_pInnovation->CreateNeuronFromID(vecNeurons[i]));
}

//finally, create the genome
CGenome babyGenome(m_iNextGenomeID++,
                   BabyNeurons,
                   BabyGenes,
                   mum.NumInputs(),
```

```
                    mum.NumOutputs());

    return babyGenome;
}
```

Speciation

When structure is added to a genome, either by adding a new connection or a new neuron, it's quite likely the new individual will be a poor performer until it has a chance to evolve and establish itself among the population. Unfortunately, this means there is a high probability of the new individual dying out before it has time to evolve any potentially interesting behavior. This is obviously undesirable—some way has to be found of protecting the new innovation in the early days of its evolution. This is where simulating speciation comes in handy…

Speciation, as the name suggests, is the separation of a population into species. The question of what exactly *is* a species, is still one the biologists (and other scientists) are arguing over, but one of the popular definitions is:

> A *species is a group of populations with similar characteristics that are capable of successfully interbreeding with each other to produce healthy, fertile offspring, but are reproductively isolated from other species.*

In nature, a common mechanism for speciation is provided by changes in geography. Imagine a widespread population of animals, let's call them "critters", which eventually come to be divided by some geographical change in their environment, like the creation of a mountain ridge, for example. Over time, these populations will diversify because of different natural selection pressures and because of different mutations within their chromosomes. On one side of the mountain, the critters may start growing thicker fur to cope with a colder climate, and on the other, they may adapt to become better at avoiding the multitude of predators that lurk there. Eventually, the two populations will have changed so much from each other that if they ever did come into contact again, it would be impossible for them to mate successfully and have offspring. It's at this point they can be considered two different species.

NEAT simulates speciation to provide evolutionary niches for any new topological change. This way, similar individuals only have to compete among themselves and not with the rest of the population. Therefore, they are protected somewhat from premature extinction. A record of all the species created is kept in a class called—wait for it—CSpecies. Each epoch, every individual is tested against the first member in each species and a *compatibility distance* is calculated. If the compatibility distance is within certain boundaries, then the individual is added to that species. If the individual is incompatible with all the current species, then a new species is created and the individual is added to that.

Testing for Compatibility

The compatibility distance is calculated by measuring how diverse the genomes of two individuals are. Once again, the innovation numbers come in handy here because we can simply match up the genes, as we did for crossover, and count the number of excess and disjoint genes. The higher this count, the greater the diversity. In addition, the weights of the connections are also compared and a total of the absolute value of differences is recorded. Consequently, we have three criteria:

- The number of excess genes (E)
- The number of disjoint genes (D)
- The difference in connection weights (W)

Once these values have been determined, the final compatibility distance is calculated using the formula:

$$\text{C.Dist} = \frac{c_1 E}{N} + \frac{c_2 D}{N} + c_3 W$$

where N is the number of genes in the larger genome (to normalize for size) and c_1, c_2, and c_3 are coefficients used to tweak the final value accordingly. If this final value is below the compatibility threshold, the genomes are said to be of the same species. If it is higher, the genomes represent different species. The method used to calculate the compatibility distance is CGenome::GetCompatibilityScore and it looks like this:

```
double CGenome::GetCompatibilityScore(const CGenome &genome)
{
  //travel down the length of each genome counting the number of
  //disjoint genes, the number of excess genes and the number of
  //matched genes
  double  NumDisjoint = 0;
  double  NumExcess   = 0;
  double  NumMatched  = 0;

  //this records the summed difference of weights in matched genes
  double  WeightDifference = 0;

  //indexes into each genome. They are incremented as we
```

```
//step down each genomes length.
int g1 = 0;
int g2 = 0;

while ( (g1 < m_vecLinks.size()-1) || (g2 < genome.m_vecLinks.size()-1) )
{
  //we've reached the end of genome1 but not genome2 so increment
  //the excess score
  if (g1 == m_vecLinks.size()-1)
  {
    ++g2;
    ++NumExcess;

    continue;
  }

  //and vice versa
  if (g2 == genome.m_vecLinks.size()-1)
  {
    ++g1;
    ++NumExcess;

    continue;
  }

  //get innovation numbers for each gene at this point
  int id1 = m_vecLinks[g1].InnovationID;
  int id2 = genome.m_vecLinks[g2].InnovationID;

  //innovation numbers are identical so increase the matched score
  if (id1 == id2)
  {
    ++g1;
    ++g2;
    ++NumMatched;

    //get the weight difference between these two genes
    WeightDifference += fabs(m_vecLinks[g1].dWeight -
                        genome.m_vecLinks[g2].dWeight);
```

```
      }

      //innovation numbers are different so increment the disjoint score
      if (id1 < id2)
      {
        ++NumDisjoint;
        ++g1;
      }

      if (id1 > id2)
      {
        ++NumDisjoint;
        ++g2;
      }

    }//end while

    //get the length of the longest genome
    int longest = genome.NumGenes();

    if (NumGenes() > longest)
    {
      longest = NumGenes();
    }

    //these are multipliers used to tweak the final score.
    const double mDisjoint = 1;
    const double mExcess   = 1;
    const double mMatched  = 0.4;

    //finally calculate the scores
    double score = (mExcess   * NumExcess / ( double)longest) +
                   (mDisjoint * NumDisjoint / (double)longest) +
                   (mMatched  * WeightDifference / NumMatched);


  return score;
}
```

The CSpecies Class

Once an individual has been assigned to a species, it may only mate with other members of the same species. However, speciation alone does not protect new innovation within the population. To do that, we must somehow find a way of adjusting the fitnesses of each individual in a way that aids younger, more diverse genomes to remain active for a reasonable length of time. The technique NEAT uses to do this is called *explicit fitness sharing*.

As I discussed in Chapter 5, "Building a Better Genetic Algorithm," fitness sharing is a way of retaining diversity by sharing the fitness scores of individuals with similar genomes. With NEAT, fitness scores are shared by members of the same species. In practice, this means that each individual's score is divided by the size of the species before any selection occurs. What this boils down to is that species which grow large are penalized for their size, whereas smaller species are given a "foot up" in the evolutionary race, so to speak.

NOTE

In the original implementation of NEAT, the designers incorporated inter-species mating although the probability of this happening was set very low. Although I have never observed any noticeable performance increase when using it, it may be a worthwhile exercise for you to try this out when you start fooling around with your own implementations.

In addition, young species are given a fitness boost prior to the fitness sharing calculation. Likewise, old species are penalized. If a species does not show an improvement over a certain number of generations (the default is 15), then it is killed off. The exception to this is if the species contains the best performing individual found so far, in which case the species is allowed to live.

I think the best thing I can do to help clarify all the information I've just thrown at you is to show you the method that calculates all the fitness adjustments. First though, let me take a moment to list the CSpecies class definition:

```
class CSpecies
{

private:

  //keep a local copy of the first member of this species
```

```cpp
  CGenome           m_Leader;

  //pointers to all the genomes within this species
  vector<CGenome*>  m_vecMembers;

  //the species needs an identification number
  int               m_iSpeciesID;

  //best fitness found so far by this species
  double            m_dBestFitness;

  //average fitness of the species
  double            m_dAvFitness;

  //generations since fitness has improved, we can use
  //this info to kill off a species if required
  int               m_iGensNoImprovement;

  //age of species
  int               m_iAge;

  //how many of this species should be spawned for
  //the next population
  double            m_dSpawnsRqd;


public:

  CSpecies(CGenome &FirstOrg, int SpeciesID);

  //this method boosts the fitnesses of the young, penalizes the
  //fitnesses of the old and then performs fitness sharing over
  //all the members of the species
  void    AdjustFitnesses();

  //adds a new individual to the species
```

```cpp
    void    AddMember(CGenome& new_org);

    void    Purge();

    //calculates how many offspring this species should spawn
    void    CalculateSpawnAmount();

    //spawns an individual from the species selected at random
    //from the best CParams::dSurvivalRate percent
    CGenome Spawn();


    //-------------------------------------accessor methods
    CGenome  Leader()const{return m_Leader;}

    double   NumToSpawn()const{return m_dSpawnsRqd;}

    int      NumMembers()const{return m_vecMembers.size();}

    int      GensNoImprovement()const{return m_iGensNoImprovement;}

    int      ID()const{return m_iSpeciesID;}

    double   SpeciesLeaderFitness()const{return m_Leader.Fitness();}

    double   BestFitness()const{return m_dBestFitness;}

    int      Age()const{return m_iAge;}


  //so we can sort species by best fitness. Largest first
  friend bool operator<(const CSpecies &lhs, const CSpecies &rhs)
  {
    return lhs.m_dBestFitness > rhs.m_dBestFitness;
  }
};
```

And now for the method that adjusts the fitness scores:

```cpp
void CSpecies::AdjustFitnesses()
```

```
{
  double total = 0;

  for (int gen=0; gen<m_vecMembers.size(); ++gen)
  {
    double fitness = m_vecMembers[gen]->Fitness();

    //boost the fitness scores if the species is young
    if (m_iAge < CParams::iYoungBonusAgeThreshhold)
    {
      fitness *= CParams::dYoungFitnessBonus;
    }

    //punish older species
    if (m_iAge > CParams::iOldAgeThreshold)
    {
      fitness *= CParams::dOldAgePenalty;
    }

    total += fitness;

    //apply fitness sharing to adjusted fitnesses
    double AdjustedFitness = fitness/m_vecMembers.size();

    m_vecMembers[gen]->SetAdjFitness(AdjustedFitness);

  }
}
```

The Cga Epoch Method

Because the population is speciated, the epoch method for the NEAT code is somewhat different (and a hell of a lot longer!) than the epoch functions you've seen previously in this book. Epoch is part of the Cga class, which is the class that manipulates all the genomes, species, and innovations.

Let me talk you through the Epoch method so you understand exactly what's going on at each stage of the process:

```
vector<CNeuralNet*> Cga::Epoch(const vector<double> &FitnessScores)
{
```

```
//first check to make sure we have the correct amount of fitness scores
if (FitnessScores.size() != m_vecGenomes.size())
{
  MessageBox(NULL,"Cga::Epoch(scores/ genomes mismatch)!","Error", MB_OK);
}


ResetAndKill();
```

First of all, any phenotypes created during the previous generation are deleted. The program then examines each species in turn and deletes all of its members apart from the best performing one. (You use this individual as the genome to be tested against when the compatibility distances are calculated). If a species hasn't made any fitness improvement in `CParams::iNumGensAllowedNoImprovement` generations, the species is killed off.

```
//update the genomes with the fitnesses scored in the last run
for (int gen=0; gen<m_vecGenomes.size(); ++gen)
{
  m_vecGenomes[gen].SetFitness(FitnessScores[gen]);
}


//sort genomes and keep a record of the best performers
SortAndRecord();


//separate the population into species of similar topology, adjust
//fitnesses and calculate spawn levels
SpeciateAndCalculateSpawnLevels();
```

`SpeciateAndCalculateSpawnLevels` commences by calculating the compatibility distance of each genome against the representative genome from each live species. If the value is within a set tolerance, the individual is added to that species. If no species match is found, then a new species is created and the genome added to that.

When all the genomes have been assigned to a species `SpeciateAndCalculateSpawnLevels` calls the member function `AdjustSpeciesFitnesses` to adjust and share the fitness scores as discussed previously.

Next, `SpeciateAndCalculateSpawnLevels` calculates how many offspring each individual is predicted to spawn into the new generation. This is a floating-point value calculated by dividing each genome's adjusted fitness score with the average adjusted fitness score for the entire population. For example, if a genome had an adjusted fitness score of 4.4 and the average is 8.0, then the genome should spawn 0.525

offspring. Of course, it's impossible for an organism to spawn a fractional part of itself, but all the individual spawn amounts for the members of each species are summed to calculate an overall spawn amount for that species. Table 11.3 may help clear up any confusion you may have with this process. It shows typical spawn values for a small population of 20 individuals. The epoch function can now simply iterate through each species and spawn the required amount of offspring.

To continue with the Epoch method…

```cpp
//this will hold the new population of genomes
vector<CGenome> NewPop;

//request the offspring from each species. The number of children to
//spawn is a double which we need to convert to an int.
int NumSpawnedSoFar = 0;

CGenome baby;

//now to iterate through each species selecting offspring to be mated and
//mutated
for (int spc=0; spc<m_vecSpecies.size(); ++spc)
{
  //because of the number to spawn from each species is a double
  //rounded up or down to an integer it is possible to get an overflow
  //of genomes spawned. This statement just makes sure that doesn't
  //happen
  if (NumSpawnedSoFar < CParams::iNumSweepers)
  {
    //this is the amount of offspring this species is required to
    // spawn. Rounded simply rounds the double up or down.
    int NumToSpawn = Rounded(m_vecSpecies[spc].NumToSpawn());

    bool bChosenBestYet = false;

    while (NumToSpawn--)
    {
      //first grab the best performing genome from this species and transfer
      //to the new population without mutation. This provides per species
      //elitism
      if (!bChosenBestYet)
      {
```

```cpp
    baby = m_vecSpecies[spc].Leader();

    bChosenBestYet = true;
  }

  else
  {
    //if the number of individuals in this species is only one
    //then we can only perform mutation
    if (m_vecSpecies[spc].NumMembers() == 1)
    {
      //spawn a child
      baby = m_vecSpecies[spc].Spawn();
    }

    //if greater than one we can use the crossover operator
    else
    {
      //spawn1
      CGenome g1 = m_vecSpecies[spc].Spawn();

      if (RandFloat() < CParams::dCrossoverRate)
      {

        //spawn2, make sure it's not the same as g1
        CGenome g2 = m_vecSpecies[spc].Spawn();

        // number of attempts at finding a different genome
        int NumAttempts = 5;

        while ( (g1.ID() == g2.ID()) && (NumAttempts--) )
        {
          g2 = m_vecSpecies[spc].Spawn();
        }

        if (g1.ID() != g2.ID())
        {
          baby = Crossover(g1, g2);
        }
```

Table 11.3   Species Spawn Amounts

Species 0

Genome ID	Fitness	Adjusted Fitness	Spawn Amount
88	100	14.44	1.80296
103	99	14.3	1.78493
94	99	14.3	1.78493
61	92	13.28	1.65873
106	37	5.344	0.667096
108	34	4.911	0.613007
107	32	4.622	0.576948
105	11	1.588	0.198326
104	7	1.011	0.126207

Total offspring for this species to spawn: 9.21314

Species 1

Genome ID	Fitness	Adjusted Fitness	Spawn Amount
112	43	7.980	0.99678
110	43	7.985	0.99678
116	42	7.8	0.973599
68	41	7.614	0.950419
111	37	6.871	0.857695
115	37	6.871	0.857695
113	17	3.157	0.394076

Total offspring for this species to spawn: 6.02704

Species 2

Genome ID	Fitness	Adjusted Fitness	Spawn Amount
20	59	25.56	3.19124
100	14	6.066	0.757244
116	9	3.9	0.4868

Total offspring for this species to spawn: 4.43529

Because the number of individuals in a species may be small and because only the best 20% (default value) are retained to be parents, it is sometimes impossible (or slow) to find a second genome to mate with. The code shown here tries five times to find a different genome and then aborts.

```
  }

  else
  {
    baby = g1;
  }
}


++m_iNextGenomeID;

baby.SetID(m_iNextGenomeID);

//now we have a spawned child lets mutate it! First there is the
//chance a neuron may be added
if (baby.NumNeurons() < CParams::iMaxPermittedNeurons)
{
  baby.AddNeuron(CParams::dChanceAddNode,
                 *m_pInnovation,
                 CParams::iNumTrysToFindOldLink);
}

//now there's the chance a link may be added
baby.AddLink(CParams::dChanceAddLink,
             CParams::dChanceAddRecurrentLink,
             *m_pInnovation,
             CParams::iNumTrysToFindLoopedLink,
             CParams::iNumAddLinkAttempts);

//mutate the weights
baby.MutateWeights(CParams::dMutationRate,
                   CParams::dProbabilityWeightReplaced,
                   CParams::dMaxWeightPerturbation);

//mutate the activation response
```

```
            baby.MutateActivationResponse(CParams::dActivationMutationRate,
                                          CParams::dMaxActivationPerturbation);
      }


      //sort the babies genes by their innovation numbers
      baby.SortGenes();

      //add to new pop
      NewPop.push_back(baby);

      ++NumSpawnedSoFar;

      if (NumSpawnedSoFar == CParams::iNumSweepers)
      {
        NumToSpawn = 0;
      }

    }//end while

  }//end if

}//next species


//if there is an underflow due to a rounding error when adding up all
//the species spawn amounts, and the amount of offspring falls short of
//the population size, additional children need to be created and added
//to the new population. This is achieved simply, by using tournament
//selection over the entire population.
if (NumSpawnedSoFar < CParams::iNumSweepers)
{
  //calculate the amount of additional children required
  int Rqd = CParams::iNumSweepers - NumSpawnedSoFar;

  //grab them
  while (Rqd--)
  {
    NewPop.push_back(TournamentSelection(m_iPopSize/5));
  }
```

```
  }

  //replace the current population with the new one
  m_vecGenomes = NewPop;

  //create the new phenotypes
  vector<CNeuralNet*> new_phenotypes;

  for (gen=0; gen<m_vecGenomes.size(); ++gen)
  {
    //calculate max network depth
    int depth = CalculateNetDepth(m_vecGenomes[gen]);

    CNeuralNet* phenotype = m_vecGenomes[gen].CreatePhenotype(depth);

    new_phenotypes.push_back(phenotype);
  }

  //increase generation counter
  ++m_iGeneration;

  return new_phenotypes;
}
```

Converting the Genome into a Phenotype

Well, I've covered just about everything except how a genome is converted into a phenotype. We're nearly there now! Phenotypes use different neuron and link structures than the genome. They can be found in phenotype.h, and look like this:

The SLink Structure

The structure for the links is very simple. It just has pointers to the two neurons it connects and a connection weight. The bool value, bRecurrent, is used by the drawing routine in CNeuralNet to help render a network into a window.

```
struct SLink
{
  //pointers to the neurons this link connects
```

```
CNeuron*  pIn;
CNeuron*  pOut;

//the connection weight
double  dWeight;

//is this link a recurrent link?
bool     bRecurrent;

SLink(double dW, CNeuron* pIn, CNeuron* pOut, bool bRec):dWeight(dW),
                                                  pIn(pIn),
                                                  pOut(pOut),
                                                  bRecurrent(bRec)

  {}
};
```

The SNeuron Structure

The neuron defined by SNeuron contains much more information than its little
brother SNeuronGene. In addition, it holds the values for the sum of all the inputs ×
weights, this value after it's been put through the activation function (in other
words, the output from this neuron), and two std::vectors—one for storing the
links into the neuron, and the other for storing the links out of the neuron.

```
struct SNeuron
{
   //all the links coming into this neuron
  vector<SLink> vecLinksIn;

  //and out
  vector<SLink> vecLinksOut;

  //sum of weights x inputs
  double        dSumActivation;

  //the output from this neuron
  double        dOutput;

  //what type of neuron is this?
```

```
        neuron_type    NeuronType;

        //its identification number
        int            iNeuronID;

        //sets the curvature of the sigmoid function
        double         dActivationResponse;

        //used in visualization of the phenotype
        int            iPosX,   iPosY;
        double         dSplitY, dSplitX;

        //-- ctors
        SNeuron(neuron_type type,
                int         id,
                double      y,
                double      x,
                double      ActResponse):NeuronType(type),
                                         iNeuronID(id),
                                         dSumActivation(0),
                                         dOutput(0),
                                         iPosX(0),
                                         iPosY(0),
                                         dSplitY(y),
                                         dSplitX(x),
                                         dActivationResponse(ActResponse)
    {}
};
```

Putting the Bits Together

The method that actually creates all the SLinks and SNeurons required for a phenotype is CGenome::CreatePhenotype. This function iterates through the genome and
creates any appropriate neurons and all the required links required for pointing to
those neurons. It then creates an instance of the CNeuralNet class. I'll be discussing
the CNeuralNet class immediately after you've had a good look at the following code.

```
CNeuralNet* CGenome::CreatePhenotype(int depth)
{
```

```
    //first make sure there is no existing phenotype for this genome
    DeletePhenotype();

    //this will hold all the neurons required for the phenotype
    vector<SNeuron*>  vecNeurons;

    //first, create all the required neurons
    for (int i=0; i<m_vecNeurons.size(); i++)
    {
      SNeuron* pNeuron = new SNeuron(m_vecNeurons[i].NeuronType,
                                     m_vecNeurons[i].iID,
                                     m_vecNeurons[i].dSplitY,
                                     m_vecNeurons[i].dSplitX,
                                     m_vecNeurons[i].dActivationResponse);


      vecNeurons.push_back(pNeuron);
    }


    //now to create the links.
    for (int cGene=0; cGene<m_vecLinks.size(); ++cGene)
    {
      //make sure the link gene is enabled before the connection is created
      if (m_vecLinks[cGene].bEnabled)
      {
        //get the pointers to the relevant neurons
        int element        = GetElementPos(m_vecLinks[cGene].FromNeuron);
        SNeuron* FromNeuron = vecNeurons[element];

        element            = GetElementPos(m_vecLinks[cGene].ToNeuron);
        SNeuron* ToNeuron = vecNeurons[element];

        //create a link between those two neurons and assign the weight stored
        //in the gene
        SLink tmpLink(m_vecLinks[cGene].dWeight,
                   FromNeuron,
                   ToNeuron,
                   m_vecLinks[cGene].bRecurrent);


        //add new links to neuron
```

```
          FromNeuron->vecLinksOut.push_back(tmpLink);
          ToNeuron->vecLinksIn.push_back(tmpLink);
      }
  }


  //now the neurons contain all the connectivity information, a neural
  //network may be created from them.
  m_pPhenotype = new CNeuralNet(vecNeurons, depth);

  return m_pPhenotype;
}
```

The CNeuralNet Class

This class is pretty simple. It contains a std::vector of the neurons that comprise the network, a method to update the network and retrieve its output, and a method to draw a representation of the network into a user-specified window. The value m_iDepth is the depth of the network calculated from the splitY values of its neuron genes, as discussed earlier. You'll see how this value is used in a moment. The enumerated type, run_type, is especially important because this is how the user chooses *how* the network is updated. I'll elaborate on this after you've taken a moment to look at the class definition.

```
class CNeuralNet
{

private:

  vector<SNeuron*>  m_vecpNeurons;

  //the depth of the network
  int               m_iDepth;


public:


  CNeuralNet(vector<SNeuron*> neurons,
```

```
            int              depth);


    ~CNeuralNet();

    //you have to select one of these types when updating the network
    //If snapshot is chosen the network depth is used to completely
    //flush the inputs through the network. active just updates the
    //network each time-step
    enum run_type{snapshot, active};

    //update network for this clock cycle
    vector<double>  Update(const vector<double> &inputs, const run_type type);

    //draws a graphical representation of the network to a user specified window
    void            DrawNet(HDC &surface,
                            int cxLeft,
                            int cxRight,
                            int cyTop,
                            int cyBot);
};
```

Up until now, all the networks you've seen have run the inputs through the complete network, layer by layer, until an output is produced. With NEAT however, a network can assume any topology with connections between neurons leading backward, forward, or even looping back on themselves. This makes it next to impossible to use a layer-based update function because there aren't really any layers! Because of this, the NEAT update function runs in one of two modes:

active: When using the `active` update mode, each neuron adds up all the activations calculated during the *preceeding time-step* from all its incoming neurons. This means that the activation values, instead of being flushed through the entire network like a conventional ANN each time-step, only travel from one neuron to the next. To get the same result as a layer-based method, this process would have to be repeated as many times as the network is deep in order to flush all the neuron activations completely through the network. This mode is appropriate to use if you are using the network dynamically (like for controlling the minesweepers for instance).

snapshot: If, however, you want NEAT's `update` function to behave like a regular neural network update function, you have to ensure that the activations are flushed *all the way through* from the input neurons to the output neurons. To facilitate this,

`Update` iterates through all the neurons as many times as the network is deep before spitting out the output. This is why calculating those `splitY` values was so important. You would use this type of update if you were to train a NEAT network using a training set. (Like we used for the mouse gesture recognition program in Chapter 9, "A Supervised Training Approach").

Here is the code for `CNeuralNet::Update`, which should help clarify the process.

```
vector<double> CNeuralNet::Update(const vector<double> &inputs,
                                  const run_type        type)
{
  //create a vector to put the outputs into
  vector<double>  outputs;

  //if the mode is snapshot then we require all the neurons to be
  //iterated through as many times as the network is deep. If the
  //mode is set to active the method can return an output after
  //just one iteration
  int FlushCount = 0;

  if (type == snapshot)
  {
    FlushCount = m_iDepth;
  }
  else
  {
    FlushCount = 1;
  }

  //iterate through the network FlushCount times
  for (int i=0; i<FlushCount; ++i)
  {
    //clear the output vector
    outputs.clear();

    //this is an index into the current neuron
    int cNeuron = 0;

    //first set the outputs of the 'input' neurons to be equal
    //to the values passed into the function in inputs
```

```cpp
while (m_vecpNeurons[cNeuron]->NeuronType == input)
{
  m_vecpNeurons[cNeuron]->dOutput = inputs[cNeuron];

  ++cNeuron;
}

//set the output of the bias to 1
m_vecpNeurons[cNeuron++]->dOutput = 1;

//then we step through the network a neuron at a time
while (cNeuron < m_vecpNeurons.size())
{
  //this will hold the sum of all the inputs x weights
  double sum = 0;

  //sum this neuron's inputs by iterating through all the links into
  //the neuron
  for (int lnk=0; lnk<m_vecpNeurons[cNeuron]->vecLinksIn.size(); ++lnk)
  {
    //get this link's weight
    double Weight = m_vecpNeurons[cNeuron]->vecLinksIn[lnk].dWeight;

    //get the output from the neuron this link is coming from
    double NeuronOutput =
    m_vecpNeurons[cNeuron]->vecLinksIn[lnk].pIn->dOutput;

    //add to sum
    sum += Weight * NeuronOutput;
  }

  //now put the sum through the activation function and assign the
  //value to this neuron's output
  m_vecpNeurons[cNeuron]->dOutput =
  Sigmoid(sum, m_vecpNeurons[cNeuron]->dActivationResponse);

  if (m_vecpNeurons[cNeuron]->NeuronType == output)
  {
    //add to our outputs
```

```
                outputs.push_back(m_vecpNeurons[cNeuron]->dOutput);
        }


        //next neuron
        ++cNeuron;
    }


  }//next iteration through the network

  //the network outputs need to be reset if this type of update is performed
  //otherwise it is possible for dependencies to be built on the order
  //the training data is presented
  if (type == snapshot)
  {
     for (int n=0; n<m_vecpNeurons.size(); ++n)
     {
        m_vecpNeurons[n]->dOutput = 0;
     }
  }


  //return the outputs
  return outputs;
}
```

Note that the outputs of the network must be reset to zero before the function returns if the snapshot method of updating is required. This is to prevent any dependencies on the *order* the training data is presented. (Training data is usually presented to a network sequentially because doing it randomly would slow down the learning considerably.)

For example, imagine presenting a training set consisting of a number of points lying on the circumference of a circle. If the network is not flushed, NEAT might add recurrent connections that make use of the data stored from the previous update. This would be okay if you wanted a network that simply mapped inputs to outputs, but most often you will require the network to generalize.

Running the Demo Program

To demonstrate NEAT in practice, I've plugged in the minesweeper code from Chapter 8, "Giving Your Bot Senses." I think you'll be pleasantly surprised by how

NEAT performs in comparison! You can either compile it yourself or run the executable NEAT Sweepers.exe straight from the relevant folder on the CD.

As before, the F key speeds up the evolution, the R key resets it, and the B key shows the best four minesweepers from the previous generation. Pressing the keys 1 through 4 shows the minesweeper's "trails".

This time there is also an additional window created in which the phenotypes of the four best minesweepers are drawn, as shown in Figure 11.22.

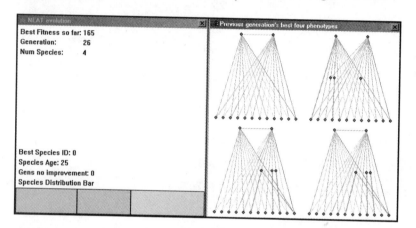

Figure 11.22

NEAT Sweepers in action.

Excitory forward connections are shown in gray and inhibitory forward connections are shown in yellow. Excitory recurrent connections are shown in red and inhibitory connections are shown in blue. Any connections from the bias neuron are shown in green. The thickness of the line gives an indication of the magnitude of the connection weight.

Table 11.4 lists the default settings for this project:

Summary

You've come a long way in this chapter, and learned a lot in the process. To aid your understanding, the implementation of NEAT I describe in this chapter has been kept simple and it would be worthwhile for the curious to examine Ken Stanley and Risto Miikkulainen's original code to gain a fuller insight into the mechanisms of NEAT. You can find the source code and other articles about NEAT via Ken's Web site at:

http://www.cs.utexas.edu/users/kstanley/

Table 11.4 Default Project Settings for NEAT Sweepers

Parameters for the Minesweepers

Parameter	Setting
Num sensors	5
Sensor range	25
Num minesweepers	50
Max turn rate	0.2
Scale	5

Parameters Affecting Evolution

Parameter	Setting
Num ticks per epoch	2000
Chance of adding a link	0.07
Chance of adding a node	0.03
Chance of adding a recurrent link	0.05
Crossover rate	0.7
Weight mutation rate	0.2
Max mutation perturbation	0.5
Probability a weight is replaced	0.1
Probability the activation response is mutated	0.1
Species compatibility threshold	0.26
Species old age threshold	50
Species old age penalty	0.7
Species youth threshold	10
Species youth bonus	1.3

Stuff to Try

1. Add code to automatically keep the number of species within user-defined boundaries.

2. Have a go at designing some different mutation operators.

3. Add interspecies mating.

4. Have a go at coding one of the alternative methods for evolving network topology described at the beginning of the chapter.

Part Four

Appendixes

APPENDIX A

WEB RESOURCES

T he World Wide Web is undoubtedly the single biggest resource for AI-related information. Here are a few of the best resources. If you get stuck, try these sources first because one or more of them is almost certain to help you.

URLs

www.gameai.com

A great site devoted to games AI run by the ever popular Steve "Ferretman" Woodcock. This is a terrific starting point for any games related AI/ALife query.

www.ai-depot.com

Another terrific resource. A great place to keep up to date with any AI-related news and it contains many useful tutorials on all things AI related.

www.generation5.org

Not strictly game related, but this Web site contains a wealth of useful information and tutorials.

www.citeseer.com

The Citeseer Scientific Literature Digital Library—an amazing source of documents. If you need to find a paper, here's the best place to start looking for it. This place is my favorite source of information on the Internet.

www.gamedev.net

This Web site has many archived articles and tutorials. It also hosts one of the best AI forums on the Internet.

www.ai-junkie.com

My own little Web site. It used to be known as "Stimulate" in the old days, but I felt it needed a new name and a new look. If you have any questions regarding the techniques described in this book, feel free to ask away at the forum.

www.google.com

Had to include this search engine here because so many people still don't seem to know how to use it! Almost everything I research on the Internet starts with this link. If you don't use it, then start!

Newsgroups

The Usenet is often overlooked by games programmers, but it can be an extremely valuable source of information, help, and most importantly, inspiration. If AI excites you, then most of the following should be of interest.

> comp.ai.neural-nets
> comp.ai.genetic
> comp.ai.games
> comp.ai.alife

APPENDIX B

Bibliography and Recommended Reading

Technical Books

Neural Networks for Pattern Recognition

Christopher Bishop

The current Bible for neural networks. Not for those of you with math anxiety, though!

An Introduction to Neural Networks

Kevin Gurney

This is a great little introduction to neural networks. Kevin takes you on a whirlwind tour of the most popular network architectures in use today. He does his best to avoid the math but you still need to know calculus to read this book.

Neural Computing

R Beale & T Jackson

Has some interesting pages.

Genetic Algorithms in Search, Optimization and Machine Learning

David E. Goldberg

The Bible of genetic algorithms. Nuff said.

An Introduction to Genetic Algorithms

Melanie Mitchell

A well-written and very popular introduction to genetic algorithms. This is ideal if you would like a gentle introduction to the theoretical aspects of genetic algorithms.

The Natural History of the Mind

Gordon Rattray Taylor

A great book on the biological basis of brain and mind. I think it's out of print nowadays; I got mine from a second-hand bookstore.

The Blind Watchmaker

Richard Dawkins

This book and one of his other books, *The Selfish Gene*, are incredible introductions to the mechanics of evolution.

Programming Windows 5ᵗʰ Edition

Charles Petzold

The Bible of Windows programming.

The C++ Standard Library

Nicolai M Josuttis

The STL Bible. This book is superb. Josuttis makes a dry subject fascinating.

The C++ Programming Language

Bjarne Stroustrup

The C++ Bible.

Papers

Evolution of neural network architectures by a hierarchical grammar-based genetic system.
Christian Jacob and Jan Rehder

Genetic Encoding Strategies for Neural Networks.
Philipp Koehn

Combining Genetic Algorithms and Neural Networks: The Encoding Problem
Philipp Koehn

Evolving Artificial Neural Networks
Xin Yao

Evolving Neural Networks through Augmenting Topologies
Kenneth O. Stanley and Risto Miikkulainen

Evolutionary Algorithms for Neural Network Design and Training

Jürgen Branke

'Genotypes' for Neural Networks

Stefano Nolfi & Domenico Parisi

Niching Methods for Genetic Algorithms

Samir W.Mahfoud

Online Interactive Neuro-Evolution

Adrian Agogino, Kenneth Stanley & Risto Miikkulainen

Thought-Provoking Books

Gödel Escher Bach, An Eternal Golden Braid

Douglas Hofstadter

The Minds I

Douglas Hofstadter

Metamagical Themas

Douglas Hofstadter

Any book by Douglas Hofstadter is guaranteed to keep you awake at night! He explores the mind, consciousness, and artificial intelligence (among other subjects) in an extremely entertaining and thought-provoking way. If you are going to buy one, go for *Gödel Escher Bach, An Eternal Golden Braid* first. I believe it's just been reprinted.

Artificial Life

Stephen Levy

If you only buy one book on artificial life, buy this one. Levy is a superb writer and although there's not a vast amount of depth, he covers a lot of ground in an extremely relaxed way. I couldn't put it down until I finished it.

Creation: Life and How to Make It

Steve Grand

A bit waffly and sometimes a little unfocused, this book is still worth reading. Grand is the guy who programmed *Creatures* and this book is an attempt to explain the mechanics of the Norms (that's what he called his creatures in the game) and also Steve's thoughts on life and consciousness in general.

Emergence (from Chaos to Order)

John H Holland

Not a bad book, it has a few interesting chapters.

Darwin amongst the Machines

George Dyson

This is similar to the Levy book but is focussed much more on the early history of computers and artificial life. Another great read.

The Emperor's New Mind

Roger Penrose

This book covers a lot of ground in an attempt to explain why Penrose believes machines will never be conscious. You may disagree with his conclusion but this book is still a very interesting read.

Bloody-Good SF Novels!

Just in case you need some lighter reading, I thought I'd include some of the great sci-fi novels I've read over the last few years—every one a page turner.

The Skinner

Neal Asher

Gridlinked

Neil Asher

The Hyperion Series of Books

Dan Simmons

Altered Carbon

Richard Morgan

K-PAX , I, II & III

Gene Brewer

And finally, any science-fiction written by Iain M. Banks

APPENDIX C

WHAT'S ON THE CD

The source code for each demo is included on the accompanying CD, along with pre-compiled executables for those of you with twitchy fingers. Each chapter has its own folder so you shouldn't have any problems finding the relevant project files.

Building the demos is a piece of cake. First, make sure you copy the files to your hard drive. If you use Microsoft Visual Studio, then just click on the relevant workspace and away you go. If you use an alternative compiler, create a new win32 project, make sure winmm.lib is added in your project settings, and then add the relevant source and resource files from the project folder before clicking the compile button.

I've also included a demo of *Colin McRae Rally 2* on the CD. In addition to being a whole load of fun, this game uses neural network technology to control the computer-driven opponents. Here's what Jeff Hannan, the AI man behind the game had to say in an interview with James Matthews of *Generation5*.

Q. What kind of flexibility did the neural networks give you in terms of AI design and playability? Did the networks control all aspects of the AI?

A. Obviously the biggest challenge was actually getting a car to successfully drive round the track in a quick time. Once that was achieved, I was then able to adjust racing lines almost at will, to add a bit of character to the drivers. The neural net was able to drive the new lines, without any new training.

The neural nets are constructed with the simple aim of keeping the car to the racing line. They are effectively performing that skill. I felt that higher-level functions like overtaking or recovering from crashes should be separated from this core activity. In fact, I was able to work out fairly simple rules to perform these tasks.

Q. Which game genres do you see "mainstream AI" (neural networks, genetic algorithms, etc.) seeping into the most, now? In the future?

A. Neural networks and genetic algorithms are powerful techniques that can be applied in general to any suitable problem, not just AI. Therefore, any game genre could make use of them. It would be ridiculous not to consider them for a difficult problem. However, experimentation is generally required. They help you find a solution, rather than give it to you on a plate.

With my experience of using neural nets, I'd say that they are particularly good at skills. When a human performs a skill, it is an automatic movement that doesn't require high-level reasoning. The brain has learned a function that automatically produces the right behavior in response to the situation. Sports games may be the most obvious candidate for this in the near future.

Support

Neural networks and genetic algorithms can be very confusing topics for the beginner. It is often helpful to discuss your thoughts with like-minded people. You can post questions and discuss ideas using the messageboard at:

www.ai-junkie.com.

Any updates to the source code contained in this book may be found here:

www.ai-junkie.com/updates

Epilogue

An apprentice carpenter may want only a hammer and saw, but a master craftsman employs many precision tools. Computer programming likewise requires sophisticated tools to cope with the complexity of real applications, and only practice with these tools will build skill in their use.

—*Robert L. Kruse, Data Structures and Program Design*

And so we come to the end of what I hope has been a stimulating and thought-provoking journey. I hope you've had as much fun reading this book as I've had writing it.

By now, you should know enough about neural networks and genetic algorithms to start implementing them into your own projects… *where appropriate.* I've italicized those last two words because I often see attempts to use neural networks as a panacea for all a game's AI needs. That is to say, some enthusiastic soul, all fired up with the excitement of newfound knowledge, will try to use a neural network to control the *entire* AI of a complex game agent. He will design a network with dozens of inputs, loads of outputs, and expect the thing to perform like Arnold Schwarzenegger on a good day! Unfortunately, miracles seldom happen, and these same people are often found shaking their heads in disbelief when after ten million generations, their bot still only spins in circles.

It's best to think of genetic algorithms and neural networks as another tool in your AI toolbox. As your experience and confidence with them grows, you will see more areas in which one of them, or both, can be used to good effect. It may be a very visible use, like the application of a feedforward network to control the car AIs in *Colin McRae Rally 2*, or it may be a very subtle use, like the way single neurons are used in *Black & White* to model the desires of the Creatures. You may also find uses for them in the development phases of your game. There are now a number of developers who use genetic algorithms to tweak the characteristics of your game's agents. I've even heard of developers letting loose neural-network controlled agents in their game's environment to test the physics engine. If there *are* any weak spots or loopholes in your code, then a neural network driven by a genetic algorithm is a great way of finding it.

If you code something you feel proud of as a result of reading about the techniques in this book, I'd love to hear from you. Seeing how different people go on to utilize these techniques is a great reward for all the hours I've spent bashing away at this keyboard. So don't be shy, contact me at fup@ai-junkie.com.

And most of all... have fun!

Mat Buckland, July 2002

Index

X

Y